EMERGENT LITERACY

Writing and Reading

Writing Research

Multidisciplinary Inquiries into the Nature of Writing

edited by Marcia Farr, University of Illinois at Chicago

Arthur N. Applebee, *Contexts for Learning to Write: Studies of Secondary School Instruction*

Carole Edelsky, *Writing in a Bilingual Program: Había Una Vez*

Lester Faigley, Roger Cherry, David Jolliffe, and Anna Skinner, *Assessing Writers' Knowledge and Processes of Composing*

Marcia Farr (ed.), *Advances in Writing Research, Volume One: Children's Early Writing Development*

Sarah W. Freedman (ed.), *The Acquisition of Written Language: Response and Revision*

Judith Langer, *Children Reading and Writing: Structures and Strategies*

William Teale and Elizabeth Sulzby (eds.), *Emergent Literacy: Writing and Reading*

IN PREPARATION

Barbara Couture, *Functional Approaches to Writing Research*

Robert Gundlach, *Children and Writing in American Education*

Martha L. King and Victor Rentel, *The Development of Meaning in Writing: Children 5–10*

Ann Matsuhashi (ed.), *Writing in Real Time: Modeling Production Processes*

Anthony Petrosky (ed.), *Reading and Writing: Theory and Research*

Leo Ruth and Sandra Murphy, *Designing Writing Tasks for the Assessment of Writing*

David Smith, *Explorations in the Culture of Literacy*

Jana Staton, Roger Shuy, Joy Kreeft, and Leslie Reed, *Interactive Writing in Dialogue Journals: Practitioner, Linguistic, Social, and Cognitive Views*

Elizabeth Sulzby, *Emergent Writing and Reading in 5–6 Year Olds: A Longitudinal Study*

Stephen Witte, Keith Walters, Mary Trachsel, Roger Cherry, and Paul Meyer, *Literacy and Writing Assessment: Issues, Traditions, Directions*

EMERGENT LITERACY:

Writing and Reading

edited by

William H. Teale

University of Texas at San Antonio

Elizabeth Sulzby

Northwestern University

ABLEX PUBLISHING CORPORATION
NORWOOD, NEW JERSEY

To Judy and Jeremy, Mitchell and Kiran—
who have helped us understand emergent literacy
from a non-academic perspective

Copyright © 1986 by Ablex Publishing Corporation

Printed in the United States of America.

Library of Congress Cataloging-in-Publication Data
Main entry under title:

Emergent literacy.

    (Writing research)
    Bibliography: p.
    Includes index.
    1. Reading (Primary)—Addresses, essays, lectures.
2. Literacy—Addresses, essays, lectures.   3. Language
acquisition—Addresses, essays, lectures.   I. Teale,
William H.   II. Sulzby, Elizabeth.   III. Series.
LB1525.E54   1986   372.4   86-1034
ISBN 0-89391-301-4
ISBN 0-89391-385-5 (pbk.)

Ablex Publishing Corporation
355 Chestnut Street
Norwood, New Jersey 07648

Contents

Writing Research

Multidisciplinary Inquiries into the Nature of Writing

Marcia Farr, series editor
University of Illinois at Chicago

PREFACE

This series of volumes presents the results of recent scholarly inquiry into the nature of writing. The research presented comes from a mix of disciplines, those which have emerged as significant within the last decade or so in the burgeoning field of writing research. These primarily include English education, linguistics, psychology, anthropology, and rhetoric. A note here on the distinction between field and discipline might be useful: a field can be a multidisciplinary entity focused on a set of significant questions about a central concern (e.g., American Studies), while a discipline usually shares theoretical and methodological approaches which may have a substantial tradition behind them. Writing research, then, is a field, if not yet a discipline.

The history of this particular field is unique. Much of the recent work in this field, and much that is being reported in this series, has been conceptualized and funded by the National Institute of Education. Following a planning conference in June 1977, a program of basic research on the teaching and learning of writing was developed and funded annually. The initial research funded under this program is now coming to fruition, providing both implications for educational improvement and directions for future research. This series is intended as one important outlet for these results.

Introduction

Emergent Literacy as a Perspective for Examining How Young Children Become Writers and Readers

William H. Teale
University of Texas at San Antonio

Elizabeth Sulzby
Northwestern University

This book is about young children and their writing and reading. It stops at the point where most books on beginning writing and reading start: when the child is around 5 or 6 years old and is able to write and read in ways that most adults recognize as actually being writing and reading. Although the period from birth to school age has long been of interest to researchers and educators concerned with oral language development, it is only relatively recently that we have come fully to realize that significant written language development is also occurring during this time.

The chapters in this volume are authored by many of the leading researchers of written language development in very young children. These researchers have investigated the not-yet-conventional ways in which these children write and read, seeking to understand the nature of these behaviors, the contexts out of which they arise, and their significance for continuing literacy development. The authors address these issues from a variety of disciplinary perspectives—anthropology, education, linguistics, and psychology—and their results speak to persons in these and related fields such as sociology, philosophy of language, rhetoric, semiotics, and artificial intelligence, who are interested in the issues of development and education in early childhood.

We have entitled this book *Emergent Literacy* and use this term throughout our discussions of the work which follows. How can we justify adopting a new term? We do so cautiously, for two reasons. First, we believe the results of the research by the authors in this volume afford a new perspective for understanding the nature and importance of children's writing and reading development during the early years. Although perhaps not so momentous as the revolutions described by Kuhn (1962), this perspective represents what may be considered a paradigm shift. Accordingly, we feel a term is needed which will unify the research strands that have arisen. Second, terms such as *language learning, language acquisition,* or *beginning reading* and *writing* bring with them histories and connotations which we think are best avoided for the present.

The papers collected in this volume present the work of scholars who have, in one way or another, contributed to the "change in perception and evaluation of familiar data" (Kuhn, 1962, p. xi) and the gathering of new data on young children's writing and reading which has taken place. As a result of such work, we are now "seeing" reading in toddlers' explorations with picture books and "seeing" writing in their scribbles.

The choice of *emergent literacy* as a term for depicting this perspective on young children's writing and reading development can perhaps best be understood by examining historically how such children's writing and reading have been treated in the areas of child development and education.[1] This historical overview focuses primarily on the United States, but similar broad trends in early childhood research and education are apparent in many countries throughout the world.

FROM BENIGN NEGLECT TO READING READINESS

The literature on learning to read and write can in fact be traced back many centuries (Mathews, 1966), but we shall confine our historical examination to the period of "modern research," that is, from the late 1800s to the present. A review of the literature published up through the second decade of the twentieth century yields one inescapable conclusion: Not much of anyone was addressing the issue of, much less researching, pre-first-grade reading and writing. Iredell (1898) certainly wrote cogently about the parallels between young children's oral language development and literacy development and about the importance for literacy learning of what occurs during the preschool years. Also, Huey (1908) devoted an entire chapter of *The Psychology and Pedagogy of Reading* to "Learning to Read at Home," in which he too stressed the importance of experiences in the early years and called for "natural ways" of ushering young children into literacy. But such statements represent exceptions rather than the rule. The inference to be drawn from this state of affairs is that, for all intents and purposes, the general belief was that literacy development did not begin until the child encountered formal instruction in school.

A companion phenomenon to "benign neglect" of preschool children was the instructional "lockstep" of the grades. This practice of offering the same instruction to all children in a given grade at the same time and in the same order led to children being "failed" or required to repeat grades in school until they "passed" (Betts, 1946; McCall, 1923). Massive numbers of children failing initial reading instruction served as impetus for educators to consider other ways of viewing beginning reading instruction.

In the 1920s a change in thinking began to be reflected in the literature. It was at

---

[1]The historical discussion which follows largely centers on reading development rather than writing development, simply because, with a few exceptions and until very recently, writing in early childhood was generally ignored.

this point that educators started to look more closely at the early childhood and kindergarten years as a "period of preparation"; the concept of *reading readiness* took root. Readiness had been discussed for years prior to this time, but during this period it began to be applied specifically to reading. The Report of the National Committee on Reading published in the 1925 *Yearbook of the United States National Society for the Study of Education* contained the first explicit reference to reading readiness (Coltheart, 1979).

It seems that the rise to prominence of reading readiness stemmed from a desire among researchers to identify the factor or factors which enabled children to be "prepared mentally" for reading. From the beginning, the endeavor was pursued along two different paths. On the one hand, there were educators who were convinced that reading readiness was essentially the result of maturation, or "neural ripeness" (Cole, 1938; Harris, 1940; Harrison, 1936; Lamoreaux & Lee, 1943); others believed that appropriate experiences could accelerate readiness (Kibbe, 1939).

Reading Readiness as Neural Ripening
During the 1920s and 1930s and even into the 1940s and '50s, work in child development, applications of child development theories in education, and popular books on child rearing were greatly influenced by the ideas of Arnold Gesell. Basically, Gesell saw development as being controlled by maturation (Gesell, 1925, 1928, 1940). To him, progress in motor or cognitive skills was the result of neural ripening or "intrinsic growth," with behaviors unfolding automatically. In fact, data on motor development in children (Dennis, 1941; McGraw, 1935) were generalized beyond their original context to support a maturationalist theory of cognitive development (Durkin, 1968). Thus, changes in children's thinking were seen to be akin to anatomical or motor development—starting from the inside and proceeding outward, largely unaffected by the environment (Hunt, 1964). Small wonder, then, that Bruner (1983) summarized this line of work by saying that, for Gesell, "the developmental question largely boiled down to when things got better or faster or stronger, or more controlled" (p. 133).

However, Gesell and the maturationalists' viewpoint was the dominant one of the period, both in academic circles and among the general public. The application of such a viewpoint to the issue of reading readiness was straightforward: Readiness to read was the result of neural ripening. The mental processes necessary for reading would unfold automatically at a certain point in development.

The implications of this theory for educational practice were also straightforward: If the child is not yet ready, wait. To everything there is a season, the maturationalists would say; but the seasons cannot be rushed. Good educational practice would, in this view, provide an environment that above all "does not interfere with the predetermined process of spontaneous maturation" (Ausubel, 1961, p. 19).

Such a developmental/educational *Zeitgeist*, combined with what Durkin (1970) has described as the predominance of the "measurement and testing movement" in education, set the stage for a study by Mabel Morphett and Carleton Washburne (1931) which had profound influence on conceptions of and educational programs in reading readiness. In September, 1928, Morphett and Washburne tested all 141 first-grade children in the Winnetka, Illinois, schools with the Stanford-Binet and the Detroit First-Grade Intelligence Test and calculated their mental ages as of the beginning of the academic year. They also tested the children's reading achievement in February and June of 1929. "Satisfactory progress in reading" was defined as completing a minimum 13 of the 21 "progress steps" in the beginning reading materials used by the children and having a sight vocabulary of at least 37 words. Correlation ratios showed that the percentage of children making satisfactory progress in February and June was considerably higher if the children had a mental age of at least 6 years, 6 months when they began school. Morphett and Washburne (1931) interpreted these results as indicating that "it pays to postpone beginning reading until a child has attained a mental age of six years and six months" (p. 501). This study was seized upon by an educational community more than willing to embrace a maturationalist viewpoint as a more humane and sensible interpretation of learning. Furthermore, in an era caught up with applying "rigorous," "objective" methods of investigation to educational issues, its statistical nature only added to its legitimacy.

Durkin (1968) explains that the Morphett-Washburne research was "a 'natural' for the 1930s" (p. 37). The popularity of the maturationalist viewpoint made the "postpone and wait" recommendation fully warranted; and Carleton Washburne's position as a leader in the progressive education movement and superintendent of the Winnetka Schools—regarded as models of individualized education—provided extra support for the "mental-age concept of readiness." Coltheart (1979) cites numerous quotations from methods texts and a history of reading instruction that indicate how widely and for how long conclusions and implications of the Morphett and Washburne study were influential in the world of education. Despite the serious questioning of this piece of research by Gates and his colleagues only a few years later (Gates, 1937; Gates & Bond, 1936; Gates, Bond, & Russell, 1939) and despite the fact that an eminent figure in reading like Emmett Betts would call the six year, six months mental-age requirement a "fairy tale" (Betts, 1946, p. 121), the neural ripening/mental–age/delay instruction orientation prevailed through four decades.

During this period of measurement and testing the "reading readiness test" also gained a hold in the educational community. Betts's 1946 edition of *Foundations of Reading Instruction* provided detailed information about 12 such tests published between 1930 and 1943, many of which survive in revised form to the present day, including the largest selling *Metropolitan Readiness Tests*. Reading readiness test results served those adhering to the maturationalist viewpoint largely as an indicator of when the child had finally acquired the mental maturity to begin reading. But examination of the tests reveals that they were not designed simply to provide an overall score indicating the child's readiness or lack thereof. Rather, they consisted of a number of subtests. The 1933 *Metropolitan Readiness Tests* for example, included subtests titled Perception: Similarities; Perception: Copying; Vocabulary;

Sentences; Numbers; Information; and the Draw-a-Man test. The other tests of this era reflected similar ideas of what could be measured and improved in order for children to *begin* to read. The *Betts Ready to Read Tests* (published in 1934) were even more detailed, having three sections each with subtests. The first section, Visual Readiness, included subtests on Letter Forms, Word Forms, and Phonetic Elements. The Auditory Readiness section included Auditory Span, Auditory Fusion, Auditory Perception, and Auditory Acuity. The final section indicated a stress on children's vision. Called Visual Sensation and Perception, it included tests of vision such as Distance Fusion, Visual Efficiency, Vertical Imbalance, Depth Perception (Coordination), Lateral Imbalance, Reading Distance Fusion, and Sharpness of Image.

Designed in this way, the tests certainly lent themselves to being used as diagnostic tools for intervention. If a child scored low in auditory discrimination, for instance, drill in this area might be prescribed. Methods textbooks used in teacher education began to include specific descriptions of how to prepare children deficient in the areas represented on the tests. Preparation, then as now, was for instruction in sequential instructional books, the *basal reader* series. During the 1930s the *reading readiness workbook* became established as a fundamental part of basal series. Betts's (1946) enthusiasm for this new development can be detected in this section:

> Since the first publication of a reading-readiness book as part of a basal series of readers in 1935, the idea of making available some type of reading-readiness materials has caught on rapidly. In addition, materials have been published for use independently of a given series of readers. While these first attempts have been somewhat crude, the whole question of preparation for reading has been thrown open. Although it would be folly to assume that an adequate reading-readiness program can be put between the covers of either a workbook or a textbook, teachers have been given further insight into the problems of readiness for systematic instruction in reading. (p. 267)

Thus, coexisting with the maturationalist viewpoint through the 1920s, 1930s, and 1940s was the school of thought that reading readiness was something that could be taught rather than merely waited for. As the reading readiness test and reading readiness workbooks became more and more established parts of the first year of school, the overriding emphasis on maturation diminished. The stage was set for the move that was to come.

Reading Readiness as the Product of Experience

The shift away from reading readiness as maturation and toward readiness as the product of experience occurred during the late 1950s and the 1960s. By 1968 Durkin wrote:

> The literature still shows some remnants of the maturational concept of readiness, but, as a whole, articles and books are now dominated by the opposite conception highlighting the contribution of environmental factors. Or to put the characterization of the current scene in the framework of the nature–nurture debate, today the spotlight happens to be on nurture. . . . (p. 48)

In addition to the growing reliance on reading readiness tests and workbooks, several factors contributed to the wholesale shift toward nurture. In the United States the launching of Sputnik in 1957 was to have a great effect on education. When the Soviets succeeded in the technological accomplishment of orbiting a satellite first, questions were raised about the adequacy of American education. One result of the commissions, inquiries, and self-evaluations that ensued was the general decision to make the curriculum more rigorous and to begin instruction as early as possible.

The rationale for the push toward earlier, as well as more, education probably also stemmed in part from increased research on young children. Infancy research was becoming widespread among psychologists by 1960. Kagan, Bruner, Brazelton, and others at Harvard, for example, were all studying very young children. The infant research was demonstrating that preschoolers knew more than they had generally been given credit for and that during the early years children could be learning many skills. Bloom's (1964) analysis of a multitude of longitudinal studies of development went even further. He concluded that the majority of human intellectual development takes place before the age of 5, with 50% of the intelligence measured at age 17 being developed by age 4 (Bloom, 1964, p. 88). Also, reports on early readers (Durkin began publishing on her California early reader study in the late 1950s) and on efforts to teach preschoolers to read (O. K. Moore's "talking typewriter," for example) were appearing. The media served to popularize this new attention to early childhood, and articles on the importance of fostering development during the early years often appeared in newspapers and magazines.

Furthermore, the influence of Bruner's (1960) *The Process of Education* should not be overlooked. It was interpreted as support for extending the teaching of subjects "downward" in the grades, the result for reading being that more of an emphasis was placed on getting children ready to read as soon as possible rather than merely sitting back and waiting.

Finally, a significant social revolution underway in the United States—the black movement—reinforced the new emphasis on environmental factors. From a variety of fields, supporters of social equality argued that large numbers of black children and children of other "minority" backgrounds came from "culturally disadvantaged" home situations and that to wait until such children got to school to help them overcome the disadvantage, much less to adopt a "delay-until-they're-ready" approach to reading readiness, was to condemn such children to educational failure. Early intervention was regarded as a key in helping achieve equality for all children.

Thus, the educational world turned its back on the neural ripening position of the maturationalists in favor of an interventionist posture. Programs such as Head Start, for instance, were intimately tied to the new emphasis on doing something about environmental factors early in the child's life so that development in an area like reading could be facilitated. The upshot of this move to conscientiously *prepare* children was actually a trend toward more direct instruction in a predetermined curriculum for early childhood and kindergarten programs. For example, although Head Start programs could have been designed along a continuum ranging from "free play" to structured approaches, most eschewed the discovery-oriented approach in favor of a moderate to high degree of structure (Lundsteen & Tarrow, 1981, pp. 62–65). In the schools, the reading readiness program and the notion of the need to teach prerequisites for reading became fixed. Furthermore, using reading readiness programs in the kindergarten literacy curriculum became a widespread practice.

The reading readiness program which became so firmly entrenched during the 1960s remains extremely prevalent in the 1980s. Every major publisher of a basal reading scheme has a readiness level for its program which is often used in kindergartens and first grades. These reading readiness programs have largely remained the same throughout the years. Generally included are activities to develop auditory discrimination and auditory memory; visual discrimination and visual memory; letter names and sounds; and word recognition as well as more general skills. Contemporary versions often provide training in the "language of instruction" as well. Also, the modern readiness program takes great care to detail explicitly how each readiness skill fits into the overall scope and sequence plan for the basal series. In accordance with this orientation and because of the current emphasis on criterion-referenced measurement of achievement, typically throughout a readiness program there is considerable testing for mastery of the particular skills which are taught.

Overall it can be said that the readiness paradigm, as institutionalized by schools and publishers in many countries of the world, implies the following:

1. Instruction in reading can only begin efficiently when children have mastered a set of basic skills prerequisite to reading. The most important skills predict subsequent achievement most strongly.
2. The area of instructional concern is reading. It is implied that composing and other aspects of writing (except for letter formation—or handwriting) should be delayed until children learn to read.
3. Sequenced mastery of skills forms the basis of reading as a subject to be taught; instruction focuses almost exclusively on the formal aspects of reading and generally ignores the functional uses of reading.
4. What went on before formal instruction is irrelevant, so long as sufficient teaching and practice presented in a logical sequence are provided when instruction begins.
5. Children all pass through a scope and sequence of readiness and reading skills, and their progress up this hierarchy should be carefully monitored by periodic formal testing.

READING READINESS: IN SUMMARY

Within 20 years of the introduction of reading readiness in the 1925 *N.S.S.E. Yearbook*, Emmett Betts would say, "Today the term 'reading readiness' is on the tip of almost every teacher's tongue. Furthermore, it is familiar to many parents" (Betts, 1946, p. 103). Thus, the concept of reading readiness and the programs and testing associated with it have been an integral part of educational practice for almost a half century. As the preceding historical overview has indicated, the concept itself has been modified over the years; however, in the 1980s reading readiness is firmly entrenched as the dominant approach to beginning literacy instruction.

The idea of reading readiness, as evidenced in the curricula of schools and preschools and in publishers' materials, affects people's thinking about literacy development in two especially significant ways. First, it leads them to conceptualize the early childhood period (and the behaviors of the child during this period) as precursor to "real" reading or writing, implying that only after the child has mastered the various subskills of reading readiness does the real part begin. Second, and closely related, it tells teacher and parent that learning to read and write begins in a schoollike setting where these readiness skills can be taught. Thus, materials designed for use with young children either in home, school, or school-like settings are inevitably modeled on formal, sequenced, direct instruction.

It might be said that reading readiness was a good concept that got applied in a bad way. There should be no quarrel with the notion that certain prior knowledge, language facility, cognitive development, and attitudinal orientations toward literacy all probably facilitate the child's learning to write and read in school-like settings. However, the reading readiness program is built upon a logical analysis of literacy skills from an adult perspective rather than upon a developmental perspective.

Research and theory in recent years indicate that we cannot cling to the conception of literacy currently institutionalized through curricula, test publishers, and schools under the name of reading readiness, if we hope to provide the best possible instruction during the child's first years in school. Current research overwhelmingly indicates the need to reconceptualize reading readiness, and indeed a new developmental perspective is in evidence. Developmental perspectives recognize children's thinking as being qualitatively different from, yet growing toward, adult modes and therefore attempt to provide instruction in accordance with a child's developing knowledges.

FROM READING READINESS TO EMERGENT LITERACY: THE CHALLENGE

For years the classroom experiences of many kindergarten and early childhood educators and results from research projects such as Durkin's (1966) have indicated that the reading readiness paradigm was theoretically and practically inappropriate. However, it has only been within the past decade that a substantial and unified challenge to the traditional approach has arisen.

The roots of this challenge can be traced to two broader trends: (a) cognitive approaches to issues of learning and development and their increasing influence on educationally related research and classroom practice, and (b) renewed interest in the first few years of life as a period of critical significance in development. These trends pointed to the importance of looking carefully at children during the early years when the foundations for all development are being laid, and to regarding children as active participants in learning–hypothesis generators and problem solvers–rather than as passive recipients of information.

The influence of these trends is nowhere more apparent than in the field of psychology of language. The year 1956 is generally regarded as marking the birth of the "cognitive sciences" (Bruner, 1983). By 1960 the Center for Cognitive Studies had been established at Harvard, and during the 1960s and early 1970s, researchers increasingly turned their attention to the close observation of young children. They developed sophisticated research techniques, adapted from a variety of disciplinary fields and intended to shed light on the mental processes involved in learning language. In short, there formed an area of study identified as *language acquisition research* that sought to describe the strategies employed in learning and using language.

This research found that, indeed, the child is an active hypothesis-generating language user. Eventually the child-as-hypothesis-tester description was modified toward the notion of child-as-constructor-of-language. In all, cognitive models proved to be far more successful at accounting for first-language learning than were stimulus–response models. Reasoning that reading was also a language process, people began to apply a similar theoretical/research approach in the attempt to understand early reading better. Findings from the language acquisition research (which had focused entirely on *oral* language) were used by researchers who hypothesized that oral language and written language proficiency might develop in parallel ways.

In the field of education, Marie Clay was a pioneer in examining young children's reading and writing in light of language acquisition research. Up to this point, ages one through five were generally regarded as the period during which oral language and reading readiness were developed, with writing and reading starting for almost all children only after they entered school. Clay began her research with 5-year-old entrants in New Zealand (Clay, 1967). Her main objective was to provide better descriptions of the early reading behaviors of children so that children with reading difficulties could be identified as early as possible. The 5-year-olds received deliberate instruction in reading, but the method used was one which "stressed fluency, meaning and 'learning as one reads,' with only slight attention to letter-sound associations and learning a basic sight vocabulary" (Clay, 1967, p. 12). This early research showed that young children could engage in important reading behaviors such as visual sensitivity to letter and word forms, appropriate directional movements, self-correction, and synchronized matching of spoken word units with written word units. Clay (1967) concluded, "There is nothing in this research that suggests that contact with printed language forms should be withheld from any five-year-old child on the ground that he is immature" (p. 24).

This work seems to have brought Clay "naturally" in touch with reading during the *pre*school years as well. Certainly the influence of Dolores Durkin's studies of early readers (Durkin, 1966) on Clay's work is in evidence. In addition, Judith

Begg and Clay (1968) published "A Note on Teaching a Preschooler to Read: Some Problems of Evaluation" shortly thereafter. The first edition of *Reading: The Patterning of Complex Behaviour* (Clay, 1972) also contained considerable reference to preschool reading experience and brought to light how Clay felt her thoughts on reading development during the early years differed from the traditional concept of reading readiness.

> . . . the transformation [to understanding the links between oral and written language] at the early reading stage takes place only in the presence of print and when the child actively seeks to discover how oral and written language are related. . . . It is the need to transform preschool skills into new ways of responding that . . . makes early reading behaviour a matter of learning and discredits the "growth from within" concept of readiness. In this book the new entrant stage of being introduced to printed language will be referred to as the "early reading behaviour stage" and the terms "preparation for reading" or "reading readiness training" or "prereading" will be avoided. (pp. 5–6)

Clearly, though perhaps not surprisingly for the 1970s, Clay rejected the neural ripening philosophy. However, her rejection of *prereading* and *reading readiness* indicated that although she recognized that becoming literate implies discontinuities in development because it requires the child to develop new ways of responding, there are important continuities between what she termed the child's *emergent literacy* (Clay, 1966) behaviors and those behaviors employed when the child is able to read independently.

Finally, we see another important seed in this volume that would eventually grow into a separate book (*What Did I Write?* 1975): the inclusion of some writing samples from young children and discussion of their significance for literacy development. Though the book is definitely one about reading, the attention to writing portends the general move by researchers toward focusing on the relationships between writing and reading in early literacy development.

Reading: The Patterning of Complex Behaviour (1972) was a significant volume for several reasons. First, it emphasized the importance of the early childhood period in the development of literacy. In particular, it illustrated that there was a great deal for researchers and teachers to learn by examining what children do with books and reading and writing, even though the children cannot yet read or write in the conventional sense. Finally, in this book the process of distinguishing between an emergent literacy approach to literacy development in early childhood and a reading readiness approach was in evidence.

At the same time that Clay was conducting her work, Yetta Goodman was examining the reading processes of beginning readers in the United States (Y. Goodman, 1967). Kenneth Goodman's model of the reading process (K. Goodman, 1967, 1968) was gaining widespread acceptance as a more adequate description of fluent reading than previous conceptualizations. Yetta Goodman hypothesized that the model was also appropriate for describing beginning reading. In the course of completing her doctoral dissertation research with first graders (Y. Goodman, 1967), Goodman found that even children who would be described as "at risk" for becoming competent readers had knowledge about many aspects of reading: They knew how to handle books and they understood the directionality of written language and the function of print in a book, for example. As she said later, "It slowly became obvious to me that children's discoveries about literacy in a literate society such as ours must begin much earlier than at school age" (Y. Goodman, 1984, p. 102). This realization and the influence of Dolores Durkin's studies of early readers (Durkin, 1966) prompted her to look at even younger children.

Thus, the early environmental print awareness studies were begun. Labels, signs, and logos common to preschool children's environments were presented to the children in varying degrees of contextualization to check on their awareness of environmental print. Results from these studies indicated that the roots of the reading process are established very early in life. Furthermore, the results supported the notions that function precedes form in learning to read and that there is a "movement from learning to read printed symbols in familiar situational contexts toward more reliance on language contexts" (Goodman & Goodman, 1979, p. 145). The print awareness work led the Goodmans to their conclusion that learning to read is natural in a literate society.

This work and subsequent research by Goodman and her students (see her chapter in this volume) directly contradicted many of the principles upon which the traditional reading readiness approach was based. The studies of Clay and Goodman from an educational perspective, and the work of others from the fields of psychology and linguistics inspired many researchers interested in child development and education to approach the study of the writing and reading of very young children. Hallmarks of this new approach have been its cognitive and developmental underpinnings. In recent years researchers have organized their work under rubrics such as *invented spelling* (e.g., Chomsky, 1971; Henderson & Beers, 1980; Read, 1970); *linguistic awareness* (or *metalinguistic awareness*) in young children (e.g., Berthoud-Papandropoulou, 1978; Downing & Oliver, 1973–1974; Ehri, 1979; Sulzby & Otto, 1982) and *print awareness* (e.g., Goodman & Altwerger, 1981; Harste, Woodward, & Burke, 1984; Hiebert, 1981; Mason, 1980). The researchers have employed a variety of techniques to gather information—ethnographic (e.g., Heath, 1980, 1983; Taylor, 1983; Teale, Estrada, & Anderson, 1981), case study (Baghban, 1984; Bissex, 1980; Sulzby, 1983) and structured interviews (e.g., Ferreiro, 1978, 1981; Harste et al., 1984; Sulzby, 1981, 1985a). They have studied children of various ethnic and social backgrounds (Ferreiro, 1981; Ferreiro & Gomez Palalcio, 1982; Goodman, this volume; Heath, 1983; Teale et al., 1981). And finally, they have conducted work in both home and school settings. The study of literacy development in early childhood has expanded to the point where in the mid-1980s we can truly say that the new perspective has become legitimized as a field attracting wide interest.

Furthermore, the conclusions emanating from the body of research cast serious doubt on the tenets outlined earlier which underlie the concept of reading readiness. Specifically, what has been learned over the last few years about literacy development in early childhood leads to the following conclusions:

1. Literacy development begins long before children start formal instruction. Children use legitimate reading and writing behaviors in the informal settings of home and community. The search for skills which predict subsequent achievement has been misguided because the onset of literacy has been misconceived.

2. *Literacy* development is the appropriate way to describe what was called *reading* readiness: The child develops as a *writer/reader*. The notion of reading preceding writing, or vice versa, is a misconception. Listening, speaking, reading, and writing abilities (as aspects of language—both oral and written) develop concurrently and interrelatedly, rather than sequentially.

3. Literacy develops in real-life settings for real-life activities in order to "get things done." Therefore, the functions of literacy are as integral a part of learning about writing and reading during early childhood as are the forms of literacy.

4. Children are doing critical cognitive work in literacy development during the years from birth to six.

5. Children learn written language through active engagement with their world. They interact socially with adults in writing and reading situations; they explore print on their own, and they profit from modeling of literacy by significant adults, particularly their parents.

6. Although children's learning about literacy can be described in terms of generalized stages, children can pass through these stages in a variety of ways and at different ages. Any attempts to "scope and sequence" instruction should take this developmental variation into account.

We said earlier in this introduction that we felt a term was needed to summarize/ capture this new paradigm for understanding early childhood reading and writing. We have decided to employ the term *emergent literacy,* to the best of our knowledge a notion first developed by Marie Clay (1966) in her doctoral dissertation research. Our choice of *emergent literacy* was made for a variety of reasons, which can be explained by examining the significance of each of the words comprising the term. Let us start with *literacy.* In research and teaching both, considerably less attention has been paid to writing than to reading (Graves, 1978), but the writing development of preschool children in particular has been neglected. However, we can now see a growing realization that in order to understand reading we must understand writing, and vice versa.

In 1970 Charles Read completed his pioneering study of young children's categorization of speech sounds as evidenced by invented spellings found in their compositions. Read's research prompted Carol Chomsky (1971) to suggest that young children should "write first, read later" and stimulated considerable work in young children's spelling in subsequent years (see Henderson & Beers, 1980). In general, this work was concerned with sound–symbol correspondences and orthographic patterns in written language rather than with children encoding intended meanings or showing evidence of composing in their writing.

Following this period, numerous parents, researchers, and teachers produced evidence that young children do indeed write, whether it be by "scribble," strings of letters, invented spelling, or other means of representation, some manifestations of which include drawing. In 1975 Marie Clay published *What Did I Write?*, cataloging a series of principles evidenced in children's early writing. Subsequent years have seen more and more attention being given to children's ability to compose text (see Farr, 1984, 1985). Even the mechanics of writing have been reexamined. In addition to spelling, letter formation has been found to emerge conceptually rather than just as rote imitation (see Simner, 1981; and note the renewed attention to Hildreth, 1932, 1936), and space as a marker for word boundaries shows evidence of being learned through a process of hypothesis-guided construction (Clay, 1975, 1979; Sulzby, 1983).

Glenda Bissex's *GNYS AT WRK: A Child Learns to Write and Read* was published in 1980. Its subtitle captures the tenor of the present times. Literacy—writing as well as reading rather than reading by itself—is what is of interest. The two processes develop in coordination with each other. Bissex, for example, chose to focus on how her child treated himself as a writer. But reading is integrally involved in becoming a writer. When children write, they read their own texts and thereby monitor their production. In fact, we now have substantial evidence to indicate that there exists a dynamic relation between writing and reading, because each influences the other in the course of development (Ferreiro & Teberosky, 1982; Sulzby, 1983) and that reading comprehension is engaged in during writing (through reading one's own writing) and is not a trivial matter (Sulzby, 1983, 1985b, 1985c).

In fact, research in early writing has helped us rethink research in early reading. Now we know that we must understand both processes if we are fully to understand written language development in the young child. Thus, the word *literacy* is of extreme importance for explaining the perspective from which the researchers represented in this volume are operating.

The term *emergent* also has special significance. Let us make clear that the term is not without considerable history. *Emergent* has long been used in the fields of philosophy, sociology, biology, and developmental psychology. Though having somewhat different connotations in each of these disciplines, it contains some core features which are elegantly suited to describe literacy in the young child. First, *emergent* connotes development rather than stasis; it signifies something in the process of becoming, as is implied by Mead (1932). As we have argued earlier, the first years of the child's life represent a period when legitimate reading and writing development are taking place. These behaviors and knowledges are not *pre-* anything, as the term *prereading* suggests. Nor is it accurate to regard this as stage 0 (zero) in literacy development as Chall (1983) proposes in her scheme of reading stages. Such a label suggests that only at stage 1, after about 6 years of age, does initial reading, i.e., "real" reading (or writing), begin. But as researchers have increasingly focused on literacy learning in very young children, more and more of these scholars have come to the conclusion that it is not reasonable to point to *a* time in a child's life when literacy begins. Rather, at whatever point we look, we see children *in the process of becoming* literate, as the term *emergent* indicates.

This is not to say, however, that reading or writing conventionally is a process different in kind from what went on in emergent literacy, before the child could write and read in the conventional sense. Throughout children's early literacy experiences, many of the motives, functions, and uses associated with writing and reading and the psycholinguistic processes employed in writing and reading are identical to those adults and other literate persons (Harste et al., 1984; Heath, 1980, 1983; Sulzby, 1981, 1983; Taylor, 1983; Teale, this volume).

At the same time we use *emergent* to suggest that development is taking place, that there is something new emerging in the child that had not "been" there before. Growth in writing and reading comes from within the child and as the result of environmental stimulation. Children do *become* literate (whereas they were not always literate), and it is this sense that *emergent* also suggests a discontinuity with what had been before. This use of *emergent* as implying both continuity and discontinuity is consistent with uses of the term in philosophy (Mead, 1932), developmental psychology and language acquisition research (Sugarman, 1983; Werner, 1957; Werner & Kaplan, 1963), and sociology (McHugh, 1968). It emphasizes that in development children are learning—changing and refining their motives and strategies and even developing new ones—but that learning builds through processes of assimilation and accommodation.

Furthermore, the growth that has been observed occurs without the necessity for formal teaching. Instead, it results from the use of writing and reading in the everyday contexts of home and community.

Finally, we have employed the term *emergent* because it is "forward looking." It suggests development, that there is a direction in which children are progressing. In the first few years of life we can see that even though development proceeds in fits and starts, with periods of vigorous growth and periods during which the child seems to be consolidating knowledge, children are continuously learning to write and read, moving toward the time during which they will do so conventionally.

We have not adopted *emergent* to defend some particular position regarding the details of the child's development. Rather, we feel it is useful as a blanket term that characterizes the manner in which young children are learning more and more about the culturally elaborated writing system that is used around them.

THIS VOLUME

We see all the contributors to this volume as conceptualizing young children's reading and writing from an emergent literacy paradigm. Though they may not use the actual term, the authors of the chapters which follow all represent a new perspective which stresses that *legitimate, conceptual, developmental* literacy learning is occurring during the first years of a child's life. That is to say, the point of view which comes forth from these chapters is that children's early reading and writing behaviors are not pre- anything, but are integral parts of a language process which is in a state of becoming. Young children's "scribbling" or "reenactments" of books may be unconventional by adult standards, but such actions play important roles in the child's continuing development.

The reader will no doubt note that the authors represented herein differ on certain details, often important details, about early childhood literacy development. Nevertheless, the overall stress on the importance and legitimacy of this period of development and the assumption that literacy is social, psycholinguistic, conceptual, and developmental in nature constitute a perspective which challenges the reader to go beyond the educational status quo and view literacy for the young child as emergent rather than either a product of maturation or a set of skills to be taught after the reading readiness objectives have been mastered.

The particular issues which occupy the authors are ones central to working out a sound theory and detailed descriptions of emergent literacy. Perhaps foremost are the questions related to development itself. How can children's progress in literacy best be described? Is the notion of developmental stages useful? What is the nature of individual differences within general patterns of development?

Closely tied to these questions is the issue of sources of development. It is clear that during the early childhood period some literacy is initiated by the adult while some is initiated by the child. The contributions of the social environment (parent–child interaction, adult modeling of writing and reading) and of the child's independent investigations of written language to development are topics of central importance in the research.

We know also that writing and reading play different roles in different families and, as a result, that young children have quantitatively and qualitatively different experiences with print. A primary objective of research in early childhood literacy development is identifying the factors that account for these differences. Therefore, investigating the roles which social, cultural, and linguistic factors play in the child's literacy experience also interests researchers greatly.

Cutting across all of these questions and areas of investigation are issues related to the methodology employed in researching young children's literacy development. Researchers operating from what we are describing as an emergent literacy perspective generally are endeavoring to keep their investigations naturalistic and, from a language perspective, holistic so that ecological validity will be maintained. But there is also concern among many researchers with issues of generalizability of results. Therefore, attempts have been made to manipulate within the ecological setting and conduct, as it were, "naturalistic experiments" (along the lines of Scribner's, 1984, naturalistic experiments on mathematical reasoning).

And finally comes the upshot of the research: the applications of the results. We think it fair to say that all of the authors represented in this volume are deeply concerned with the interface between research and policy, whether it be day care, preschool, or school policy, home intervention policy, or larger issues of governmental/social policy. In the chapters that follow each author has something to say about the implications of the research for policy. Many times the recommendations that are made challenge certain classroom practices which are currently widespread. Other times the authors offer provocative conclusions which prompt reexamination of long-held beliefs upon which educational or social programs have rested. In these and other ways the authors have attempted explicitly to link research and practice.

Thus, the chapters in this volume examine the beginnings of literacy from a number of perspectives and in a variety of ways. However, the thread which runs through them and which separates these authors' orientation to literacy development in early childhood from much previous work on young children's reading and writing can be characterized as an *emergent literacy* viewpoint. We feel that this perspective can reveal a great deal about children's literacy development during the first few years of life. Furthermore, such insights offer valuable information to aid in the attempt to achieve the objective of universal literacy.

REFERENCES

Ausubel, D.P. (1961). Learning by discovery: Rationale and mystique. *Bulletin of the National Association of Secondary-School Principals, 45,* 18–58.

Baghban, M.J.M. (1984). *Our daughter learns to read and write: A case study from birth to three.* Newark, DE: International Reading Association.

Berthoud-Papandropoulou, I. (1978). An experimental study of children's ideas about language. In A. Sinclair, R.J. Jarvella, & W.J.M. Levelt (Eds.), *The child's conception of language* (pp. 55–82). New York: Springer-Verlag.

Betts, E.A. (1946). *Foundations of reading instruction.* New York: America Book.

Bissex, G.L. (1980) *GNYS AT WRK: A child learns to write and read.* Cambridge, MA: Harvard University Press.

Bloom, B.S. (1964). *Stability and change in human characteristics.* New York: Wiley.

Bruner, J.S. (1960). *The process of education.* Cambridge, MA: Harvard University Press.

Bruner, J.S. (1983). *In search of mind.* New York: Harper & Row.

Chall, J.S. (1983). Stages of reading development. New York: McGraw-Hill.

Chomsky, C. (1971). Write now, read later. *Childhood Education, 47,* 296–299.

Clay, M.M. (1966). *Emergent reading behaviour.* Unpublished doctoral dissertation, University of Auckland, New Zealand.

Clay, M.M. (1967). The reading behavior of five-year-old children: A research report. *New Zealand Journal of Educational Studies, 2,* 11–31.

Clay, M.M. (1972). *Reading: The patterning of complex behaviour.* Auckland, New Zealand: Heineman Educational.

Clay, M.M. (1975). *What did I write?* Auckland, New Zealand: Heinemann Educational.

Clay, M.M. (1979). *Reading: The patterning of complex behaviour* (2nd ed.). Auckland, New Zealand: Heinemann Educational.

Cole, L. (1938). *The improvement of reading: With special reference to remedial instruction.* New York: Farrar & Rinehart.

Coltheart, M. (1979). When can children learn to read—And when should they be taught? In T.G. Waller & G.E. MacKinnon (Eds.), *Reading research. Advances in theory and practice, Vol. 1.* New York: Academic Press.

Dennis, W. (1941). Infant development under conditions of restricted practice and of minimal social stimulation. *Genetic Psychology Monographs, 23,* 143–189.

Downing, J. & Oliver, P. (1973–1974). The child's conception of "word." *Reading Research Quarterly, 9,* 568–582.

Durkin, D. (1966). *Children who read early.* New York: Teachers College Press.

Durkin, D. (1968). When should children begin to read? In H.M. Robinson (Ed.), *Innovation and change in reading instruction: The sixty-seventh yearbook of the National Society for the Study of Education (Part II).* Chicago, IL: The National Society for the Study of Education.

Durkin, D. (1970). What does research say about the time to begin reading instruction? *Journal of Educational Research, 64,* 52–56.

Ehri, L.C. (1979). Linguistic insight: Threshold of reading acquisition. In T.G. Waller & G.E. MacKinnon (Eds.) *Reading research: Advances in theory and practice, Vol. 1.* New York: Academic Press.

Farr, M. (1984, April). *State of the art: Children's early writing development.* Paper presented at American Educational Research Association Annual Meeting, New Orleans, LA.

Farr, M. (Ed.) (1985). *Advances in writing research,* Vol. 1: *Children's early writing development.* Norwood, NJ: Ablex.

Ferreiro, E. (1978). What is written in a written sentence? A developmental answer. *Journal of Education, 160,* 25–39.

Ferreiro, E. (1981). The relationship between oral and written language: The children's viewpoints. In Y.M. Goodman, M.M. Haussler, & D.S. Strickland (Comps. & Eds.), *Oral and written language development research: Impact on the schools.* Urbana, IL: National Council of Teachers of English.

Ferreiro, E., & Gomez Palacio, M. (1982). *Análisis de las perturbaciones en el proceso aprendizaje de la lectoescritura* [Analysis of variations in the process of literacy development]. (5 volumes). Mexico City: Office of the Director General of Special Education.

Ferreiro, E., & Teberosky, A. (1982). *Literacy before schooling.* Exeter, NH: Heinemann Educational.

Gates, A.I. (1937). The necessary mental age for beginning reading. *Elementary School Journal, 37,* 497–508.

Gates, A.I., & Bond, G.L. (1936). Reading readiness: A study of factors determining success and failure in beginning reading. *Teachers College Record, 37,* 679–85.

Gates, A.I., Bond, G.L., & Russell, D.H. (1939). *Methods of determining reading readiness.* New York: Bureau of Publications, Teachers College, Columbia University.

Gesell, A. (1925). *The mental growth of the pre-school child.* New York: Macmillan.

Gesell, A. (1928). *Infancy and human growth.* New York: Macmillan.

Gesell, A. (1940). *The first five years of life.* New York: Harper & Bros.

Goodman, K.S. (1967). Reading: A psycholinguistic guessing game. *Journal of the Reading Specialist, 4,* 126–135.

Goodman, K.S. (1968). *Study of children's behavior while reading orally.* (Final Report, Project No. S 425). Washington, DC: U.S. Department of Health, Education, and Welfare.

Goodman, K.S., & Goodman, Y.M. (1979). Learning to read is natural. In L.B. Resnick & P. Weaver (Eds.), *Theory and practice of early reading.* Hillsdale, NJ: Erlbaum.

Goodman, Y.M. (1967). *A psycholinguistic description of observed oral reading phenomena in selected young beginning readers.* Unpublished doctoral dissertation, Wayne State University, Detroit.

Goodman, Y.M. (1980). The roots of literacy. In M.P. Douglass (Ed.), *Claremont Reading Conference Forty-fourth Yearbook.* Claremont, CA: The Claremont Reading Conference.

Goodman, Y.M. (1984). The development of initial literacy. In H. Goelman, A. Oberg, & F. Smith (Eds.), *Awakening to literacy.* Exeter, NH: Heinemann Educational.

Goodman, Y.M., & Altwerger, B. (1981). *Print awareness in pre-school children: A working paper. A study of the development of literacy in preschool children.* Occasional Paper No. 4, Program in Language and Literacy, University of Arizona, Tucson.

Graves, D.H. (1978). *Balance the basics: Let them write.* A Report to the Ford Foundation. New York: Ford Foundation.

Harris, A.J. (1940). *How to increase reading ability.* New York: Longmans Green.

Harrison, M.L. (1936). *Reading readiness.* Boston, MA: Houghton Mifflin.

Harste, J.C., Woodward, V.A., & Burke, C.L. (1984). *Language stories and literacy lessons.* Portsmouth, NH: Heinemann Educational.

Heath, S.B. (1980). The functions and uses of literacy. *Journal of Communication, 30,* 123–133.

Heath, S.B. (1983). *Ways with words: Language, life and work in communities and classrooms.* Cambridge, MA: Cambridge University Press.

Heath, S.B., & Thomas, C. (1984). The achievement of preschool literacy for mother and child. In H.

Goelman, A. Oberg, & F. Smith (Eds.), *Awakening to literacy*. Exeter, NH: Heinemann Educational.

Henderson, E.H. & Beers, J. (Eds.) (1980). *Developmental and cognitive aspects of learning to spell.* Newark, DE: International Reading Association.

Hiebert, E.H. (1981). Developmental patterns and interrelationships of preschool children's print awareness. *Reading Research Quarterly, 16*, 236–260.

Hildreth, G. (1932). The success of young children in letter and number construction. *Child Development, 3*, 1–14.

Hildreth, G. (1936). Developmental sequences in name writing. *Child Development, 7*, 291–303.

Huey, E.B. (1908). *The psychology and pedagogy of reading.* New York: Macmillan.

Hunt, J.McV. (1961). *Intelligence and experience.* New York: Ronald Press.

Hunt, J.McV. (1964). The psychological basis for using preschool enrichment as an antidote for cultural deprevation. *Merrill Palmer Quarterly, 10*, 209–248.

Iredell, H. (1898). Eleanor learns to read. *Education, 19*, 233–238.

Kibbe, D.E. (1939). *Improving the reading program in Wisconsin schools.* Madison, WI: Department of Public Instruction.

Kuhn, T.S. (1962). *The structure of scientific revolution.* Chicago, IL: The University of Chicago Press.

Lamoreaux, L.A., & Lee, D.M. (1943). *Learning to read through experience.* New York: Appleton-Century-Crofts.

Lundsteen, S.W., & Tarrow, N.B. (1981). *Guiding young children's learning.* New York: McGraw-Hill.

Mason, J. (1980). When do children begin to read: An exploration of four-year-old children's letter and word reading competencies. *Reading Research Quarterly, 15*, 203–227.

Mathews, M.M. (1966). *Teaching to read: Historically considered.* Chicago, IL: University of Chicago Press.

McCall, W.A. (1923). *How to experiment in education.* New York: Macmillan.

McGraw, M.B. (1935). *Growth: A study of Johnny and Jimmy.* New York: Appleton-Century.

McHugh, P. (1968). *Defining the situation: The organization of meaning in social interaction.* Indianapolis, IN: Bobbs-Merrill.

Mead, G.H. (1932). *The philosophy of the present.* Chicago, IL: Open Court.

Morphett, M.V., & Washburne, C. (1931). When should children begin to read? *Elementary School Journal, 31*, 496–508.

National Society for the Study of Education. (1925). Report of the National Committee on Reading. *24th Year Book of the National Society for the Study of Education.* Bloomington, IN: Public School Publishing.

Read, C. (1970). *Children's perceptions of the sounds of English: Phonology from three to six.* Unpublished doctoral dissertation, Harvard University, Boston, MA.

Read, C. (1975). *Children's categorization of speech sounds in English.* Urbana, IL: National Council of Teachers of English.

Scribner, S. (1984). Studying working intelligence. In B. Rogoff & J. Lave (Eds.), *Everyday cognition: Its development in social contexts.* Boston, MA: Harvard University Press.

Simner, M.L. (1981, April). *Printing errors in kindergarten and the prediction of academic performance.* Paper presented at the Biennial Meeting of the Society for Research in Child Development, Boston, MA.

Sugarman, S. (1983). Empirical versus logical issues in the transition from prelinguistic to linguistic communication. In R.M. Golinkoff (Ed.), *The transition from prelinguistic to linguistic communication.* Hillsdale, NJ: Erlbaum.

Sulzby, E. (1981). *Kindergarteners begin to read their own compositions: Beginning readers' developing knowledges about written language project.* Final report to the Research Foundation of the National Council of Teachers of English. Evanston, IL: Northwestern University.

Sulzby, E. (1983). *Beginning readers' developing knowledges about written language.* Final report to the National Institute of Education (NIE-G-80-0176). Evanston, IL: Northwestern University.

Sulzby, E. (1985a). Children's emergent reading of favorite storybooks: A developmental study. *Reading Research Quarterly, 20,* 458–481.

Sulzby, E. (1985b). Kindergarteners as writers and readers. In M. Farr (Ed.), *Advances in writing research, Vol. 1: Children's early writing development.* Norwood, NJ: Ablex.

Sulzby, E. (1986). Children's elicitation and use of metalinguistic knowledge about "word" during literacy acquisition. In D.B. Yaden & W.S. Templeton (Eds.), *Metalinguistic awareness and beginning literacy: Conceptualizing what it means to read and write.* Portsmouth, NH: Heinemann Educational.

Sulzby, E., & Otto, B. (1982). "Text" as an object of metalinguistic knowledge: A study of literacy development. *First Language, 3,* 181–199.

Sulzby, E. & Teale, W.H. (1983). *Young children's storybook reading: Longitudinal study of parent–child interaction and children's independent functioning.* Proposal to the Spencer Foundaton. Evanston, IL: Northwestern University.

Taylor, D. (1983). *Family literacy: Young children learning to read and write.* Exeter, NH. Heinemann Educational.

Teale, W.H., Estrada, E., & Anderson, A.B. (1981). How preschoolers interact with written communication. In M. Kamil (Ed.), *Directions in reading: Research and instruction. Thirtieth Yearbook of the National Reading Conference.* Washington, DC: The National Reading Conference.

Werner, H. (1957). The concept of development from a comparative and organismic point of view. In D.B. Harris (Ed.), *The concept of development.* Minneapolis, MN: University of Minnesota Press.

Werner, H. & Kaplan, B. (1963). *Symbol formation.* New York: Wiley.

Children Coming to Know Literacy

By Yetta M. Goodman*
University of Arizona

Yetta Goodman's metaphor of the roots of literacy has helped to focus attention on the beginnings of writing and reading, and it has provided a conceptual scheme for understanding the nature and process of literacy development in early childhood. In this chapter, Goodman has integrated her research with that of her students and colleagues in order to elucidate further the roots of literacy metaphor and to extend it across children of various sociocultural, linguistic, and ethnic backgrounds.

LITERACY DEVELOPMENT

Literacy is a cultural phenomenon. It develops as society has a need for language communication across time and space. It expands as society becomes more complex and needs literacy to perpetuate its history, its economy, its politics, its education, its literature, its religions and philosophies, its recreation, and whatever other functions it can serve.

Children in a literate society grow up with literacy as an integral part of their personal, familial, and social histories. Interacting with their literate environment, children invent their own literacies, and their inventions often parallel the inventions of literacy by society as a whole. Eleanor Duckworth (1978) has discussed the significance of children's inventions in this way:

> I see no difference in mind between wonderful ideas that many other people have already had, and wonderful ideas that nobody has yet happened upon. That is, the nature of creative intellectual acts remains the same, whether it is an infant who for the first time makes the connection between seeing things and reaching for them . . . or an astronomer who develops a new theory of the creation of the universe. (p. 28)

Written language is one expression of language, and is the major medium through which literacy is represented. The different functions literacy serve as a symbolic system for humans and the values it holds for the members of a society will affect the way in which children learn written language. Because it is language, children will learn it in ways similar to oral language. However, because it is written, the ways in which written language differs from oral language in terms of its

---

*With Ann Marek, who helped with writing and integrating the various aspects of the research.

different functions, purposes, and forms will influence its development in young children.

Over the last few years, I have presented research findings and conclusions about literacy development in children (Goodman, 1980, 1982, 1983, 1984; Goodman & Altwerger, 1981). The purpose of this chapter is to update my previous statements by integrating results from research projects which have used procedures similar to mine and which help me support and expand conclusions that I have reached. This triangulation of research data from 78 children, representing different populations and settings, provides "conclusions (which) are more stable than any of the vantage points from which they were triangulated" (Guba, 1978, p. 64).

I will organize my conclusions around five roots of literacy (Goodman, 1980), which have become for me a metaphor for the beginnings of reading and writing in children. Originally, the metaphor was an attempt to model or organize how reading and writing develop in the young child. Its purpose remains the same, but the metaphor also provides a vehicle to continue to expand and explain my understandings about literacy in the young people of a society. Labels such as "early reading and writing" or "beginning reading and writing" have been unsatisfactory to explain the complexity of the development of literacy in children. Such terms have allowed teachers and curriculum developers to believe that the beginnings of reading and writing can be stated as a specific point in time that is visible and measurable. Even with all the research and anecdotal knowledge about oral language, no one has ever been able to pinpoint the exact moment when a child begins to talk or listen. In the same way, no one knows when a child begins to write or read. The roots of literacy metaphor suggests the complexity of the interaction of functions, forms, and conceptualizations that become part of children's knowledge about literacy as they develop. The metaphor can also be extended to suggest that the roots are deeply buried in the soil of the literate environment. The roots can be studied in the environment in which they occur, but their growth and development are not observable on the ground surface.

I will organize the conclusions of the various research projects as they relate to each of the five roots of literacy. First, however, each research study will be described, followed by data and conclusions from the five research reports.

REVIEW OF PROCEDURES

Each of the studies to be discussed used one or more of the four procedures outlined in Goodman and Altwerger (1981). The procedures were developed in order to gain insight into children's responses to and knowledge about print in their environment, the knowledge children have about book handling, and concepts children have about reading and writing. Each procedure is explained in this section; see Goodman and Altwerger (1981), or Fagan, Jensen, and Cooper (1985) for specific details.

Environmental Print Awareness Procedures: Signs of the Environment

The print awareness tasks have been designed to reveal subjects' abilities to read print in the environment through using the support of contextual cues. Labels, carefully selected to represent common household items and familiar environmental print, are mounted on tag board and presented one at a time to the subjects. Items include cereal, toothpaste, and soup labels; stop and school signs; and McDonald's and Coca-Cola logos, among others.

The actual label is shown to the child first (for example, the entire front panel from a Rice Krispies box). At a second session with the subject, the same labels are presented, retaining their stylized print and color, but with all other surrounding print and designs removed. In a final session, the child is presented with the graphic unit of the label printed by hand in black ink on a white index card. At this third level of decontextualizaton, no supporting context—pictures, design, or color—remains.

Each level of task is presented one week apart, and the order of the items is changed each session.

Preschoolers' Book-Handling Knowledge

The book-handling task was developed by Goodman and Altwerger as an adaptation of the work by Clay (1972) and Doake (1981). Subjects are presented with a child's book and asked to read for the researcher. If the child cannot read or refuses to read, the researcher reads the book for the child. During the reading, questions are asked of the child which provide insight into the child's understanding of directionality, written language terminology (such as *page, letter,* and *word*), book format (such as title page and author's name), and other procedures for reading a book (reading page by page, knowing what print should be read and what print is extraneous, etc.).

Metalinguistic Awareness Interviews: Concepts About Reading and Writing

Interviews are conducted to reveal the child's perceptions and attitudes about reading and writing. Questions which explore the child's concepts about the processes of reading and writing and the functions for written language include: Do you know how to read/write? Is it possible to learn to read by yourself? Why do people read/write?

Subjects' responses are video- or audiotaped and later transcribed and analyzed.

Writing Sample

Part of the interview procedures include eliciting a writing sample from the subject in order to explore young children's use and understanding of print-oriented terminology. Subjects are asked to write and draw, and then they talk about their productions. After the subjects write and draw, the researcher asks the child: Read me what you wrote. Show me your writing. Show me your drawing. Is drawing the same as writing? How are they the same/different?

The child's responses are video- or audiotaped and later transcribed. The actual writing and drawing samples are also collected and become part of the data.

RESEARCH STUDIES

Following are brief abstracts of the five studies which will be triangulated to state my conclusions about the roots of literacy.

Print Awareness in Preschool Children (Goodman and Altwerger, 1981)

This study was conducted in Tucson, Arizona, to investigate preschoolers' responses to print in the environment, their concepts about reading and writing, and their knowledge about print in books. The four evaluations described earlier were administered to each of 11 children. There were four 3-year-olds, three 4-year-olds, and four 5-year-olds. All children attended a day-care center where minimal direct teaching was conducted. The children represented a variety of racial and ethnic backgrounds as well as a range of economic levels. All of them spoke English, and several were bilingual.

Transitions Into Literacy: A Psycholinguistic Analysis of Beginning Reading in Kindergarten and First-Grade Children (Haussler, 1982)

This study was undertaken to "describe and analyze the relationship of the development of print awareness in eight children to their development of beginning reading of texts" (Haussler, 1982, p. 5).

Haussler used the Environmental Print Awareness and Metalinguistic Awareness procedures described previously. To assess book-handling knowledge, she used Marie Clay's (1972) "Concepts About Print" tests, *Stones* (1979), and *Sand* (1972). Though Clay's instruments are similar to those outlined by Goodman and Altwerger, there are some differences. Clay's instruments, for example, include a test of whether children can discern misspelled words (*huose* for *house*) or out-of-order phrases and sentences.

Eight children from a combination kindergarten–first-grade classroom in Tucson, Arizona, were selected for Haussler's study. None of the eight could read connected discourse at the beginning of our study; four were highly "print aware" as measured by the Signs of the Environment task, and the other four were on the lower end of the print awareness scale. The development of these children was followed for a year with data collected in the school setting.

Print Awareness of the Preschool Bilingual Spanish–English Speaking Child (Romero, 1983)

In 1983, Romero conducted her study of the print awareness knowledge of 25 four- and five-year-old Spanish/English bilingual children to see if differences among the children were related to home environmental factors. These children were enrolled in a Title I Parent and Child Education (PACE) program in Tucson Unified School District No. 1. Romero's study included the Signs of the Environment and Preschoolers' Book-Handling Knowledge procedures. She adapted the environmental print awareness task by including packages with Spanish labels. Also, she utilized both a children's book written in English and its Spanish translation for the Book-Handling Knowledge task. Romero used either Spanish or English during her interactions with the children, depending upon their language dominance.

Indices of Literacy in Preschool Children: A Preliminary Research Report (Long, Manning, Manning, Martin, Williams, and Wolfson, 1982)

In this study, the four tasks outlined in Goodman and Altwerger were administered, though there were slight procedural changes. For example, the Signs of the Environment task was modified to include actual objects (such as a two-liter bottle of Coca-Cola and a miniature stop sign). In addition, labels were presented without color in one task.

The subjects in this study included nine 3-year-old black children from the city of Birmingham, Alabama, and eight 3-year-old white children from a rural area of Alabama. The socioeconomic level of these children ranged from lower class to lower-middle class.

Print Awareness in Papago Kindergarten and First-Grade Children (Goodman and Marek, 1984)

This study was undertaken to extend the findings of the Goodman and Altwerger (1981) study to another population of children. The procedures in this study were basically the same as those reported in Goodman and Altwerger. All four tasks were administered to 11 Papago children attending an elementary school on the Papago Indian Reservation. There were five 5-year-olds, five 6-year-olds, and one 7-year-old. The 5-year-olds were in kindergarten; the other children were in first grade.

DEFINITION OF READING AND WRITING

The conclusions which follow are based on my definition of reading and writing. In general, it is now understood that children do not view the world or the concepts within the world in the same way as adults do. The conclusions discussed later are based on the belief that when children are reading and writing they are *making sense out of or through print*. Eventually, readers and writers of English intuitively come to know that written language in English is based upon certain alphabetic principles. However, this knowledge is not a prerequisite for children's learning to read and write. Children perceive written language and provide evidence that they are aware that there is a message in that transaction when they read "brake the car" in response to a stop sign or "toothpaste" in response to a Crest toothpaste label. Children believe that they have written a message for themselves or for others when they produce what looks like a scribble or a string of letters to the observing adult and say, "This says 'I love you, Gramma!'" These children are obviously involved in reading and writing. But researchers, teachers, and others concerned with literacy have tended to ignore these important beginnings in reading and writing, and we do not have a good label to use to describe these literacy events. Terms such as "early reading and writing" or "beginning reading and writing" all represent fairly well-defined concepts in the field which has heretofore ignored certain significant aspects of early literacy. Some scholars have tried new terms such as "emergent reading" (Holdaway, 1979; Sulzby, 1983), and I have offered "the roots of literacy." Regardless of the label, it is important when concerned with issues of literacy development to keep in mind the definition of reading and writing expressed earlier— *human interaction with print when the reader and writer believe that they are making sense of and through written language.*

THE ROOTS OF LITERACY

The beginnings of reading and writing occur in individuals when they develop the awareness that *written language makes sense*. Children show this awareness when they point to some print and ask, "What does that say?" Or, they may write in a scribble or letter string form and show their work to another person, saying, "I wrote a letter for you," or asking, "Will you read this to me?" The children in these settings know that written language symbolizes language or ideas—an invitation, a thank-you, an expression of love, or a story or note to be kept.

Almost simultaneous with this initial discovery that written language expresses meaning, written language users begin to wonder *how written language makes sense*. They become aware that written language takes certain forms and they begin to experiment with those forms. They make some marks to represent themselves or other important persons, and those markings take a different form from their drawings, although they may then embed these written symbols into a house or a scene. Their writing resembles the writing of the adult community, so that a Hebrew 4-year-old and a Bengali 4-year-old produce different kinds of scribble writing. Children already know that most things in their lives are organized systematically, and they begin to look for and experiment with the organization of the complexities of written language. They continuously attempt *to make sense of and through written language* in order to comprehend or express meanings, ideas, or emotions.

As children explore their literate environment, they develop their roots of literacy (Goodman, 1980). These roots include: print awareness in situational contexts; print awareness in connected discourse; functions and forms of writing; oral language about written language; and metalinguistic and metacognitive awareness about written language.

In the discussion that follows, each of these five roots will be explained and supported by conclusions based on a compilation of the data analyzed from the five studies reported earlier.

ROOT I:
DEVELOPMENT OF PRINT AWARENESS IN SITUATIONAL CONTEXTS

The development of print awareness in environmental contexts is the root of literacy most common to all learners and the most well developed in the preschool years. In the print-rich environment of most present cultures, young children are continuously interacting with, organizing, and analyzing the meanings of the visible language. The child develops a model, a world view or a schema, which includes rules about the features of written language in situational contexts.

I believe that the development of knowledge about print embedded in environmental settings is the beginning of reading development, which in most cases goes unnoticed. Neither the children nor their parents are aware that reading has begun, because reading is a receptive process. Like listening, it cannot be observed directly, but can only be inferred from other behaviors. It is not until the child responds to oral language very deliberately and overtly that people believe the child has listened (i.e., understood). Beginning reading, like beginning listening, takes place in a familiar, predictable setting for the child. Since this setting includes color, shape, body movement and familiar oral language, many adults assume that the child is not reading print but using the other contextual cues to make sense. I don't deny that the beginning reader is using other cuing systems. I wish only to argue that the child is also using the print as a cuing system. Listening takes place in a familiar context in which all cuing systems available are used by the child to understand oral language. The written language environment provides similar cuing systems for the child learning to read and write.

At the same time children produce language, they play with pencils and marking pens. They write on envelopes, scraps of paper, and sometimes even on floors and walls. In their play, they are creating writing, which may resemble something we may call scribbles or letter strings but is a serious expression of meaning for the beginning writer.

Print awareness seems to be a common phenomenon among the subjects reported in the research studies described in this chapter. No important differences were reported among different socioeconomic, racial, or linguistic groups. The following conclusions are based on the various studies about print awareness in situational contexts:

1. At least 60% of all of the 3-year-old subjects in these studies can read environmental print when it is embedded in context. By ages four and five, an average of 80% of the subjects could read environmental print.

2. At any point of decontextualization, fewer subjects are able to read environmental print.

3. All subjects read either by providing the exact information related to the print in the item or by stating generic terms for specific names—for example, saying "toothpaste" for "Crest." They also may provide terms for related names such as "McDonald's" for "Burger King" or indicate an item's function in the society,

such as saying "It's good for you" in response to "Milk." Rarely does a subject make remarks completely unrelated to the item. This result suggests the subject's ability not only to decode print to meaning but also to categorize and relate print to life's experiences.

4. An average of 50% of the 4- and 5-year-olds are able to read print in partial context when only the logo is presented to the subjects apart from the entire item.

5. Children tend to use "say" or "says" as the reading word metaphor. That is, they will respond, "That says toothpaste" or ask, "What does that say?" as they point to print.

6. In most cases they do not consider their interaction with print a reading event. Despite their ability to read environmental print, three quarters of the subjects report that they cannot read.

7. There seems to be no difference in the ability to read environmental print based on ethnic, geographic, racial, or linguistic differences. The differences that do occur are due to chronological age, with an increase in the percent of children who read environmental print at successively older ages.

ROOT II:
DEVELOPMENT OF PRINT AWARENESS IN CONNECTED DISCOURSE

Children are involved with connected discourse in written language that is not situationally embedded. This kind of written language includes books, magazines, newspapers, and letters. The variety of written language available to any child will depend on the family and community culture. A particular child's experience with connected written discourse will, therefore, probably be more idiosyncratic than that child's experience with situationally embedded print, which is more universally a part of all children's environments. In some homes, books are readily available, and adults and siblings can be seen reading aloud to each other, talking about events from books. "I'm the middle-sized Billy Goat Gruff today," says Reuben to his father. Or, when he sees a bowl of blueberries on the table, he recites, "Plink, plank, plunk," echoing Little Sal's and Little Bear's experiences in *Blueberries for Sal* by Robert McCloskey.

In many other homes, the daily newspaper may be used to find out about the television programs to watch, to look for bargains at the local supermarket, or to catch up on the latest football scores, or to anticipate the weather conditions. In still other homes, a religious work may occupy a special place on the mantle and may be read aloud daily with great emotional intensity, followed by an interpretive discussion.

Some homes may receive mail which is shared, while in others mail may be opened and read when children are not around to annoy or disturb. Although children's experiences with the reading of books seem to vary, most have a good deal of book experiences by the time they enter first grade. Reading may take place silently, orally, individually or in groups (Heath, 1983; Taylor, 1983). A child may sit in a lap and have a very personal experience with a caregiver and the book being read. Or preschoolers may sit together in a group of 20 or 30 others, listening intently and watching as an adult holds the book in various ways to share the illustrations.

Each kind of material with which a child may transact probably has more than one function. Books may be fun and filled with stories, or they may be read out loud by someone in a formal manner, and the material being read may be incomprehensible to the child. Children learn early whether the connected discourse has significance for their daily life's experiences.

At age 3, some children examine each page of a story as an independent entity, talking about each page as if it were unrelated to the one that came before or the one that comes after. At ages four, five, and six, many children open books in the appropriate direction and know that the story moves along from page to page, even though they still may be unaware of the function of print in books. They show awareness of the directionality of print from left to right across the page, and back to the left again, moving from top to bottom. As they have greater experience with written language in connected discourse, children begin to know that print is the communication device, just as it is in situationally embedded print.

Children begin to read without being fully aware of word boundaries, or punctuation; nor do they understand the concepts represented by the terms *letter, word,* or *number* in the same ways that adults do. But children's responses do show evidence that they know about the overall organization of what they are reading—they can predict how stories or letters will start and what kind of language to expect in a newspaper.

The five studies described earlier support the following conclusions about awareness of connected discourse:

1. The ability to handle books appropriately seems to be universal for all the children studied. This is not just true across socioeconomic, linguistic, and racial groups: it is also true across age groups. The handling of books includes knowing what books are and what they do; knowing that books are to be read; knowing how to turn pages; knowing the direction books tend to go; and knowing about the function of the print on the pages.

2. Children learn between the ages of 3 and 5 that print carries the message. Younger children believe that pictures carry the message in the book.

3. Children understand the proper orientation of books—how to hold a book, how to open it, and how to turn the pages. They are aware that a book has a story, a narrative or sequence of events, that proceeds through the book from page to page until the end.

4. The children demonstrate their understanding of general terms like *read, page, story,* and *book* by responding appropriately to directions like: Show me the front of the book; show me the first part of the story; and, where do I begin to read? However, they usually cannot verbalize conventional, adult definitions for these terms. They are often unable to demonstrate conventional understandings of the

more specific terms like *letter, capital, number,* and *word,* and they seldom are able to provide definitions.

5. Regardless of their sophistication with book handling, the subjects generally say that they can't read, that they will need help to learn to read, that they won't learn to read until they go to school, and finally, that learning to read is going to be hard.

ROOT III:
DEVELOPMENT OF THE FUNCTIONS AND FORMS OF WRITING

Writing is conceived of as being different from reading by the subjects in these studies. This is indicated in their comments about writing and in their willingness to produce writing. It may be that since writing is produced and visible, it is more salient or obvious to the language user. This opportunity for observation plagues language researchers, too. Research in both oral and written language has tended to focus on what can be observed and measured rather than on the receptive processes themselves. As we gain greater insight into the processes of reading and writing, it becomes apparent that writing and reading are not mirror images of each other. There are both similarities and differences in reading and writing processes, depending on the particular functions and purposes each serves, although each no doubt has impact on the other. I believe that the various functions and forms of writing develop in direct proportion to the functional experiences children have while engaged in writing, rather than in relation to biological stages or critical moments of learning.

The conclusions about writing can be reflected as follows:

1. Almost all the subjects respond that they can write. This is clearly different from the subjects' responses to whether they can read and must reflect differences in the way the children and the community in which they live interact about reading and writing.

2. Fifty percent of all 3-year-olds make letters or symbols which look like letters in addition to scribble forms.

3. The subjects seem to produce different kinds of representations when asked to draw or write, although the distinction between writing and drawing is not very clear in their discussions.

4. The children seem to be able to discuss the functions of writing to a greater degree than they discuss the functions of reading.

The fact that writing is something the children are involved in producing and that they can see others produce seems to have an effect on their views about what reading and writing are, their ability to participate in reading and writing events, and their knowledge of the function of reading and writing.

ROOT IV:
THE USE OF ORAL LANGUAGE TO TALK ABOUT WRITTEN LANGUAGE

Children develop oral language about written language as they have active and intimate experiences with written language. In the home and other caretaking settings, children develop principles and concepts about the functions of written language, the relationships among written language, oral language, and ideas, and the organization or linguistic system of language. They also begin to develop the labels related to these principles and concepts. During literacy events which have real purposes and functions for the children, the oral language children use about written language develops over a period of time, and moves toward conventional forms.

Children also have numerous opportunities for encountering oral language about written language isolated from its use. Preschools, television shows, and commercial materials developed for preschoolers which parents are encouraged to buy provide children with the names of letters, sounds for letters, terms such as *word* and *number,* and so forth. Such an emphasis is similar to formalized instructional settings. As noted in the section on reading connected discourse, most of the children did not know the conventional, adult definitions of such terms as *letter, number,* or *word.* What is important to understand, however, is that the naming of letters, numbers, and words apart from the use of written language seems to be conceived by many children as a task unrelated to reading or writing.

All the children, however, used terms such as *pencil, read, write, draw,* and *book* in the contexts of the procedures and were able to respond to the procedures as if they knew how the oral language related to the written language.

ROOT V:
METACOGNITIVE AND METALINGUISTIC AWARENESS ABOUT WRITTEN LANGUAGE

This last root focuses on the ability of children to analyze and explain the process of language itself—to talk about language as if it were an object of study. My definition of metalinguistic awareness is narrowed to overt statements that show evidence of the child's analysis of the written language process. This does not mean that the analysis has to be correct by adult standards, but it must show evidence that the child can talk about how language works. For example, 4-year-old Kristy told a researcher in the Goodman and Altwerger (1981) study that she knew which names were her friends Denise, Donald, and Donna, because "they got the same D's, the same of these (points to N's), and they got the same of A's like this and this (points to A's in Donald and Donna)." Her attempts to explain the differences further showed different levels of control: "Denise gots . . . D . . . L . . . I messed up . . . D . . . E . . . U . . . I . . . S . . . L . . ." Kristy is intuitively aware of the differences among the three names. She knows one labeled cubby from another. She can tell which labeled snack bag belongs to which of her friends. She is consciously able to analyze the differences by pointing to D's and N's in the names, which is her way of analyzing the differences at this point. Her metalinguistic knowledge is beginning, but her responses are not conventional.

1. Kids provide metalinguistic statements about language. They can use terms such as *book* and *story* appropriately and make statements about reading and writing when written language is not in view.

2. These comments or statements about written language, however, do not seem to have a direct relationship to the degree of sophistication in their reading and their writing. Some children who are reading and writing even in a traditional sense may provide much less metalinguistic knowledge than other children who may be aware of the function of print in the environment but still believe that the pictures in the book hold the communicative message of the connected discourse.

3. Metalinguistic statements represent personal or public concepts about written language. They either reflect children's idiosyncratic statements about their observation of language, such as Anders when he pointed to the *A* on the Safeway bag and said, ''That says me.'' They may represent what they have heard and understood from the community as 4-year-old Sarah did when she looked at Milk and said, ''Milk . . . M–I–L–K spells *milk* . . . It could say *mother* (points to *M*) . . . that's how you make *mother,* but I know that's *milk.*''

LITERACY DEVELOPMENT: SUMMARY

This chapter has brought together a group of research studies concerned with literacy development in young children, organized around the metaphor of the five roots of literacy. My concern with literacy development is an applied one: How can what we know about how children learn written language help us to develop curriculum involving the teaching of written language? If we do not recognize the significance of these beginnings, we cannot support and build on the strengths children are developing in their search for meaning through written language.

All the evidence indicates that children are inventing, discovering, and developing literacy as they grow up in the literate society. They develop many insights about the functions of written language for themselves and for adults important to them. They discover that written language makes sense, and as members of a literate society they make sense of and through written language. Furthermore, they develop concepts or principles about how written language makes sense. The studies I have interrelated show that children become knowledgeable about the various systems of language used in writing and reading. The subjects develop notions about the graphophonic, semantic, syntactic, and the pragmatic systems of written language. They provide evidence that they know some of these systems operate differently in written and oral language, and they show an understanding that reading and writing are symbolic systems. They are aware that reading and writing represent ideas, knowledge, and thoughts as well as representing some aspects of oral language.

The importance of understanding the kinds of knowledge children are developing about reading and writing is in the insights this understanding provides for teachers, curriculum developers, teacher educators, and researchers. Since children are actively developing their own schemata about written language, it becomes important for those in teaching and curriculum development to build on this knowledge base and to exploit children's search for meaning through written language.

Teacher educators must help preservice and inservice teachers become aware of the knowledge and theories revealed in research about children's development of written language prior to school and to help them respect the ways in which children learn written language. Many preschool and early elementary school programs and approaches to the teaching of reading and writing must change drastically to take advantage of what children know about reading and writing. Teachers must be helped to observe and evaluate children's written language development within the literate contexts that provide the social environments through which children learn so much about written language.

The growing knowledge must help researchers become aware of the significance of contextual differences, the influences of the tasks and the researchers themselves on the results of examining children's knowledge about literacy.

The value society places on literacy is growing. If we are going to achieve greater literacy for all, then we must have the understandings necessary to observe literacy develop in the very young child. We must legitimize all children's abilities to develop and build their own roots of literacy.

REFERENCES

Clay, M. (1972). *Sand, a diagnostic survey: Concepts about print test.* Auckland, New Zealand: Heinemann Educational.

Clay, M. (1979). *Stones.* Auckland, New Zealand: Heinemann Educational.

Doake, D. (1981). *Book experience and emergent reading in preschool children.* Unpublished doctoral dissertation, University of Alberta, Canada.

Duckworth, E. (1978). *The African primary science program: An evaluation and extended thoughts.* Grand Forks, ND: North Dakota Study Group on Evaluation, University of North Dakota Press.

Fagan, E.R., Jensen, J. & Cooper, C. (Eds.). (1985). *Measures for research and evaluation in the language arts.* (Vol. II). Urbana, IL: ERIC-NCTE.

Goodman, Y. (1980). The roots of literacy. In M. Douglass (Ed.), *Claremont Reading Conference Forty-Fourth Yearbook.* Claremont, CA: The Claremont Reading Conference.

Goodman, Y. (1982). El desarrollo de la escritura en niños muy pequeños. In E. Ferreiro & M. Gómez Palacio (Eds.), *Nuevas perspectivas sobre los procesos de lectura y escritura.* Mexico: Siglo Veintiuno Editores.

Goodman, Y. (1983). Beginning reading development: Strategies and principles. In R.P. Parker & F.A. Davis (Eds.), *Developing literacy: Young children's use of language.* Newark, DE: International Reading Association.

Goodman, Y. (1984). The development of initial literacy. In H. Goelman, A. Olberg, & F. Smith (Eds.), *Awakening to literacy.* Exeter, NH: Heinemann Educational.

Goodman, Y., & Altwerger, B. (1981) *Print awareness in preschool children: A study of the development of literacy in preschool children* (Occasional Paper No. 4). Tucson, AZ: University of Arizona, Program in Language and Literacy, Arizona Center for Research and Development, College of Education.

Goodman, Y., & Marek, A. (1984). [Print awareness in Papago kindergarten and first-grade children]. Unpublished raw data.

Guba, E.G. (1978). *Toward a methodology of naturalistic inquiry in educational evaluation.* (CSE Monograph Series in Evaluation No. 8). Los Angeles, CA: UCLA Center for the Study of Evaluation.

Haussler, M.M. (1982). *Transitions into literacy: A psycholinguistic analysis of beginning reading in kindergarten and first-grade children.* Unpublished doctoral dissertation, University of Arizona, Tucson.

Heath, S.B. (1983). *Ways with words.* Cambridge, MA: Cambridge University Press.

Holdaway, D. (1979). *The foundations of literacy.* Sydney, Australia: Ashton Scholastic.

Long, R., Manning, G., Martin, K., Williams, C., & Wolfson, B. (1982). *Indices of literacy in preschool children.* Unpublished research report, The University of Alabama, Birmingham, AL.

Romero, G.G. (1983). *Print awareness of the preschool bilingual Spanish-English speaking child.* Unpublished doctoral dissertation, University of Arizona, Tucson.

Sulzby, E. (1983). *Beginning readers' developing knowledges of written language.* (Final Report to the National Institute of Education, NIE G80-0176). Evanston, IL: Northwestern University.

Taylor, D. (1983). *Family literacy: Young children learning to read and write.* Exeter, NH: Heinemann Educational.

2

The Interplay Between Information and Assimilation in Beginning Literacy*

Emilia Ferreiro
Center of Research and Advanced Studies
National Polytechnic Institute, Mexico

In this chapter, Emilia Ferreiro presents two case studies of young children's literacy development over approximately two years. By her focusing upon the children's developing knowledge about the writing of the proper name, we have an excellent opportunity to observe the processes of assimilation and accommodation in action. What adults tell and show children about writing and reading is sometimes "taken up" by the child and at other times rejected outright. Thus, Ferreiro applies Piagetian interpretations to literacy development and provides clear pictures of (a) children as active participants in learning, and (b) the reasonableness of young children's writing and reading strategies which may, from an adult perspective, seem strange—both key factors in the concept of emergent literacy.

INTRODUCTION

"Considerable attention has been paid to the spontaneous drawing activities of young children, but their first writing efforts have all but escaped the notice of child psychologists. The probable reason is that writing, much more than drawing, is considered a subject of school instruction. The concept of writing as a developmental process in preschool age children is comparatively new." This was written many years ago in an article by G. Hildreth (1936) whom we now consider a pioneer in this field. Although published in 1936, the same words can be reproduced almost without change nowadays.

Hildreth analyzed in her article the developmental sequence that can be observed in the way children write their proper names. The writing of the proper name will also be the main focus of the analysis presented in this chapter. However, the way to understand "writing as a developmental process" will not be the same. Hildreth focused exclusively on the *figurative* aspects of the written productions: Motor control, the use of the writing instrument, speed, tendency to horizontal or vertical movements, tendency to make discrete symbol units, constriction in space, letters correctly formed, correct spelling of the name, reversals, and so on.

* The data reported in this chapter come from a research project that was financially supported by a joint grant of the Ford and Spencer Foundations (Ford Foundation Project 78–203).

Undoubtedly, the figurative aspects are important. They were very often considered the only relevant aspects of written productions. However, since the time we started our research on the developmental process of writing, we considered it as a psychogenetic process, in the Piagetian sense. It became soon evident that focusing on the figurative aspects obscured more important features of the development. We were therefore obliged to put those figurative aspects on the back shelf in order to let the *constructive* aspects emerge to light. The constructive aspects are the ones that really "escaped the notice of child psychologists" (even those that became influenced by Piagetian theory!).

The analysis that follows is completely centered on these constructive aspects, and no definition could be clearer than this. Our research supports the notion that the writing system—as a socially constructed object—is an *object of knowledge* for the child (Ferreiro, 1978, 1984; Ferreiro & Teberosky, 1982). The link between print and oral language is not immediately grasped by any child. Even those that grow up in an environment rich in literacy experiences—as the children analyzed in this chapter—have considerable trouble understanding the relationship between oral language and the graphic forms. In order to understand the set of conventional graphic forms and their rules of composition as a particular representational system, the children build up various hypotheses that are not idiosyncratic but developmentally ordered.[1]

Literacy development takes place, no doubt, in a social environment. But social practices as well as social information are not received passively by children. When they try to understand, they necessarily transform the content received. Moreover, in order to register the information, they transform it. This is the deep meaning of the notion of *assimilation* that Piaget has put at the core of his theory.

In this chapter, we will try to follow the ups and downs of the development of specific knowledge about the writing system that is more closely dependent on the information provided by the environment. To do this, we will choose as a guideline the writing of the proper name. As will be seen, the information provided by the environment (mainly the family, in the cases we will present) is sometimes quickly accepted, sometimes ignored, and sometimes frankly rejected. Our task is to understand why this happens.

We will follow with a great deal of detail the evolution of two children. Both have parents with university degrees, parents for whom reading and writing are part of their everyday life and who have a genuine interest in the development of their children (in particular, they follow with great interest their intellectual development). These children have many books at their reach: books bought for them, books that are read to them, books in their parents' desks, books that are used at home. In addition, there are magazines, journals, and letters that are received at home because some relatives live in foreign countries. These children possess paper

---

[1] We used the term *hypotheses* in a broad sense to refer to ideas or systems of ideas constructed by children in order to explain the nature and the way of functioning of a given knowing object. Of course, young children do not use these ideas as hypotheses in a strict sense.

and various types of instruments for drawing and writing. Moreover, these parents are sensitive to the children's questions; they stimulate these questions, and they are ready to answer them.

SANTIAGO

Santiago is the only child in the family. At the age of two (obs. 1–2;0) he is already an active consumer of story books. His father reads to him almost every day, but Santiago thinks—as all children who try to understand this particular speech situation—that when reading, one reads the pictures. Nevertheless, he is able to make a distinction between the text and the pictures, calling the texts "what is written" (*lo escrito*). Pointing to the text in a story book, he says—in his baby-talk— "this is written" (*esto está escrito*).

When he is 2 years, 3 months old (obs. 2) he continues to think that when reading, one reads the pictures, but he starts to interpret commercial labels. Pointing to the label on the front of a bottle of Pepsi Cola, he says, "Here it says Pepsi Cola" (*Aquí dice Pepsi Cola*). Then he looks at the top and says, "Here it also says Pepsi Cola" (*Aquí también dice Pepsi Cola*). His mother asks him where it says that, and he answers, "In the little blue part" (*En lo azulito*) (the letters are blue). She asks him about the red part that has no text, and he answers, "There it doesn't say" (Ahí no dice).[2]

Two months later (obs. 3–2;5) Santiago affirms that when reading, one reads the texts of the books, not the pictures, "because there are letters" (*porque hay letras*). The term "letters" is used for letters but also for numbers in books and in various objects. A few days later (obs. 6–2;5), one of his friends is reading a book. Santiago asks him, "Where are you reading?" His friend—who is at the level through which Santiago has just passed—answers that he is reading the pictures. Santiago contradicts him: "No, here, where the letters are" (*No, acá donde hay letras*). At about this time the following dialogue takes place between Santiago and his mother (obs. 5–2;5). He asks his mother to read him a story about little cats. Holding the book, she asks, "Where shall I read it?" Santiago points to the text. Pointing to the picture of the little cats, she asks again, "Can I do it here?" Santiago answers promptly, "No, these *are* the little cats" (*No, esos son los gatitos*, with strong emphasis on the verb).[3]

The facts just referred to provide the context within which a decisive intervention

---

[2] For Santiago, letters are already substitute objects. This is not the general case for 2-year-old children. For an analysis of the transition between letters as objects to letters as substitute objects, see Ferreiro (1984).

[3] For a convenient interpretation, it must be taken into account that in Spanish there is a difference between the verbs *ser* and *estar* that is not present in English. The verb *ser* is used to assert either what a person or an object actually is, or a permanent quality they have. The verb *estar* is used to assert either a nonpermanent quality or a spatial position of a person or an object. For instance, "This is a cat" should be translated with the verb *ser;* "The cat is here" should be translated with the verb *estar*. Santiago used a form of the verb *ser*.

by a member of the family takes place, an intervention that will have consequences in the rest of the evolution (obs. 4–2;5). Santiago wants to write and asks for some models. Someone in the family answers by writing Santiago's name (in capital letters) and the first letters of some other names belonging to persons well known by Santiago. Santiago is told, "This is Santiago's, this is Ruben's," etc. (*Esta es la de Santiago, esta es la de Rubén*). Santiago seems excited by this information. Within the next few days, he asks for a similar writing example. Two days later, he is able to recognize many letters using this "belonging-to rule" and asks for more information of the same kind. The result is the following: When he is 2 years, 7 months old (obs. 12), Santiago recognizes without error 14 different letters as belonging to a known person.

The list is the following:

R = "Rubén's" (his father)   S = "Santiago's"
P = "daddy's" (*la de papá*)   C = "Carmela's"
M = "mommy's"   E = "Ernesto's"
A = "Anne's"   F = "Fernando's"
I = "Irma's"   N = "Nelson's"
L = "Luis's"   T = "Tere's" or "Teresa's"
O = "Omar's"   G = "Gabriel's"

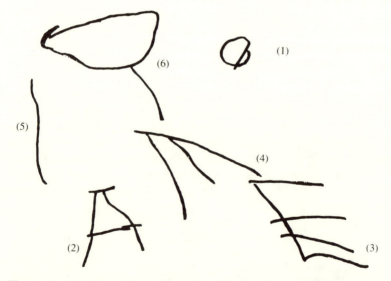

Figure 1. Santiago—2 years 7 months old. (1) "La de Omar"; (2) "La de Anne"; (3) "La de Ernesto"; (4) "La de mamá"; (5) "La de Irma"; (6) "La de papá"

Santiago has already established a firm basis for recognizing letters. Moreover, he is able to make a distinction between "the letter of (someone)" and the texts where "it may say" such a particular name. Let us consider the following dialogue with the researcher.

What is this? (Letter S)	"That's Santiago's" (*La de Santiago*).
Does it say Santiago?	"No, it's Santiago's" (*No, la de Santiago*).
What about this one? (Letter R)	"That's Rubén's" (*La de Rubén*).
Does it say Rubén?	"No, it's Rubén's" (*No, la de Rubén*).

Santiago knows that the first letter alone is not sufficient to "say" the entire name, but he does not understand why people put *the others' letters* in order to say a particular name. For instance, when we write CARMELA, Santiago recognizes each one of the letters as "Carmela's, Anne's, Rubén's, mommy's, Ernesto's, Luis', Anne's. Why did you put all of them together?" (*La de Carmela, la de Anne . . . Para qué las pusiste todas juntas?*).

Exactly the same happens when his own name is written. When we proceed to write (slowly) SANTIAGO, he proceeds to say: "Santiago's, Nelson's, Tere's, Irma's, Anne's, Gabriel's, Omar's."

Why am I putting all of them together?	"In order to have three because I will be this old" (showing 3 fingers) (*Para que sean tres porque yo cumplo así*).
What does it say here? (SANTIAGO.)	"Santiago . . . and daddy has gone to work" (*Santiago . . . y papá se fue a trabajar*).
What else?	"Mommy and daddy" (Mamá y papá).

The first conflicting situation is already showing up: This "belonging to" rule allows Santiago to be quite sure about identifying the letters (it provides him also with a valid reason to discriminate between arbitrary graphic forms). But only one letter is not enough "to say" a particular name. More letters are needed, but these *other letters* are also the property of other persons. The first letter allows him to predict what the text says (the first letter on the left- or on the right-hand side, as we will later see), but as soon as he takes the first letter to predict the meaning of the entire text, he is forced to leave aside the fact that the others "belong" to other persons (Nelson's is there, but it does not say Nelson; Gabriel's is there but it does not say Gabriel; and so on). To what extent are the letters "of the others" a constitutive part of the proper name?

Another related problem is the following: What is the reason for the amount of letters required for each particular name? In the case of his own name, Santiago looks for a reason (the same reason many other children look for): As many letters as years he has or is going to have in the near (and highly desirable) future. However, if this is the reason, there are more letters than expected. What else can it "say" in the residual letters? In the example just presented, Santiago solves the problem by adding "mommy and daddy." In the same interview, Santiago is asked again what the written text SANTIAGO says, and this time he answers, "Santiago washed his hands, he went to play, he ate a cracker" (*Santiago se lavó las manos, fue a jugar, comió una galletita*); while he is saying all these phrases, he follows with his finger the text several times from right to left and from left to right.

What else can we learn from this new information? Obviously, that Santiago can move freely—from right to left and from left to right—on a written text. But this is not the most relevant fact. The thing that is really important is that Santiago finds in the text too many letters. It is his own name, written as adults have shown him to do it, but it is a model that he finds impossible to assimilate for two reasons; in qualitative terms, because of the presence of the letters "of the others" in the proper name; in quantitative terms, because there are more letters than needed. Trying to "absorb" these residual letters, he looks in two alternative directions; either the text includes the names of persons closely related to himself (and who can be more closely related to him than mommy and daddy?), or else what is written includes things that Santiago does, along side his own name ("Daddy," plus the things that Daddy does, appears as an intermediate solution).

Neither of those solutions is satisfactory, and there are good reasons for such dissatisfaction. If what is written is the many things Santiago does, why does Santiago's "letter" appear only once? If Santiago is written only once, what is written in the written text that allows it to "say" everything that Santiago has done? (As we shall see immediately after this, Santiago—like all children—has the idea that the prototype for "something to be written" is the noun, and particularly, proper names). The other alternative is not much more promising: If Santiago is in the company of "mommy and daddy," why are their letters not in the text?

This conflicting situation is not the only one identified at that moment. In the same interview the following dialogue takes place:

What is this? (Letter R)	"Rubén's" (*La de Rubén*).
Is your daddy's the same as this one?	"Yes."
You said that this one (P) was your daddy's, and this one (R) was Rubén's. Is that possible?	"Yes, my daddy is Rubén" (*Sí, mi papá es Rubén*).
Why does your daddy have two letters?	"Because . . ." (*Porque sí*).
Anne has only one, Omar has only one, Irma has only one . . .	"Because" (*Porque sí*).
Santiago has only one . . .	/no answer/
Which one is your daddy's? Only one or both?	"Both" (*Las dos*).

One would be tempted to conclude that Santiago is thinking of the two names that correspond to a single person ("daddy" and "Rubén"). However, the following complementary data shows that we should be cautious in jumping too quickly to such an interpretation. Santiago is talking with his friend Gabriel who, pointing to a

P, says, "It is Daddy's." Santiago answers promptly, "It is not Daddy's, it is *my* daddy's" (*No es la de papá, es la de mi papá;* obs. 10–2;6, that takes place during the same month of the interview analyzed in the preceding dialogue sample).

In Santiago's mind, the letters are not linked to names but to persons, as being the property of particular persons. In that way, "daddy" can be a privileged owner (accepted as such). The conflict is solved with an ad-hoc exception to the general rule. But it is only a local solution and, as happens with any local solution, will leave the way open for the conflict to emerge again.

A third conflicting situation is also solved locally: In front of a letter without a known owner, Santiago decides that it is "nobody's" letter (*de nadie*). For instance, W is "Nobody's. It is mommy's upside down" (*La de nadie. Está al revés de mamá;* obs. 12–2;7).

There is a fourth conflicting situation that is left without solution: The family has, so far, given information about known human owners for different letters, but U was provided as "the one of fingernail" (*la de uña*), pointing to the figural similarity between fingernail and U. During the same interview we are analyzing (obs. 12–2;7), the following dialogue takes place:

What are letters for?	"For people" (*Para las gentes*).
Is this one (U) for people?	"Yes, no . . . yes, no . . ."
What can it be for?	"I don't know" (he remains doubtful).
Are there letters that are not for people?	"No."
All of them are for people?	"Yes."
The one for fingernail also?	"Yes . . . no. . . . yes . . . no . . ." (low voice, for himself, being doubtful and in conflict).

To sum up the situation at this point of Santiago's literacy development: He has quickly absorbed the information provided by the family, but he has reformulated it. The family has given information about the first letter of proper names, but Santiago has understood it as owners of letters. Each person may have his or her own letter, as a part of his/her own identity. This letter cannot be shared. For that reason, when the family gives the information that L—previously identified as "Luis," is also the letter of Leonardo, Santiago rejects this information and is quite disturbed (obs. 8–2;6).

The information provided by the environment has allowed Santiago to find a reason to discriminate among the arbitrary letter forms, but this same rationality has its own limits: It is bothersome (but not more than that) to accept that there are letters that belong "to nobody"; it is somewhat disturbing to accept that someone (but not anybody) has the right to have two letters instead of only one; it is much more disturbing to accept that there is one letter "for fingernail," all the others being "for people"; it is extremely conflicting to accept that the letters of the others are a constitutive part of the proper name. With all the available information, but also with all these conflicts, Santiago will pursue his exploration into literacy.[4]

How does Santiago interpret texts, with all the available information?[5] Two procedures of interpretation coexist, side by side, without coordination: one, taking the first letter, as a starting point considering it as the cue letter of a given person; the other, taking the context as a starting point. Two different interpretative hypotheses correspond to these procedures: One, that only proper names are written in the texts; the other, that common names are written (either those of the objects on which the text is printed, or those of the objects pictured next to the text). The following examples illustrate both procedures of interpretation.

When he is 2 years, 6 months old (obs. 10), Santiago asks what it says on a label attached to bananas. The answer he is given is, "It says Juanita Banana." One week later (obs. 11–2;6), Santiago observes a taxi on the street and, pointing to the sign attached to the roof, says, "Here it says taxi, and in the little papers on the bananas it said Juanita Banana" (*Ahí dice taxi, y en los papelitos de los plátanos decía Juanita Banana*). Playing with some little cars (obs. 12–2;7) he says, "This is a little truck" (*Esta es una cañometa;* "cañometa" is his own way of uttering the noun *camioneta*). Someone asks him what make it is. Santiago turns it, points to the letters that are on the back side, and says "Cañometa." Also at age 2;7 (obs. 13) he is shown a book with animal pictures without a text. He names the animals as "It is an elephant, it is a donkey . . ." (*es un elefante, es un burro . . .*). We make a card with the text ELEFANTE and put it below the image of an elephant. Santiago says: "You put elephant" (*Le pusiste elefante*). Then, we change the card's place, putting it below or besides other animals, asking in each case what it says there. Santiago changes the attributed meaning, depending on the context: "Lion. Donkey. Horse." It again becomes "Elephant" when the card is put in its original place. The same card on the armchair says "armchair," and when it is hung up in the air it says "wall" (the nearest object).

Through all these examples it is possible to observe the procedure of context-dependent interpretation at work, without taking into account the qualitative properties of the text (that is, the letters themselves that Santiago is able to identify). The hypothesis that the letters carried by an object must be interpreted as the name of that object persists for many months: when he is 3 years, 1 month old (obs. 25),

---

[4] Before proceeding, let us say that in the same interview that fixes a turning point in Santiago's development, he is able to produce, but with great difficulty, some of the letters he knows (see Figure 1). He can also adjust the spatial orientation of his interpretation in order to keep the idea that letters are "for people" (for instance, looking at the text *UIO* he says: "the fingernail's, Irma's, Omar's." However, when asked what is said in the entire text he answers that it says "Omar," going from right to left). Finally, let us point out that at the same time he starts to distinguish between numbers and letters. Numbers are "nobody's" and they are not "for reading." Nevertheless, the distinction between numbers and letters is not yet well established because, suddenly, he asks (spontaneously): "Isn't it true that letters are numbers?" (*Verdad que las letras son números?*").

[5] The word *text* is used in this chapter to refer to written strings of letters, either in print or handwriting.

Santiago is given a toy as a gift. He looks at it and says, "Here there are letters. They say what it is" (*Aquí hay letras. Dicen lo que es*). In fact, what was written in the text was the word MEXICO.

It is important to take into account that in all previous examples there is a clear differentiation in the utilization of the indefinite article: The article appears to refer to the object or to the image (*es una cañometa, es un elefante* . . .) but it disappears when he interprets the text. We have shown elsewhere (Ferreiro & Teberosky, 1982, chap. 3) that this discriminatory use of the article is one indicator of a tremendous evolutionary importance.

Let us now see some examples of the other procedures of interpretation, in similar contexts and at the same ages. We present to Santiago some children's playing cards that have images with their corresponding names. We ask him what it says on each one (obs. 17–2; 10). Santiago anticipates a proper name for each one of the texts, making use of the first letter as a cue, and adjusting the direction of the reading to the letter cue: in PAYASO ("CLOWN") it says "Omar" (pointing from right to left); in GAUCHO it also says "Omar" (from right to left); in GITANA it says "Gabriel" (from left to right), in NENE ("BOY") it says "Nelson," and in BAILARINA ("GIRL DANCER") it says "Beto." So, he can attribute a boy's proper name to the picture of a girl, without being perturbed by it. During the same interview we present him with a cigarette box, asking what the text might say. Over the word MARLBORO, Santiago thinks that "Omar" is written, pointing to the final O, and in another similar text, he asserts that "*mamá*" is written, pointing to the initial M.

The two interpretation procedures we have illustrated with examples may be summed up as follows: By taking into account the context (the object or the image), the text says "what it is"; by taking into account the text, the first thing to do is to search for the owner of the first letter, in order to know which is the proper name that is written, and, in this case, the context must be left aside.

At the age of 2 years, 10 months (obs. 17), we register some nonsystematic attempts to deal separately with the belonging-to rule (or rule of ownership) already established for individual letters and the presence of these same letters in the composition of other names. At certain moments, Santiago attempts a syllabic decomposition of a name in order to know how many letters are necessary: He asks for three to write "San–tia–go" and two for "Ru–bén" (his father). In this context it seems clear that the three letters for his own name ought to have a different (although complementary) meaning than the previous three, "because I will be three years old." In the same interview, he seems to lose the previous distinction between "the letter of (someone)" and "it says (the proper name of the same person)":

(The researcher writes *S.*)	"This one alone says San–tiago" (*Esa sola dice San–tiago*)
Don't you need any more?	"No."
What about this one? (T)	"That's Tere's" (*La de Tere*).

What does it say?   "It says Tere" (*Dice Tere*).

Is Tere written there?   "Yes."

(The dialogue continues in the same terms with four other letters of different persons).

It is interesting to note that, at this moment of his development, Santiago, instead of making progress in the writing of letters that he has just begun to draw but was far from mastering, starts to draw pseudoletters.[6] For these pseudo-letters he invents absurd names as owners of them (using always the formula; "It's so-and-so's," with invented names). Moreover, and even stranger, he also writes his own name with three pseudoletters, making then a syllabic reading "San–tia–go," one syllable for each letter (obs. 18 and 19–2;11).

What meaning can we attribute to this seeming regression, or "going back?" It is not the case that Santiago has forgotten the already established "rule of ownership." On the contrary, he has enlarged the number of letters recognized with this same rule. A few days after this (obs. 23–2;11) we ask him to write Rubén's letter, that of the fingernail, Beto's, and Ernesto's, and he draws all these letters correctly (see Figure 2).

Our interpretation of these facts is the following: Santiago does not succeed in reconciling the ownership rule with the fact that the same letters are used to constitute other names. As he cannot solve the problem, he tries to isolate both aspects: Only one letter to each person, and the entire name in only one letter, working only at the qualitative level. On the other side, he tries to understand why adults use so

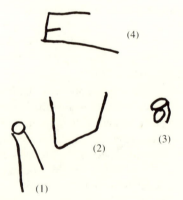

Figure 2. Santiago—2 years 11 months old. (1) La de Rubén; (2) La de uña; (3) La de Beto; (4) La de Ernesto

---

[6] In literacy development we should be careful to distinguish between the drawing of letters and the writing. We keep the term *writing* when a given meaning is intended to be attached to the production or when the child himself uses such a term. Letters can also be treated merely as graphic forms that children try *to draw*. Some children use the expression "to make letters" (*hacer letras*) as distinguished from "to write" (*escribir*).

many letters for a single name, and in this case he works only at the quantitative level, making his first syllabic analysis of words. (We know very well, from our previous research, the great importance of the discovery of the syllabic hypothesis). The pseudo-letters he is inventing allow him a momentary dissociation between quantitative and qualitative aspects of the written product (because the qualitative ones are so closely linked to the ownership rule).

Nevertheless, this dissociation cannot be a solution. Santiago knows very well that adults write with "real letters." A first attempt to coordinate both quantitative and qualitative aspects is observed when he comments, spontaneously: Pointing to an O, he says "it is the [ow] of Omar, Ooooo–mar," and pointing to a C he says, "it is the [kɔ] of Carmela" (obs. 20–2;11).[7] So, letters start to be something more than someone's letter: They start to take the sound value of the first syllable of the name.

The two following observations make it clear that Santiago is not ready to leave aside the idea that letters cannot be shared. Santiago draws a kind of P and says, "It's daddy's" (*Es la de papá*). His mother replies that it also is the letter of Paula. Santiago, disturbed and perplexed at the same time, looks for a compromise solution. Pointing to the round part of the letter, he says, "That's daddy's" (*la de papá*) and pointing to the straight part of the same letter, he says, "That's Paula's" (*la de Paula*) (obs. 24–3;0). So he divides the letter into two parts, to be able to attribute a name to each part, instead of having the same letter for two different nouns. One month later (obs. 27–3;1) Santiago refuses to accept that the letter of Ana could be the same as the one of Anne (in spite of the sound proximity of both names). Neither can he accept that Z could be the letter of Zorro, because "It's Nelson's."

How long will it take Santiago to accept that a given letter may belong to various names? Exactly one calendar year. Only when he is 3 years, 7 months old (obs. 40) does he start asking, first with resignation and then with genuine interest, "Whom else does this letter belong to?" (*De quién más es esta letra?*).

Why has Santiago absorbed the information provided by the family about the way of identifying letters so quickly and avidly, and why is he rejecting so obstinately the information also provided by the family about the fact that letters belong to more than one proper name?

Here we are at the center of our problem. Any one of the classical "factors" can be invoked. It is not the case that Santiago has lost interest in literacy (quite the contrary). He has rather precocious intellectual development (he has the notion of numerical invariance at 4 years, 1 month, which is much earlier than the average age). There are no family or school pressures to oblige him to go even more quickly. But, even being an extremely intelligent and stimulated child, Santiago cannot avoid the cognitive regulations that are basic to any reorganization in this domain. *Santiago cannot accept that one letter belongs to more than one person, because this would disorganize the entire constructed system.* The rule of ownership

---

[7] [Kɔ] is not the name of the letter *C* in Spanish, but the strong part of the first syllable of *Carmela*."

(given, as we have seen, by the family in terms of the initial letter of proper nouns, but assimilated by Santiago as letters with only one owner) allows him to find a good reason to start the discrimination task between arbitrary graphic forms. In addition, this rule allows him to know what is said in a given text, using the first letter as a cue. If a letter belongs to more than one person, one cannot foresee what is said in a given text, even after a meticulous exploration of the letters. It is this that acts clearly as a disorganizer, and this is the very reason of Santiago's efforts to avoid the intrusion of a perturbing element of such magnitude.

However, this cannot explain why Santiago absorbed so quickly the first type of information. We already know—from our previous research—that nouns (particularly proper nouns) are the prototype of "what is written." Young children can be doubtful about the possibility of other word classes to be written, but they are sure about nouns (see Ferreiro, 1984).

So, we will propose that the way in which the information about letters was given by the family could be easily assimilated, because it corresponds to an already well-established children's idea. This implies that the way in which information is given determines its possibilities of assimilation. To be assimilated, the information must be integrated to a previously constructed system (or to systems in process of building up). It is not information, as such, that creates knowledge. Knowledge is the product of construction of the knowing subject. Santiago shows us how difficult this building up of knowledge may be—in spite of all available information.

Let us go back once again in Santiago's history. Before he was able to accept that one letter belongs to two different names, we have the following data. When he is 3 years, 2 months old (obs. 26), he comes back to the idea that only one letter is not sufficient "to say" a given name. He keeps the idea that texts carried by objects "say" its name. He tries to compose some written names making a correspondence between the amount (or the size) of the letters to the size of the referred objects. The following examples show each one of these characteristics (obs. 26–3;2).

(1) (We present Santiago a set of plastic letters.)

"It's Mommy's (M), it's Omar's (O), Gabriel's (G), Santiago's (S)."
(He puts all the letters on a line; then he adds I).
"It's Irma's. It says Irma" (pointing to the composed text MOGSI)
"If we put this one it says Anne" (MOGSIA).

And this way? (We take out A, leaving MOGSI.)

"It says Irma."

And this way? (We take out I, leaving MOGS.)

"It says Santiago."

And this way? (G alone.)

"It says Gabriel but . . . with only one letter? Let's add Diego's and Anne's" (GDA).

Now, does it say Gabriel?	"No, more are needed" (*No, le faltan más*). (He adds S, the result is *GDAS*). "Now it's OK (*Así ya está*). "Now it says Gabriel" (*Así ya dice Gabriel*). "Gabriel with Santiago" (for "Gabriel" he points from left to right and for "Santiago" he points from right to left). "Because Gabriel always plays with me" (*Porque Gabriel siempre juega conmigo*).
(2) (We present Santiago a card with the picture of a dog and a text below.) What is it?	"A dog" (*Un perro*).
What has been put here? (pointing to the text)	"Dog, just like it's called" (*Perro, lo mismo que se llama*).
(3) What's the little baby who was born in your house called? (his cousin)	"He's called Paulito."
Which one of all these letters could be Paulito's?	"This little one" (*Esta chiquita*, a small *x*, the smallest in the set of plastic letters).
(We suggest the following game: For some picture cards, he should pick out the texts that go with them the best. We show him a picture of three hens and a chick.) What may I put for these?	"Little chick and hens . . . This one for the little one" (*Pollito y gallinas . . . Este para el chiquito*, choosing a text of only two letters).
For the little chick?	"Yes."
And for the hens?	"A big one" (*Uno grande*).
One or many for the hens?	"Many" (*Muchos*). "This, this, this" (he chooses three texts having more or less the same length, with 8–9 letters each one). "This one for that one, this one for that one, this one for that one." (He

	puts each text below each hen; he puts then the two-letters text below the little chick.)
What does it say all together?	"Hen and little chick . . . are friends" (*Gallina y pollito . . . son amigos*).
Where does it say that they are friends?	"Tu–qui–tiqui" (One syllable over each text; they are nonsense syllables. He tries to avoid the situation; he refuses to pursue the game.)

The data we have just presented are very revealing. We have cited the philosophical statement made by Santiago before ("Here are letters. They say what it is"), at 3 years, 1 month. Now he adds this other statement, also of a philosophical nature: Letters say "the same as it (the object) is called." This is, no doubt, one of the specific functions attributed to a written text by young children (cf. Ferreiro, 1984).

Letters serve the function of representing that fundamental property of the objects that drawing is not able to represent, namely, *their names*. It is a function foreign to our customary view of the writing system as a way of communication, but it is *a function of one system of representation by reference to other representation systems*. In fact, children start (sometimes simultaneously, as Santiago did) dealing with three different systems of representation: drawings, letters, and numbers. One of their problems is to understand what is the *specificity* of each one of those systems with reference to the others, as representational systems (i.e., what they enable one to represent, what they cannot enable one to represent, and how they represent what they are supposed to represent).

Having accepted again that only one letter is not enough "to say" a given name, Santiago must accept that the letters "of the others" participate in the constitution of his own name. How can one understand this participation? Santiago starts elaborating his idea as follows: The letters "of the others" are there only as "friendly company," to fulfill the requirement of minimum amount of letters (at least four is what Santiago requires at this moment). It is the first letter (the first from the right or from the left side) that gives his value to the totality. With the same letters—simply adding or taking out one—we obtain a different written name.[8] Each

---

[8] Although we are not dealing here with data about the identification of numbers, it is interesting to note that a few months later (obs. 41–3;7) this procedure to compose names is applied also to numbers. Santiago rejected numbers as being "for reading" at 2 years, 7 months. This notwithstanding, he accepts them one year later. Playing with plastic letters and numbers, he composes the string EYI87 and tells us that it says "Ernesto." Adding one N (NEYI87), "it says Nelson." Modifying the string in this way YI87 it says "seven," and like this GNEYI8 it says "eight." It seems evident that the different representational systems are not built up in isolation, but with several kinds of interactions between them (including interferences). A last remark: It is not the case that the interpretation "seven" for the string YI87 was forced by the fact of the impossibility of finding an owner for Y, because at that time Santiago's stock of letter cues was considerably enlarged, and Y was identified as "Yolanda's letter."

letter is being considered from a double value system: either as "another letter" (any one) that ensures the requirement of the minimum *quantity* allowing a reading act; or as a particular letter, in initial position, the *qualitative* value of which determines the interpretation of the entire text. Depending on its position in the string, a given letter may assume its qualitative value or a purely quantitative one. It is the first successful attempt to conciliate quantitative and qualitative properties. This coordination between both properties is crucial in literacy development.

What is happening, in the meantime, with Santiago's proper name? When he is 3 years, 6 months old (obs. 37), Santiago starts to sign his own drawings (Figures 3 and 4). He writes from left to right, but then he reads in either direction. This "signature" is composed of 3 or 4 letters, followed by a straight line and a dot, both interpreted by Santiago as "It is when it is finished" (*es cuando terminó*). (Santiago is one of the few children studied by us that, at this developmental level, utilizes punctuation marks.) When the written name is composed of 3 letters, he reads it syllabically: "San–tia–go"[9] (pointing and uttering one syllable for each letter). When it is composed of 4 letters, he keeps the syllabic decomposition of the name, but adds "did it" (*lo hizo*) for the residual letter (*San–tia–go–lo hizo* or *Lo hizo–San–tia–go*, depending whether the text is interpreted from left to right or from right to left). The variations in the amount of letters seems to be related to the following considerations: Santiago would prefer 4 letters as the minimum quantity of a written name, but when making a syllabic analysis of his name (that allows him to interpret each one of the constitutive letters) there should be only 3. The oscillation between both criteria is reflected in the variations in the amount of letters.

At 3 years, 9 months (obs. 44), he puts three letters for his own name, but now the three are pertinent, not only the first one. He writes SIO, one letter for each one of the syllables of San–tia–go (Figure 5).

At 3 years, 10 months (obs. 48), he asks someone in the family to write his name. Then he tries to read it syllabically, "stretching" the final part as much as possible: "San–tia–g–o" (on the first four letters SANT).[10] He then proceeds to cross out the four remaining letters (IAGO).

Here we are facing a new conflicting situation. Once again, Santiago rejects the information provided by the family environment. But this time the reasons to reject it are different, and we should understand them in order to have a real understanding of the development we are dealing with. Santiago has made a great progress in his literacy development: Trying to understand the meaning of each one of the letters that compose his own name, he has divided it into syllables and he has attributed to each letter the value of one syllable (see Ferreiro, 1985, for a more detailed analysis of the cognitive problems involved in the beginning of the syllabic period). In doing this, for the first time Santiago is linking specifically the parts of the written name to the parts of the uttered name.

---

[9] Editors' note: Unlike the typical English pronunciation [sæn–tiy–ɔ–gow], the name *Santiago* consists of three syllables when pronounced in Spanish [sæn–tyɔ–gow].

[10] He says: [sæn] (pointing to S)–[tyɔ] (pointing to A)–[g] (pointing to N)–[ow] (pointing to T).

Figure 3.   Santiago—3 years 6 months old.

This type of syllabic analysis is not limited to the proper name. At the same age (obs. 44–3;9) we collect the following data: We ask Santiago to look for written cards that can "go well" with different pictures. Santiago tries several times a syllabic justification of the chosen texts. For instance, LA is good for "si–lla" (chair) because there are two letters for two syllables; BO is suitable for "si–llón" (armchair) for the same reason; GATO could be acceptable for "per–so–nas" (people), this time using G for the first syllable, A for the second, and the remaining two letters for the third syllable; SILLA could be acceptable for "pa–ya–so" (clown), using the same procedure as in the previous case.[11] This syllabic analysis is **purely** quantitative, because Santiago does not pay attention to any letter in particular (for instance, in SILLA he anticipates "payaso," in spite of the fact that it starts with "his own" letter). This syllabic analysis coexists with other possible criteria of interpretation, in particular, with the possible correspondence between the amount of

---

[11] When children are using syllabic analysis *to justify* a choice already made, they try very often a compromising solution, as Santiago does in the last two cases.

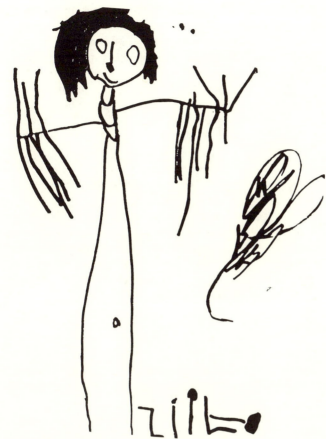

Figure 4.   Santiago—3 years 6 months old

letters and the size of the referred object. So, for instance, Santiago thinks that the card for elephant must have "many many letters" (*muchísimas letras*) because elephant is "the biggest in the world!" (*lo más grande del mundo!*).

During the same interview, we ask Santiago to write the names of the fruits and vegetables of a toy market and he says, "It is best to write speaking" (*mejor escribiré hablando*), and that means to utter the words syllabically. When he says one syllable, he writes one letter. For instance, io is what he writes for "pi–ñas" (pineapples). But sometimes only part of a letter is used to represent a syllable.

Figure 5.   Santiago—3 years 9 months old

When Santiago wants to write "na–ran–jas" (oranges), for example, he writes Si; the S for the first syllable; the stem of the i, for the second; and the dot of the i for the third syllable! The written texts he produces are, then—in this case as in all the others—impossible to interpret, if we do not know the process of construction.

The market play was so exciting for him that two days later, he plays spontaneously. This time he makes texts with four or five letters that are then justified syllabically, but he succeeds in isolating some phonemes in order to arrive at the end of his productions (obs. 45–3;9). For instance, he reads "ca–la–ba–s–as" (pumpkins), "na–ran–ja–s" (oranges), "man–za–n–as" (apples). The syllabic hypothesis (that is, that each letter has the value of one syllable) cannot yet be applied to control the production; it is applied only to justify a production already made. None of the letters are pertinent (in so far as sound-symbol correspondence is concerned) to the syllables they represent.

Some other relevant facts take place during this same period. Let us remember that when he was 2 years, 7 months old, a given text changed its meaning depending on the image with which it was associated (for ELEFANTE it was possible to read "donkey," "lion," etc.) When he is 3 years, 9 months, the situation is different: Once he has given a certain interpretation, there is a conservation of the attributed meaning in spite of the text's being shifted (obs. 44):

(The text SILLA was attributed by Santiago to a clown's picture. We ask if it is possible to put the same card for another clown.)	"Yes."
What would it say?	"Clown, the same" (*Payaso, lo mismo*).
(The text GATO was previously attributed to a chair's picture. We put it under the picture of some people.)	
What does it say?	"Chair" (*silla*).
This one (text DUC, attributed to a tiger) is not good for this one (picture of a milkman)?	"No, because it says tiger and that's not a tiger" (*No, porque dice tigre y eso no es tigre*).
If I put it here, wouldn't it say milkman?	"No, it won't say that" (*No, no va a decir*).

Some months before, we also registered spontaneous comments like the following: "*churrito . . . charrito . . . chorrito . . .* they have the same letter" (*tienen las mismas letras*) (obs. 29–3;3); "*asa* and *taza* have the same letters" (obs. 29–3;4). He starts to show great interest in writing with a typewriter. Making explorations with this instrument, he discovers that letters have two forms (capital and lower case) and starts to talk about "Nelson's other one, Anne's other one" (obs. 31–3;4).[12]

At the same age that Santiago shows conservation of the meaning attributed to a text through the variations of context, he arrives, spontaneously, to a very important deduction: If the letters are the same (all of them, and not only the first one), it must say the same. This same conclusion applies for numbers as well as for letters. When he is 3 years, 10 months old, Santiago observes the prices of two commercial products (two cans of the same product) and says, "They have the same numbers, they cost the same" (*tienen los números iguales, cuestan lo mismo*) (obs. 48). Three days later, he observes the labels of two coffee cans and makes the following comment: "They have the same letters, they say the same" (*tienan las mismas letras, dicen lo mismo*) (obs. 49).

When he is almost 4 years old, Santiago seems to have all the elements that will allow him to understand the nature of the writing system used by his environment. In other words, he is in a definite period of reorganization of his own hypotheses about the nature of the system. He knows already that it is necessary to look at all the letters that compose a text, and not only at the first one. He is now able to keep an attributed meaning through contextual changes. He has succeeded in making logical deductions of the greatest importance (if "they have the same letters, they say the same," even without knowing what the text says). He has built up the syllabic hypothesis (each letter represents one syllable), a hypothesis that nobody has taught him, a hypothesis that Santiago has built up by himself, as have all the children we have studied. This syllabic hypothesis allows children to start understanding the relationship between the constructed totality (the written name) and its constitutive parts (its letters in a given order), and puts them on the way to understanding the relationship between letters and the sounds of speech.

Nevertheless, this same syllabic hypothesis opens the way to new conflicts, particularly with the proper name as it is written by adults. Santiago will again find that there are residual letters in his own name when the three syllables are accounted for. This notwithstanding, his written name will be there as it is, resisting Santiago's syllabic hypothesis and forcing him, finally, to another type of analysis of the word in order to account for all the letters. Let us see what Santiago is doing with this name when he is 4 years, 1 month old (obs. 52). He tries several readings of the conventional writing of his name, always jumping some intermediate letters in order to reach the end. For instance:

---

[12] To work with the typewriter has other consequences and a new disruption into the organization of numbers and letters. For instance, before *e* was converted into "Ernesto's other one" he called it "Ernesto's number" (obs. 28). Some other mixing up between numbers and letters is due to figural similarity. For instance, finding the number 6 in front of a building, he says: "It has Gabriel's letter (obs. 31). In another situation he comments: "The *o* of Omar sometimes is zero" (*La o de Omar a veces es cero*) (obs. 33). Until 3½ years, lower-case letters whose form is very different from the corresponding capitals (for instance, *a* and *g*) are named "the letters of the typewriter" (*letras de la máquina*) but sometimes are named "the numbers that are in the typewriter" (*números que están en la máquina*) (obs. 37).

S	A	N	T	I	A	G	O

(written model)

| s | a | n | t | i | a | g | ———————— | o |

| s | a | n | t | i | a | g | ———————————— | o (readings) |

As he always finds some residual letters, he gives up and reads it "nonstop"; instead of pointing to individual letters, he places his finger at the beginning of the uttered word, runs it smoothly left to right, and finishes with the finger and the voice over the last letter.

At that moment Santiago is perfectly conscious of the difference between what he was doing before in order to predict the meaning of the texts and what he is trying to do now. Consider the following dialogue (obs. 52–4;1):

(We show him a match box pointing to the text it has.)	"Letters" (*Letras*)
What do those letters say?	"I can't read" (*No puedo leer*).
But you may guess, . . .	"No, I can't guess" (*No, no puedo adivinar*).
Before you were guessing. Did you forget how to guess?	"I didn't forget but now I'm a big boy" (*No me olvidé pero ahora soy grande*).

During the same developmental period, he is able to give easily the first phoneme of many names: "león" (lion) starts "with /l/," "perro" (dog) starts "with /p/." And, a little bit later (obs. 54–4;3), he can identify in a new way the already known letters:

R = "the /r/, to make Rubén" (*la /rr/, para poner Rubén*)
D = "the /d/ of Diego"
J = "the /j/ of Juan"
T = "the /t/ of Tere and of toro" (bull)

At this particular time we collect, among his papers, some sheets of papers with proper names well written, with all the letters, but not distributed in linear order (obs. 53–4;3) (see Figure 6). Santiago starts always from left to right but sometimes at the top and sometimes at the bottom of the sheet of paper. When he reaches the edge on the right-hand side of the page, he either resumes again at the left side, or moves from right to left, below or over the preceding letters.

From now on, his progress is very fast: Three months later, Santiago writes complete letters and different types of texts (that we will not analyze here). His name always appears well written, if we leave aside the figural aspects (because he continues from right to left when he reaches the limit of the page, and the initial letter appears sometimes with an incorrect orientation) (Figure 7).

This last remark allows us to emphasize the necessary distinction between constructive and figurative aspects of children's written productions. From the figurative point of view, Santiago's written productions are still rather deficient—

(1)

(2)

Figure 6.   Santiago—4 years 3 months old: (1) Pablo; (2) Rubén

Figure 7.   Santiago—4 years 6 months old

and they will continue to be the same for some more months. But from the constructive point of view, they are perfect. In spite of the fact that Santiago writes sometimes from right to left or from bottom to top, that the orientation of some of the letters is inverted, and that the organization of the graphic space is imperfect, from the time Santiago was 4½ years old he was writing according to the alphabetical principle, without syllabic residuals, and using the letters with his phonetic conventional value (with spelling variations compatible with the system, even if they do not always correspond to the standard spelling of each word).

MARIANA

The evolution of the girl we are now going to analyze is different from Santiago's pathway. She also belongs to a family which provides great stimulation concerning literacy. She has a sister some years older. Since she was 2 years old, the family has read stories to her. She also begins with the idea that what is really written are names (particularly proper names), as is shown in the first data we obtained from her:

> Mariana picks up a book without pictures. She opens it, and running her hand along the page from top to bottom, says, "Here it says Little Red Riding Hood" (*Acá dice Caperucita Roja*). She turns to another page, repeats the same gesture and says, "Here it says wolf" (*Acá dice lobo*), and again, with another page, "Here it says grandmother" (Acá dice abuelita) (obs. 1–2;11).

> She takes her mother's pocket telephone directory and asks her, "May I read it to you?" (*Te lo leo?*). Then she follows the lines from page to page while she is uttering proper names. (obs. 2–3;0).

> Her mother is writing. Mariana says, "Can you give me your writer? (*Me prestas tu escribir?*).[13] The mother gives her the pen. Mariana draws a wavy line on a card. Her mother asks what it says there. Mariana answers, "It says Valeria (her sister's name). May I make another person?" (*Te hago otra persona?*) She makes a similar line and starts another activity, leaving the line without interpretation (obs. 2–3;0).

At that age, Mariana—as did Santiago at the beginning of his evolution—thinks that it is possible to read (or to tell) the pictures as well as the text of a book (obs. 2–3;0). When she tries to read she follows the lines sometimes from left to right, sometimes from right to left.

When she is 3 years, 2 months (obs. 4), we ask her to write her name. She draws some slightly wavy lines with different colors, saying that "Mariana" is written in each one of them (Figure 8). Spontaneously, she adds similar lines where it says "Valeria" (her sister) and, referring to a small isolated line, she believes it says "Alejandrita" (a small cousin). She does not recognize her written name when we present it with capital letters.

After few months (obs. 7–3;6) Mariana now says that she knows how to write

---

[13] Mariana is using the infinitive form of the verb (*escribir* = to write) as a noun.

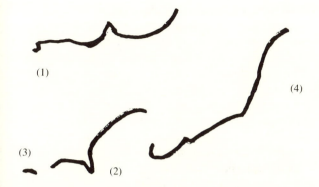

Figure 8. Mariana—3 years 2 months old. (1) "Mariana"; (2) "Mariana"; (3) "Alejandrita"; (4) "Valeria"

her name. She makes five capital letters (PSQIA) while repeating "Mariana" several times (Figure 9). Then we cover part of this text, to see how Mariana's interprets the visible parts. (Each time we asked her, "What does it say here?"[14]), her answers were the following:

PS///	"Two Mariana" (*Dos Mariana*)
//QIA	"Three Marianas" (*Tres Marianas*)
PSQIA	"Many" (*Muchas*)

She, then, shows indifferentiation between the parts and the totality: All the letters make up her name, but her name is also in each one of the letters.

Two months after this (obs. 8–3;8), her mother writes a post card to be sent to her grandmother. When it is finished, she gives the card to Mariana, saying, "Put your name here." For the first time Mariana insists that her mother write her name on another piece of paper. Then she copies her name very carefully, erasing at several points, and rewriting, until she is satisfied with the result. (The model provided by the mother was in capital letters).

Santiago was attending a kindergarten without any specific instruction about written language, but Mariana went to one where they started with writing exercises (with script letters). One day, coming back from school, Mariana says, "My

Figure 9. Mariana—3 years 6 months old

---

[14] Cf. Ferreiro and Teberosky (1982), chap. 6 for a detailed analysis of the developmental answers obtained with this procedure.

teacher has already learned how to write my name!'' (*Mi maestra ya aprendió a escribir mi nombre!*).

Before proceeding with the evolution of the written name, we need to add some complementary data. Like Santiago, Mariana thinks that, in the texts that go with the pictures of playing cards, ''it must say what name it is'' (*tiene que decir cuál es el nombre*). In all the cases, she anticipates nouns without articles, taking into account the picture. For instance, in GITANA it says ''girl'' (*niña*), in NENE it says ''boy'' (*niño*), etc. (obs. 7–3;6). When we offer her some pictures and texts to be glued on a page, she glues some texts, without any specific instruction, near the pictures and says, ''I will glue the name'' (*voy a pegar el nombre*). She does not provide a text for the pictures that already have letters in them (the picture of a commercial can, for instance), because ''they already have names'' (*ya tienen nombres*). When she chooses the texts, she pays attention to the relative length of the text and the picture, without paying attention to the letters themselves. If two different texts are attributed to pictures that are called the same, these two texts say the same name, in spite of the objective differences (obs. 10–3;9). She spontaneously starts to make syllabic analyses somewhat connected with the act of writing. She says, ''I know how to write *cinturón, cin–tu–rón*'' (belt), and at the same time, she makes writing gestures with her finger in the air. Her mother asks how she writes her name, and she repeats the gesture, saying, ''Ma–ria–na'' (obs. 9–3;8).[15]

This syllabic procedure clearly show up in the following interview (obs. 10–3;9). We present Mariana with a big sheet of paper on which there are pictures cut out and glued. We ask her to put ''the names'' (*los nombres*) on the paper. She writes two letters while saying ''cu–cha–ra'' (spoon) (see Figure 10). She is not satisfied because the length of the text does not coincide with the length of the picture; therefore, she adds some other letters. She writes from left to right, but then she reads from right to left, with nonstop pointing, ''cuchara.'' The same happens with the following picture. She makes two letters that correspond to ''ta–za'' (cup)—one letter for each syllable. She observes the relationship between the length of the picture and the length of the text, and says, ''No, too much is left out'' (*No, falta mucho*), and adds letters until she reaches the edges. Going always from right to left, she tries various interpretations, without success: ''ta–za . . . . . taaaasza . . . . . taaazaaa . . . .'' She gives up, without obtaining a satisfactory reading interpretation.

At this point, we find the first conflictive situation. In this case the conflict is between two quantitative aspects: The written ''name'' ought to have the length of the picture but, at the same time, each letter ought to stand for one syllable. Both requirements are impossible to reconcile. Mariana starts to write with the syllabic parts of the name in mind and puts only two letters; then she goes to the picture and thinks that more letters are needed to reach the edges. She adds letters, and only then she discovers the impossibility of applying a syllabic interpretation to the result.

---

[15] Editors' note: Like *Santiago, Mariana* is pronounced with three syllables: [ma–rya–na].

Figure 10.   Mariana—3 years 9 months old

This same conflict appears with her own name, the length of which is determined by an "outside" source as the amount of letters adults decided to give it. Mariana has made several attempts to copy her name. She knows how to copy it, but she cannot interpret it because she makes a syllabic interpretation of each letter, and there are too many letters left over. Her sister explains to her that she must take the letters two by two (two for each syllable) with one exception: For the intermediary syllable—*ria*— "you need three." Mariana accepts the explanation, but places the exception at the end: She points to two letters for the first syllable, two for the second one, and the residual three for the last syllable. A few days after this, we observe her repetition of the same procedure (obs. 12–4;2).

Because the rule of "two letters for each syllable" allows Mariana a better understanding of the composition of her own name, she applies it to all her pieces of writing. We present her with a picture of a rooster over a fence. She says, "I don't know how to write gallo. I don't know the [gɔ]" (*No se escribir gallo. No se la* [gɔ]—obs. 11–4;0). [16] We encourage her to do it anyway she can. She starts from right to left, putting letters and numbers that she sometimes names correctly: "o

---

[16] [gɔ] is not the name of a letter, but the first syllable of the word.

. . . three . . ." (*la o . . . el tres* . . .). She makes a piece of writing for "gallo" and, below, two others: one for vertical sticks and the other for horizontal sticks of the fence (Figure 11). She reads "pa–los" (sticks) in the last piece of writing (O3Oi), pointing to two letters for each syllable, from right to left, and joining them with small lines. She also reads "pa–los" on the following text (3OAi), applying the same reading procedure. When she gets to the first text (AOi3Oi), she realizes that there are residual letters, if the text is going to be read as "ga–llo" and finds immediately a wonderful solution: "Here it says *ga–lli–na*" (hen).

Let us stop here for a moment to inquire about what kind of qualitative information was acquired by Mariana because, unlike Santiago, she seems exclusively centered on quantitative aspects (*how many* letters are needed in order to say such and such name, and not which ones). From the time she was 3 years old, Mariana has known letters' and numbers' names, but she applies them without consistency to graphic forms. Any letter can be called "ce," "ge," or "u," as well as "*cero*" (zero) or "*cuatro*" (four) (obs. 5–3;3). The generic conventional denominations ("numbers" and "letters") also lack stability between 3 and 4 years of age. Coming back from school when she is 4 years, 2 months old (obs. 13), she says spontaneously to her mother, "I learned one letter for reading" (*Me aprendí una letra de leer*). Her mother asks if there are letters that are not for reading, and Mariana answers, "Yes, the letters for counting" (*Si, las letras de contar*) (i.e., numbers). It is only between 4;3 and 4;6 that Mariana is able to correctly recognize and name letters and numbers. Letters are "for reading" (*para leer*); numbers are "for counting . . . for putting it down . . . for knowing it" (*para contar . . . para ponerlos . . . para saberlos*), but they are not good for reading. From now on, she rejects putting together numbers and letters in a given piece of writing.

What is happening at school? We have no direct observations, but her workbook is full of pages that are exactly alike: Each page has a picture and a corresponding text that is repeated many times. And this happens as well in Spanish as in English, because English instruction also takes place through written texts in her kindergar-

Figure 11.   Mariana—4 years old

ten.[17] What does Mariana do with the English written texts? She has no problem: She reads them syllabically, in Spanish, taking two letters for each syllable. So, for instance (obs. 11–4;0), *an apple* is converted into "man–za–na" (2 letters for each syllable, but 3 for the last one); *car* is converted into "co–che," grouping the first two letters (between finger and thumb as she says the first syllable; then the thumb stays on the last letter while the index finger is kept in the air as she says the last syllable). There are several pages in Spanish with written names and their definite articles, followed by drawings. Mariana reads those texts according to the idea shared by all the children: What is written is the name *without* the article. So, in the text *los osos polares* (the polar bears) it only says "oso" (bear); in the text *los tiburones* (the sharks) it only says "pez" (fish), taking into account only the drawings she made. (obs. 17–4;11).

These are typical examples of *distorted assimilation,* to use the classical Piagetian terminology. The distance between the available information and children's ideas is too big: Children are not able to understand, because accommodation is impossible when assimilation is not also possible. The result is a distortion of the object (in this case, the written text), which is completely assimilated to the interpretative schemes of the subject, without taking into account its specific properties.

The school is trying to teach one thing and Mariana is learning another. In a very naive way, the school is making the assumption that Mariana, like any other child, can learn immediately that written texts are related to the utterance in a very precise manner: If two sounds are the same, we give to them the same representation; if they are not the same, we give a different representation. This notwithstanding, Mariana is searching in other directions. Let us see what they are. We present her the written noun GALLO (rooster) (obs. 14–4;3). We ask her whether we would need more letters or fewer letters in order to write *gallina* (hen). Mariana answers, "Fewer. Because the hen is smaller" (*Menos. Porque la gallina es más chica*). Taking the written model as a starting point, she writes GALL. We ask her to write *pollito* (chick), and Mariana says, "With the same letters, but fewer" (*Con las mismas, pero menos*) and writes GAL (Figure 12a).

During the same interview, we ask how many letters are necessary to write her mother's name (that has two syllables). Mariana thinks that we need 7 letters. In

(12a)   (12b)

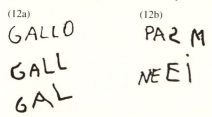

Figure 12.   Mariana—4 years 3 months

---

[17] Mariana is not a bilingual child, but she attended a kindergarten where English was taught (3 hours a week), the language being introduced simultaneously in oral and written form to children that were not yet able to speak English.

order to write her own name, she anticipates 4 letters (even after copying it many times). For her father's name she anticipates "as many as one thousand!" (*como mil!*). Identical syllables do not receive the same representation. We write PA, say that there it says "pa," and ask how could we write "papá." Mariana adds two different letters (SM) and reads "pa–pá" (two letters for each syllable). The same happens when we write NE asking what must be done in order to obtain "*nene*" (Figure 12b).

We can assert, then, that at this developmental point Mariana is almost exclusively centered on the quantitative aspects of writing. The same syllable, repeated twice, is allowed to be represented by different letters. If there are two letters for each syllable, it is all right. Any two letters.

We say that Mariana is almost exclusively, but not entirely, centered in the quantitative aspects, because at that age she pays careful attention to a qualitative dimension that we did not have the need to emphasize in the case of Santiago. In order to have a text that may "say" something different from another text, there ought to be an objective difference between them. This difference may be quantitative (introducing variations in the quantity of letters) or qualitative (changing the letters and/or their position in the string). Mariana realizes one or the other possibility, at different moments. When she tries to write "hen" and "chick," taking the model GALLO as a starting point, she introduces quantitative differences that reflect the size differences in the referred objects. In this case she keeps "the same" letters for a specific reason: The shared letters represent the similarity of meaning between the three written names (that correspond to the same family), and the difference in the quantity of letters represent the ordered size differences between the three animals whose names are written.

In the case of the three written strings for a rooster on a fence (Figure 11), the quantitative differences are not motivated by the differences in size but by differences in the quantity of syllables of those names. With a very limited stock of graphic forms (only 4 different forms), Mariana creates differences between the written words changing the position of the elements in the string. The two strings written as "pa–los" are different because the sticks are different (vertical or horizontal); the difference created in the representation is only a qualitative one.

From this it follows that we need to make a distinction between the different ways of establishing qualitative or quantitative differentiations.[18]

1. *Intrarelational quantitative differentiation.* It is expressed as the minimum quantity of letters that a string ought to have in order to allow a reading interpretation (leaving aside any other consideration). This way of differentiation between "readable" and "nonreadable" strings evolves toward the consideration of two intrinsic limits: Both a minimum and a maximum that determine the span of the quantitative variations allowed.

---

[18] I am proposing here a new classification of ways of differentiation as built up by children. The relationship between these ways of differentiation and levels of conceptualization is rather complex and is not developed here. A point of caution: This classification does not imply that quantitative and qualitative differentiations having the same name appear simultaneously in the developmental process.

2. *Interrelational (nonsystematic) quantitative differentiation.* It is established by the amount of letters that a text must have in regard to an external referential point that is not stable. For instance, in Mariana's case, her mother's name must have more letters than Mariana's and fewer than her father's name; the name "chick" must have less than "hen" and "hen" must have less than "rooster." The amount of letters depends on the external referential point that is chosen. This referential point may be the referred object itself or else another written representation (more letters or fewer letters than another already written name, in order to have a different representation).

3. *Interrelational systematic quantitative differentiation.* It is established by the amount of letters that a text ought to have with reference to an external referential framework that is considered as fixed (as many letters as syllables or as many letters as phonemes in a given name). In this case two systems are put in relationship: The sound system and the graphic system. The correspondences made are always valid.

Let us see the same three ways of differentiation from the qualitative viewpoint.

1. *Intrarelational qualitative differentiation.* It is established by the requirement of internal variation, following which a written text cannot have the same repeated letter. A written name must be written with different letters. Spanish-speaking children usually adopt a clear limit: The same letter can appear no more than twice in the same string (and, if possible, never in a row). This rule is adopted by Mariana when she writes "gallo" and "palos."

2. *Interrelational (nonsystematic) qualitative differentiation.* In order to have different interpretations, there must be an objective difference in the texts themselves. If a text "says" such and such a name, the following text must present a qualitative difference (i.e., this latter text cannot have the same letters in the same order). It is clear that an interrelational quantitative differentiation automatically creates an interrelational qualitative one. It is this same way of differentiation that is shown in Mariana's pieces of writing that we have mentioned before.

3. *Interrelational systematic qualitative differentiation.* It is established by the possibility of determining what letters, and in what order, make up a given name, with reference to a fixed external referential framework. In this case, letters are not just any letters (changing if the referential point changes) but have stable values (syllabic or phonetic ones). The requirement of similar graphic units for similar sound units does not oblige adoption of the conventional sound values of letters, but usually that is what happens, because children do not entirely invent the system of writing: They discover the laws of a system that is socially constructed (a system that they do not assimilate until they have covered the hard task of reconstructing it that we are presenting here).

Where can we place the "ownership rule" used by Santiago? We may think that it is a qualitative differentiation of the third type, because this rule creates a fixed referential point. But we will maintain that it is of the second type for the following reasons. This rule does not allow a comparison between the letters—as a system— with the "system of known persons." Applying this rule, Santiago obtains pairs without any relationship between them: the relation between Santiago and "his" letter, the relation between Rubén and "his" letter, and so on. The relationship between the owners themselves is as opaque (or indeterminate) as the relation between the letters themselves. Because it is a system of one-to-one relationship, exceptions are avoided: A single letter cannot have more than one owner, because this will destroy the one-to-one correspondence and may force considering a possible reason for such an "anomaly" that goes far beyond what is needed by the one-to-one correspondence. There is no stable relationship between two systems, only a stable relationship between elements that are incomparable between themselves. In addition, in Santiago's case the relationship between the letters and an external referential point is limited to the initial letter of a string. It does not matter what other letters he adds. The qualitative differentiation is limited to a precise point in the string; it cannot go further.

With the new theoretical elements of analysis, let us go back to Mariana's evolution of her written name. At 4 years, 3 months (obs. 14), Mariana recognizes her name written in capital letters. As we already have seen, she reads taking two letters for the first syllable, another two for the second one, and the residual three letters for the last syllable. Now, when we proceed to cover parts of this text we obtain the following answers:

M	A	/	/	/	/	/	"Ma-riá"	(one syllable to one letter)
/	/	/	/	/	N	A	"riá-na"	(idem, but from right to left)
M	A	R	I	/	/	/	"Ma-riá"	(two letters to one syllable)

Mariana oscillates between two possible rules: one syllable to one letter or one syllable to two letters. She is now convinced that in the parts of the written name are the syllabic parts of her name, but how does one know exactly where they are? By the time she is 4 and a half years old, Mariana knows how to write her name, without copying it. (obs. 15–Figure 13).

She is so proud of her accomplishment that she shows it to us, kisses it, and says, "This is the way my name goes, isn't it?" (*Verdad que así se escribe mi nombre?*). This notwithstanding, when we ask her, a few minutes later, how many letters are in her name, she answers: "Five, I think . . . /m/, ma, ri, a, na. Four? . . . Ma-ri-a-na." Mariana can already write her name conventionally, but she does not yet understand why it is written the way it is. The proof of this is the following: When she tries to read it, she says

M A r i A n A	(written name)
ma-ri- a - n - a - n - a	(reading interpretation)

This also shows that Mariana has come back to one-to-one correspondence (Why two letters for a single syllable? It is more logical to have only one unit on the representational side for each unit at the spoken level). Trying to "stretch out" her name

Figure 13.   Mariana—4 years 6 months old

Mariana has broken the diphthong ([rya]) in the second syllable. Doing this, she has obtained one more syllable (''Ma–ri–a–na''), but this is not enough to control all the letters. For the residual ones Mariana repeats the two last phonemes, without treating them as such. Two months later, things remain the same (obs. 16–4;8). This time she writes her name mainly with script letters and with one permutation in the order of the letters: MairaNa (Figure 14). All the reading interpretations she tries are unsuccessful:

M	a	i	r	a	N	a	(written name)
m	a	r	i	a	n	a	.	.		.	.
m	a	r	i	a	n	n	n	a	(reading interpretations)
m	a	r	i	a	n	a	a	a	a

Between the first and the second attempt she reads ''nonstop,'' but it is not at all satisfactory to her, because this type of reading implies no more than the global recognition of her written name, and this is not Mariana's problem: her problem is to figure out the significance of each one of the parts that make up this totality.

At the same developmental period (obs. 15–4;6) she applies the same syllabic hypothesis to other written productions. When preparing the texts for some cards for a market of fruits and vegetables, she can apply the syllabic hypothesis not only to control her production but also to anticipate how many letters she will write. For instance, she writes ROUO for ''ji–to–ma–tes'' and MOU for ''li–mo–nes.'' She pays special attention to the interrelational qualitative differentiation (nonsystematic, because the letters she is going to write down for a given name are determined by those she has already put in the previous strings). She also pays attention to the interrelational quantitative differentiation that is becoming a systematic one (she puts one letter per syllable, but not always).[19] Because she keeps the requirement of three letters per word, she also has problems with two-syllable words. For instance, for ''piñas'' she puts OMR with the interpretation ''pi-n-ñas.''

Conflicts centered on criteria for quantitative control remain and are even more acute than before: She needs as many letters as syllables, but at least three letters to have a string that is interpretable. Both criteria lead to contradictory results. We also detected other conflicts that appear when she searches for a correspondence between quantitative aspects of the representation and quantifiable aspects of the referred object. When she is 4 years, 8 months (obs. 16), this conflicting situation becomes apparent in three specific cases: when writing a plural noun; when writing the di-

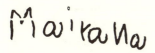

Figure 14. Mariana—4 years 8 months old

---

[19] On two occasions she writes 4 letters for 3-syllable words, making the necessary adjustments when she reads: OMOM is ''na–ran–ja–jas'' or ''na–ran–j–jas''; UROA is ''chi–cha–r–os.''

minutive form of a noun; when writing two nouns that correspond to real objects with a great size difference. It is worth taking a look at these three cases:

1.   We ask her to write *gato* (cat). She writes MI while saying "ga–to." She looks at the result and thinks that one more letter is needed (to keep with the minimum quantity requirement). She reanalyzes syllabically the word and concludes: "None are missing" (*no me falta ninguna*). We ask her to write *gatos* (cats), showing a picture of three cats. She picks another card. In one side of this card she writes the number 3 and, in the other side, she copies her previous text (MI). Then she reads it as "ga–to" and is not satisfied. She says: "I had to continue. Ga–a–tos. Three. Ga–tos. No! Two! Two more letters. These are not the right ones" (*Es que éstas no son*). Then she changes the text MI to the text SU.

2.   Mariana has learned at school to write OSO (bear). We ask her to write it. Then we ask her if we need more or fewer letters to write *hormiguita* (little ant). She answers: "Less! Because it is very small! Only two." She writes SO and reads "Hor–mi . . . ." She adds another letter (SOS) and reads "Hor–mi–ga." We remind her that "hormiguita" was the real word. She adds another letter (SOSE) and she reads "Hor–mi–gui–ta." But now she compares this text of four letters with the first one (only three for OSO). She is perplexed and so disturbed that she rejects both written productions.

3.   We ask her to write *pato* (duck). Mariana writes four letters (ESOS); then she reads it as "pa–to–pa–to." She crosses the final *S* (the minimum quantity being three at the moment); then she reads "pa" on the first letter and the second syllable "to" on the remaining two letters. We ask her to write *patito* (little duck). She thinks that it should have fewer letters, so she writes ES, but she is not satisfied for two reasons: one, because the amount of letters is less than the required minimum; second, because the syllabic reading converts it into "pa–to." She comes back to her initial string (ESO) and says: "pa–ti–to." "Its name is here, the patito's" (*Aquí está su nombre, el del patito*).

Mariana has not succeeded in solving the conflicts that writing poses to her. She is focusing on the quantative aspects that she still does not manage to control satisfactorily. During all this time she disregards the qualitative information that comes through school instruction and even the qualitative information she could obtain from her own written name.

Mariana is not slow in her intellectual development: In fact, she is as precocious as Santiago. When she is 4½ years old, she has conservation of numerical invariance.[20] And this is not so strange, if we take into account the fact that she was spontaneously working on one-to-one correspondence activities in various domains, particularly in literacy (because the syllabic hypothesis is no doubt a specific case of this one-to-one correspondence).

---

[20] We are referring here to the notion that the amount of objects in a set remains the same, if none are added or taken away and in spite of figurative changes introduced in the set by any other transformation (see Piaget & Szeminska, 1941).

Her written name, as a piece of information provided by her cultural environment, is still resisting her assimilatory schemes. At the age of 5 years, 2 months, she built her name with wooden ABC blocks as MAIRANA. Then she proceeded to copy it mirror writing each letter (Figure 15).[21] Interpretation problems remain the same:

```
M     a     i     r     a     n     a    (text)
  ma-ri      -a   . . . . . . . . . . . . . . . . . .
  ma    -     ri   . . . . . . . . . . . . .  (readings)
  ma        -ri  - a  . . . . . . . . . . . . .
```

For the first time, her attempts to read show us a qualitative conflict, instead of a purely quantitative one: Mariana is bothered when she uttered the syllable ''ri'' pointing to an *a* and the syllable ''a'' on the letter *i*. It is for those reasons that she goes back to her previous rule: ''two letters for each syllable'' (when she reads ''ma'' on the two first letters and ''ri'' on the next two). However, this is not satisfactory, and she tries a mixed solution: ''ma'' on the first two letters, ''ri'' over *i* and ''a'' on *r*. To say ''ri'' over *i* is fine, but to utter ''a'' on an *r* is not at all good, because she is now starting to give the vowels their conventional sound value.

Two months later (5;4), Mariana again writes her name with the letters in the right order, both conventionally as well as in mirror images (Figure 16). When we work with the parts of her name the conflict dominates the situation:

```
M a / / / / /      ''Ma''
M / / / / /        ''Ma''
M a / / / / /      ''Mári . . . marí . . . marí . . . ma-rí. . . . mári''
M a r i / / /      ''ma-ri-a-na . . . No, no! Marí . . . María . . . Marí. . . .
                     Mári . . .''
M / / / / /        ''Ma''
M a / / / / /      ''Mari''
M a r i / / /      ''Mari''
```

Figure 15. Mariana—5 years 2 months old

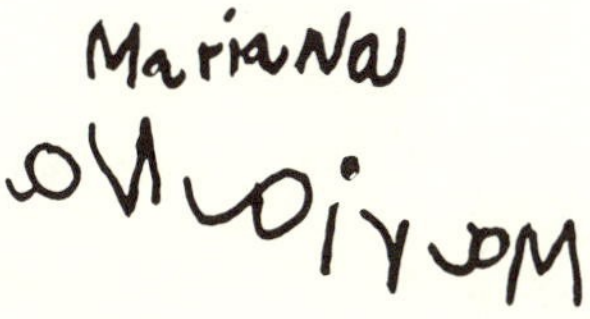

Ma ríʌNɑ

Figure 16. Mariana—5 years 4 months old

[21] It should be pointed out that Mariana has always used her left hand to write but she utilizes her right hand for many other activities. This fact does not explain all her reversals nor the changes she made in the direction chosen for reading or for writing. Santiago was right-handed, but he also produced reversals and changes in the direction he chose for reading or writing. All the children we have studied longitudinally have produced—at different moments and in various amount—some reversals. We only mention it. The details of such phenomena are marginal to our present analysis.

Mariana

Figure 17.   Mariana—6 years old

She realizes that she is not able to find a solution, and quite upset, she says, "You never asked me such a question before!" (*Es que nunca me habían preguntado esa pregunta!*). (Of course, from time to time, over the previous two years, we worked with her on exactly the same problem with the same technique.)

Unfortunately, at this time we were obliged to stop the longitudinal study. She knew how to produce and to name the vowels and some consonants, but it was only knowledge about isolated letters that she had. When she made up a text the same letters assumed other values. We have no systematic data on the following months, but we know that around the age of 6 (obs. 22–6;0) Mariana was able to write messages and letters that she signed without difficulty (Figure 17).

CONCLUDING REMARKS

We have presented with a great deal of detail certain aspects of the literacy evolution of two precocious middle-class children. However, we were not presenting all the data we have from these children. We have expressly chosen the data that we consider to be most closely related to the production of their own names and to the way they understand them. Why so many details? There are reasons for this. We shall mention some of them. In general terms our aims were the following:

1. Through a detailed analysis of the facts, we tried to show the deep meaning of the dynamics of equilibration that Piaget has formulated as a general model of the acquisition of knowledge. Taking Piaget's equilibration theory as a general theoretical framework for our interpretation has enlarged our perspective about literacy. This theory has not exempted us from doing empirical research. On the contrary: It has forced us to find new technical procedures that allowed us to make apparent facts that are difficult to obtain by observation alone: to combine observation with experimentation; to make a rigorous analysis of the details of the facts; to make theoretical assumptions about the data we were processing so that they, in turn, would guide the new data collection.

2. We also wanted to demonstrate that, if conflicts are at the center of the evolution (because the main reason for the construction of new and more coherent systems is indeed the need to overcome contradictions; see Piaget, 1977), development cannot be described as a succession of accomplishments. To grow into literacy is not a restful traveling from one stage to another. Many ups and downs are found on the way, the precise meanings of which need to be understood. As any other growing in cognitive domains, it is an exciting adventure, full of unknowns, with many turning points where anxiety is difficult to keep under control.

3. We wanted to give a concrete example of our way of working in longitudinal case studies. More often than not, concrete examples are much clearer than general statements about methodological issues.

4. The evolution of children growing under similar cultural conditions may considerably differ from one another. But, at the same time, it shows that even though the evolutions of these two children appear to be so different in the way of working with the available information, both are very much alike from the point of view of the dynamics of development (aside from the precise content they happen to be working on). Both Santiago and Mariana try to reconcile contradictory evidence; both pass through periods of acute conflicts; both select (from the information available) that which they are able to assimilate; both disregard information for very precise reasons; both are not satisfied until they find a general coherent interpretative system.

5. Finally, we wanted to emphasize how necessary this kind of detailed data processing is, if we intend to conceive ways of intervention that take into account the problems as defined by children. It is not suggested that all children face exactly the same coordination problems, but it is suggested that all of them will have trouble when trying to coordinate quantitative and qualitative aspects of writing, that all of them will pass through a sequence of intra- and interrelational criteria of differentiation, that all of them build up interpretative systems that are not mirror replications of what has been taught to them.

REFERENCES

Ferreiro, E. (1978). What is written in a written sentence? A developmental answer. *Journal of Education, 160,* 25–39.

Ferreiro, E. (1984). The underlying logic of literacy development. In H. Goelman, A. Oberg & F. Smith (Eds.), *Awakening to literacy.* Exeter, NH: Heinemann Educational.

Ferreiro, E. (1985). Literacy development: A psychogenetic perspective. In D. Olson, N. Torrance, & A. Hildyard (Eds.), *Literacy, language and learning: The nature and consequences of reading and writing.* Cambridge University Press.

Ferreiro, E., & Teberosky, A. (1982). *Literacy before schooling.* Exeter, NH & London: Heinemann Educational.

Hildreth, G. (1936). Developmental sequences in name writing. *Child Development, 7,* 291–303.

Piaget, J. (1977). *The development of thought: Equilibration of cognitive structures.* New York: Viking.

Piaget, J., & Szeminska, A. (1941). *La genèsé du nombre chez l'enfant [The child's conception of number].* Neuchâtel & Paris: Delachaux & Niestle.

3

Writing and Reading: Signs of Oral and Written Language Organization in the Young Child*

Elizabeth Sulzby
Northwestern University

In this chapter Elizabeth Sulzby draws on her longitudinal study of writing and reading development funded by the National Institute of Education and proposes that, during the course of literacy development, children are sorting out oral and written language relationships. Although this chapter focuses on three children at one point in time, the findings are interpreted in light of the two years during which these and other children were studied. A high point of the chapter is the discussion of the forms that children's writing can take, including examples from six additional children. The author argues that emergent literacy as a perspective and an area for research is needed to fill out general developmental theory and reading/ writing theory.

Current research in young children's writing and reading development suggests that it is erroneous to think that children in literate societies acquire writing and reading as "written language" after they have acquired "oral language." The thrust of my research for the past eight years has been to investigate young children's writing and reading development and the relationships between oral and written language that this development reveals.

In this chapter, I present data from a project in which I explored children's knowledge about writing from a paradigm that varies from conversation to reading one's own written compositions. These data are presented to illustrate children's understandings of relationships between oral and written language and reflect patterns found in the project as a whole (Sulzby, 1983a, in press-c).

In my research I have found that children show signs of knowledge of written language in oral delivery form and show signs of oral language in written delivery form. Furthermore, most middle-income and at least some low-income children sort out these differences more and more conventionally as they grow older and have more experiences with reading and writing tasks.

Thus the idea of a transition from oral to written language appears to be an

* Support for the research herein was furnished primarily by the National Institute of Education (NIE-G-80-0176). The storybook reading research has been supported additionally by the Spencer Foundation. I thank these agencies and numerous people involved in the research. Particularly important in the examples included here are "Miriam Kendall," the teacher, her children, and the school personnel who welcomed us and my colleagues in data collection, Susan Anderson, Beverly Cox, and Beverly Otto.

oversimplification as well as erroneous. Nevertheless, the acquisition of conventional literacy does come long after children are judged to be quite competent in oral language situations. I argue that an important part of what children are acquiring is an understanding of the relationships that can exist between oral and written language in their culture.

I have assumed, however, that so-called mainstream middle-class students in United States communities are exposed to rather conventional distinctions between oral and written language, but that they incorporate the distinctions that adult society presents only in relation to their own developing concepts. Thus I have used tasks that are arrayed according to conventional distinctions and have watched for children's adaptations of linguistic modes that could reveal the relationships they see between the modes. From this point forward, I write as if the mainstream literate distinctions hold, even though this is clearly an oversimplification.

From a linguistic and psychological perspective, oral and written language appear to have some differences that are relatively culture-free; other differences are dependent upon the cultural context. First, I will distinguish between those features, and then I will relate them to the young child learning to read and write conventionally in a modern literate society.

ORAL AND WRITTEN LANGUAGE—ORAL AND WRITTEN DELIVERY FORMS

First I must distinguish between oral and written language and oral and written delivery forms. I assume that people acquire what linguists call "language" and that language consists of both oral and written language.

When people speak, they most typically are speaking in what I call "oral language." That is, they are engaged in face-to-face verbal discourse. That discourse can be dialogic, monologic, or some combination of patterns, but it typically reflects that basic nature of oral language—the message is transient and cannot be reviewed; the message is highly dependent upon the present physical, linguistic, and paralinguistic context. Oral language is typically delivered orally, although as we shall see, this is not a necessary condition.

Indeed, people can speak "written language." When people read aloud, they are speaking written language. Similarly, when people dictate or speak the words of a written composition during composing, they are speaking written language. However, our modern societies include more complex linguistic forms and functions; features of written language become part of speech that is delivered orally. For example, speakers often give speeches that have features more appropriate to written form.

Some features are specific to writing. Writing has a permanence that speech does not and, unless destroyed, writing can be reviewed. It maintains "stability"—it is frozen in time and location. Writing is linear; the wholeness or interrelatedness of ideas or events have to be described in units that appear in linear order. Other features of writing are more conventional than they are necessary, but they serve to allow writing to do its communicative task more effectively. Writing is relatively "decontextualized," to use the term popularized by Olson (1977). Its wording requires specification for the audience/reader (Menig-Peterson & McCabe, 1978; Sulzby, 1985b; Tinzmann, Cox, & Sulzby, 1983). The order of information needs to be presented when needed by the audience/reader (Flower, 1979).

Young children import features of written language into their speech. Researchers are becoming increasingly aware of the phenomenon called "reading prosody" or "reading intonation" that can be heard when young children are looking at the pictures of a storybook (Sulzby, 1983b; 1985a). Second, children (as well as adults) make "errors" in written composition by taking conventions more appropriate to oral situations and importing them into written situations. Finally, children use oral language in order to find out more about written language; they ask questions in oral interactive form about the written forms they are exploring.

THEORETICAL BASIS OF THE RESEARCH

My perspective toward emergent literacy builds upon two primary sources: from developmental theory, the theories of both Piaget and Vygotsky; and, from the field of reading, interactive theories which are currently being expanded to include reading and writing. I believe a theory must be grounded so, like Piagetian scholars, I spend much time in close observation of individual children, attempting to see the world of literacy from the child's viewpoint, suspending empirical and theoretical presuppositions while looking, then modifying both my research and emerging theory in response to these observations.

I believe that a theory of emergent literacy must account both for the individual child's invention and exploration and for the limiting features of biology, structure, and convention. Piaget stressed development as a limiting case and showed that young children's concepts are their own constructions, as Ferreiro (this volume) has begun to illustrate in written language. Children construct ideas about reading and writing that are not taught to them, are not modeled for them, and are not yet conventional. My interpretation is that these ideas continue to exist in some form in a repetoire of knowledges about written language.

We do see, however, that much information is presented to children about written language; thus the social interaction theory of Vygotsky becomes an important tool. Vygotsky described the zone of proximal development as a range of social interaction between an adult and child in which the child can perform with degrees of assistance from an adult that which s/he cannot yet perform independently. Much has been made of this idea in describing parent–child interactions, including interactions with literacy. The zone of proximal development ends at the level at which the child can operate independently. In addition to the independent level and the zone of proximal development, though, the child has the ability to revert below the typical independent level to more primitive behaviors to serve higher-order goals, as when young children who can use invented spelling to write revert to scribbling to compose a story. The child also has the ability to pretend and to explore with or without direct social interaction with the adult. Thus in my work, I use tasks that are arrayed across the hypothesized zone of proximal development and also include encouragement techniques that urge the child to "do it your way," "pretend," or "do it like grown-ups do it," "the best you can; it doesn't have to be just like grown-ups do it."

I have used the phrase, "children's developing knowledges about written language," with an *s* on knowledges in order to stress that children are exposed to information about literacy in great variation, and they show even more variation in their responses to what they are exposed to. I argue that this variation is important and is dealt with in at least two ways. First, there is the organizing nature of conventional adult literacy that children are exposed to in social interaction. Ferreiro (this volume; and Ferreiro & Teberosky, 1982) has stressed the importance of the conventional model for providing children with conflictive situations that lead to further development. Second, and in contrast to the Piagetian view, this variation implies that literacy is not acquired in a neat, universal sequence. Children are learning about letters, sounds, words, and production and comprehension of written language simultaneously and in various orders. This latter point leads to the importance of an interactive model of reading/writing.

Interactive theories (Rumelhart, 1977; Lesgold & Perfetti, 1981) assume that people process information about all "levels" of knowledge about reading/writing simultaneously. Unfortunately, until recently such theories could not deal with early literacy, because it was assumed that young children had to acquire the so-called "lower" levels such as letter identification, letter–sound relationships, letter patterns, and words, before they could comprehend written language. Now, researchers are amassing evidence that so-called "higher" levels such as text production, text comprehension, monitoring and self-correction strategies are also being developed in young children at the same time that children are beginning to develop concepts about letters, sounds, and words. I argue that children's knowledges are not organized like adult, conventional knowledge; thus the interactive theories have the wrong details for a picture of young children, even though the idea of parallel processing of levels of knowledge appears to be sound.

Finally, I believe that a theory of emergent literacy must encompass the whole child. The child learns content in a social context and the affective part of learning is just as important as the content. Thus, in my studies, the interaction with the adult examiner is important and the speech of both partners is the unit of analysis, both for tracking oral and written language relationships and in documenting the rapport and spontaneity between partners.

FROM CONVERSATION TO READING YOUR OWN COMPOSITIONS (BEGINNING READERS' DEVELOPING KNOWLEDGES ABOUT WRITTEN LANGUAGE)

During 1980–1982 I conducted a two-year longitudinal study of 5- and 6-year-old children's literacy development, with the primary focus on their kindergarten year. The data that I present here come from a study conducted in April of the kindergarten year. The subjects were nine children selected for intensive case study, with three each being judged to be high, moderate, and low in emergent literacy. Each child was assigned to one researcher who worked with the child for the entire 2-year period. By the time these data were collected, the children had been observed at least weekly in their classroom activities and had taken part in seven sessions in which they wrote in response to the researcher's elicitations.

Prior to this session, the children had taken part in two other sessions using the same tasks. In these tasks we had asked children to compose a written text (a) by storytelling to see if the content was "the way you want it to be from beginning to end," (b) by dictating to a scribe, and (c) by writing the text themselves. In the first two sessions, children were asked to compose about a topic, learning to ride a "big wheel," about which we had previously elicited conversation. This conversation gave us evidence that the children all had experienced this event and that it was a realistic topic for composition. For the session I describe here, we provided a new experience to the children as a stimulus and recorded their speech during the experience.

A problem we ran into in the "big wheel" sessions had been children's tendency not to specify the events of the story in a decontextualized manner and not to include the structural features of a well-formed story. Two findings were important. First, children contextualized their stories to the situation specified in the directions and to the aspects of a story specified in the directions (Cox, 1983; Cox & Sulzby, 1984). This kind of effect has also been reported in detail by King and Rentel (1981, 1982) and, anecdotally, by Harste, Burke, and Woodward (1981). In examining the children's compositions for details specifically related to the well-formed story by story grammar standards, we found that children typically omitted the setting and referred to the protagonist and to the topic by pronouns.

It appeared clear that children could contextualize their stories to the language we used in directions, but we also speculated their individual experiences in learning to ride a big wheel or other child's riding toy varied. Some of the children appeared to have great memories for the details of the attempt of first learning to ride, and others appeared to have it coded in memory as something that "just happened," even though other parts of the experience, like who helped them or the events of buying the toy, were recounted in great detail. We had found this kind of variation of the "semantic content" of this event with a different group of kindergarteners as well (Sulzby, 1981, 1985b).

Bearing these considerations in mind, for this study, we made a full record as each child took part in the new experience we provided. The experience was structured so as to elicit all parts of a simple story as outlined in story grammar terms, using the outline by Stein and Glenn (1979) as a guide: setting, initiating event, internal response (including a goal), attempt, consequence, and reaction.

In the new experience, the children were introduced to a setting, in which they themselves became the protagonists as the event unfolded. After they entered the setting, a new, or initiating event with elements of suspense was announced, and there was a pause for children to have an internal response. Additionally, an externally imposed goal was announced, and children were given directions about how to attempt to attain the goal. However, a complication was built into the attempt situation so that a stereotyped, "I did it," rendition would be highly unlikely. Finally, separate consequence and reaction situations were built into the design of the stimulus experience. In order to make it more likely that the child would include these parts in the composition, we specified a nonpresent audience.

Task Situation

The experience was a race with silly, wind up toys. Groups of three children were seen at a time and were told that the researchers had a surprise for them. They were led to a spot on the floor of the school cafeteria on which a race track had been outlined with masking tape. The track had three lanes, one for each child. Children typically predicted, voluntarily, that they were going to race. Then one researcher, who led the experience, announced in a dramatic fashion that the children would do something a bit different. The children were told that the researchers had four boxes with surprise racers inside. The children were to draw numbers to see which racer each would get.

This activity was structured to elicit language of surprise and exploration when the child opened the box and began to explore the eccentricities of the racer inside. Each toy had a fluke that made it intrude into the other children's lanes. One black, hairy spider had floppy legs that sent it harem-scarem across the floor; a toy helicopter proceeded in one direction then another and another; a toy airplane turned slow somersaults that ended in its changing direction; and a plastic frog with a baby on its back could only be propelled by pumping a plastic syringe, which guided it unpredictably across the tile floor.

The lead researcher waited until the children had explored how their toys worked and then announced the rules of the race. Each child was to manage his or her own racer and had to get it down the lane to the finish line, without picking up or carrying the racer. The racer had to cover the entire race track; if the racer went into another child's lane, the child guiding the racer had to get it back across the lane marker at the same spot that it went out and then continue on toward the finish line.

As the children raced, the adults yelled encouragements but did not interfere with the children's activities or speech. The children were praised no matter what order they finished in, first, second, or third. The researchers waited as the children finished whatever comments they had about the race, and then announced that each child would get a ribbon and would get to decorate the ribbon. Again, the goal was for the children to continue to recapitulate the events conversationally and to comment on the new activity.

After all parts of the experience were finished, the lead researcher then guided a more structured discussion of what happened during the race. This discussion was similar in structure to the way teachers conduct "circle time" or "sharing time" in kindergarten or first-grade classrooms (cf. Green & Wallat, 1981; Mehan, 1979; Markowitz & Moses, 1981; Sulzby & Anderson, 1982). The lead researcher concluded the discussion by announcing that the children were again going to write stories as they had done previously. As in previous sessions, topic and audience considerations were drawn to the children's attention. The directions were worded as follows.

> THE SPECIAL PART ABOUT TODAY'S STORY IS THAT WE WANT YOU TO MAKE THE STORY FOR SOMEONE WHO WASN'T HERE. . . . YOU NEED TO MAKE THE STORY SO THAT A PERSON WHO WASN'T HERE WOULD UNDERSTAND WHAT HAPPENED AND WHAT A GOOD TIME WE HAD.

Each child was then led to a separate table by an individual researcher who reiterated the entire set of directions, elicited a told story, a dictated story, and a handwritten story. For each task, the researcher restated the general directions, along with modifications for each mode, and always reinstated the audience considerations.

The entire sessions were tape-recorded, with two recorders placed at either end of the race track and moved to surround the sites of the ribbon decoration and the concluding group discussion. Children's composing sessions were tape-recorded individually. Tapes were transcribed and checked twice initially and numerous times thereafter. The resulting typed protocols included the scribe's copy of the dictation and the child's handwritten story, along with comments about nonverbal behaviors added by the researcher.

Full results of this study are reported in Sulzby (1983a, in press-c). For this chapter, I have used examples to illustrate selected parts of children's understandings of oral and written language.

Children's Use of Oral Language Appropriate to Oral Situations

The first way we looked at the resulting data was to ask ourselves if what we were calling signs of written language in children's oral language was simply these children's typical usage, independent of the speech situation. Thus it was very important to be certain that children's speech differed in oral and written language situations. While we had evidence from previous studies and classroom observations, the evidence gathered in this session appeared to be stronger and to show more variation with different oral situations.

One of the instances in which oral language could be used in ways that seemed appropriate for oral rather than written language are interview sessions. Interviewing often set the context for the kind of language structuring that teachers use in classroom lessons, the structure that Mehan (1979, 1982) calls the IRE sequence. That is, the adult examiner would initiate, or ask a question (I), the child would respond (R), and the adult would give some kind of evaluation (E). Evaluations could take many forms, be it simply an "Hmm," and going on to the next question, praising the child, or asking the child to explain further. It does, however, keep the adult in charge of keeping the discourse alive.

The second class of instances in which oral language should be used is conversation. Analyzing the structure of interviews in previous studies led us to consider how we could elicit conversation from children that would be more like casual acquaintances or friends talking together; we attempted to structure situations that would elicit such conversations. In such conversations, either partner would be free to raise a topic and the other could choose whether or not to pick up that topic and extend it. Also, each person's speech would be highly contingent upon the other person's. Units of speech could be elliptical or could be the "uh's," "um's," or "uh-huh's" of acknowledgment that signals willingness for the conversation to continue. Within limits of politeness, speech units can overlap, can dangle as incomplete fragments, or can be interrupted. Utterances could be highly contextualized, depending upon the conversational or physical context for specification rather than putting the specification in the utterance itself. Finally, the significance of each speech utterance can be marked through prosodic features (see Sulzby, in press-a; also Genishi & de Paolo, 1982; Labov & Waletsky, 1967; Peterson & McCabe, 1983; Wade, 1983).

Besides the IRE-type interviews and conversation, a third important category of oral situation is when speech accompanies activity. In these situations, the speech is backgrounded to the activity which is foregrounded. Such speech typically is not interactive but is private. It may be composed of sentences, fragments, or of interjections. Again, we designed our situation to include instances in which speech could accompany activity.

In the prolonged example that follows (1.1–1.5) three children were being introduced to the idea of the race. The speech situation gradually changes from the adult-led IRE sequence structure to speech that is more conversation between equals to the final situation in which the speech activity is not conversation but speech accompanying action. A section illustrating the adult's use of contextualized language in an oral monologue bridges between the examples to maintain the account for the reader and to introduce ideas that will be built upon in sections on written language characteristics. In this example, there are three children, Doug (5–8), Nicole (6–1), and Mike (6–0), and three adults, ES, BO, and BC. In example 1.1, the adult has led the children toward the race track setting and has begun to talk about the surprise.

Example 1.1

ES:	. . . figure out what it is we're going to do today.
Mike:	A race.
ES:	Wow! You're really smart. Now, sit down, sit down. Let's think a minute. Does that look like a race track?
Children:	Yes.
	Yes.
	Yeees.
ES:	Yeah? You ever been in a race?
Doug:	No.
Mike:	Well—but my daddy had—I raced in at home.
ES:	Yeah? How about you, Doug?
Doug:	No.

ES: Never had a race?
Doug: Mmhm.

At this point, the adult had held the floor open for Doug in a manner similar to IRE structure but had deliberately been using casual speech, "You ever been in a race?" and "How about you?" The children begin to pick up on the cues and take part in a more conversational manner, beginning as Nicole interrupts the adult.

Example 1.2

ES: No? And you neither, Mike? Not on your big wheel—or your bicycle or—
Nicole: (Interrupting)—I sometimes race my friends—on my bike.
ES: On your bicycle?
Nicole: I have—I have a two-wheeler.
ES: Yeah! Oh, you do?
Nicole: I have a two-wheeler.

The adult then went into an oral monologue to explain the race. The monologue included some features of written language but also included many features appropriate to oral language, such as stress and gestures. The latter reached its apex when the adult acted out being one of the funny racers.

Example 1.3

ES: Okay? Now, there may be an accident, okay? Your racer might go across—the line—the wrong way. Or might go outside—or it might go—start to go in somebody else's lane. And if it does that, you have to stop it and put it back in right at that place. Let me show you what. Let's pretend that I'm a racer. Let's pretend that Mike winds me up and I'm his racing toy. And I start and I go across like that. (Sounds of shoes scurrying across the floor)
Child: *Yeah!*
ES: I crossed the line. *Well,* I can't start back in up *here.* That would be cheating. I have to go back across the line right where I came out (sounds of shoes scurrying)—so I have to keep in my lane, and I have to go forward in that lane. Okay. *Now!* Let's see—what kind of funny racer each one of you gets. Okay, are we ready?

In this instance, while the adult is carefully specifying the rules of the game, much of the specification comes through contextualized wording and through activity. In "and I start and I go across like that," the speech is highly contextualized. However, after the demonstration, the adult recapitulates in the specific wording more appropriate to written language, "I crossed the line," however, she continued with contextualized language with accompanying stress on *here.*

In example 1.4, the adult had already introduced the racers and the children were exploring them. This exploration was marked by lots of laughter and speech accompanying activity. In the example when the adults questioned the children, they felt

free to ignore the questions, continue with their activity, and initiate exchanges on
their terms, as Mike does in example 1.4.

Example 1.4

BO:	How do you make them go?
	(Clip-clopping noises)
Child:	(Laughs)
ES:	What you doing, Mike? (More clopping noises, then prolonged laughter from children and adults)
Mike:	Where's the box?
BO:	No, we're not going to put them in the boxes now.
Nicole:	I thought we were going to *race* the boxes.

Finally, in example 1.5, we overhear the children's speech during the activity.
This language was typical of children's speech during the race, with high emotive
character, marked by squeals, excited-sounding or regretful cries, yells of encouragement, or excited descriptions of the actions of the racers. Note the degree of
contextualization in the wording of this speech.

Example 1.5

ES:	On your marks, get set, go! (Sounds of movement and squeals)
Nicole:	(In a loud, disgusted-sounding tone) What's the *matter* with this thing?!
Child:	(Murmurs)
Child:	It's going the wrong way! I guess I'll have to turn it this way.
Nicole:	(Loudly, frustrated-sounding tone) I can't *steer* the thing!
Adult:	Uh-oh.
ES:	(Referring to Mike's progress) Hey, what luck!
All:	(Laughter)
BO:	Oh, my goodness!

From these examples and those of other children in the study, we concluded that
we had structured situations that captured children using oral language characteristics in oral situations. We had also learned, from previous studies, that many of the
features found in such oral situations, in particular the contextualized wording, intruded inappropriately into written situations, like dictation and written composition. However, other features found here, like conversational turns, interruptions,
and prosody marked by high affect, were rarely found in dictation and written composition.

There is another important oral language situation that I have not discussed here.
That is the context in which oral language is used to discuss language—the
metalinguistic context. This context is amply illustrated in the examples that follow,
particularly in instances of asides and meta-statements (see also Sulzby, in press-b).

Oral and Written Language Distinctions: Storytelling and Dictation

In the preceding section, I discussed the importance of children being able to use oral language characteristics appropriately in oral situations. Now I increase the scope to look at children varying from oral to written situations and using language appropriate to each situation.

In this study, children were asked to tell stories and to dictate them as things that people sometimes do when they write stories, for the purpose of getting the story "just the way you want it to be," "from beginning to end." (The final task was handwritten composition, as the children knew from the directions and from previous sessions using this structure.)

The storytelling task was described as telling the story to the examiner who would listen. The child was to tell the story "from beginning to end." Our expectations from previous research were that some children would not do this but would need interrogation from the adult examiner in order to produce the material that other children would readily produce as an oral monologue (see Cox & Sulzby, 1982; Sulzby, 1981).

The task in dictation also required the child to produce the story "from beginning to end." In dictation, the examiner's role was described to the child as being that of a scribe instead of that of a listener as in the storytelling task. The adult scribe would write down what the child dictated. The child was told that the story didn't have to be just like it was in storytelling: "You may want to make some things different now that you are dictating this story." We expected children with some awareness of the constraints of writing to change their speech in relation to the scribe's writing, whereas some children would still use language more suited to the storytelling situation. In both tasks, we expected some children to need conversational exchanges.

The structure of our directions could be expected to draw a relatively minor distinction between storytelling and story dictation, certainly less than that between dictation and voluntary narratives like those elicited by more naturalistic techniques in which writing was not an eventual goal (see Botvin & Sutton-Smith, 1977; Peterson & McCabe, 1983). Indeed, we expected from previous research and from our theoretical considerations that some children would treat the tasks as essentially the same: a chance to tell a story. However, we further expected that children with more awareness of the nature of written language would take the scribe's needs to write into account in dictation, whereas in storytelling they of course would not.

Oral monologues and written monologues can be examined from many different perspectives and differences and similarities can appear across those perspectives. Gradually, we have begun to untangle those perspectives by focusing on them one (or a few) at a time. In some comparisons, judges have listened to the audiotapes to see if prosodic features can be used to reveal distinctions (see Sulzby, 1982, in press-a). In others, the written transcripts have been analyzed for features of story grammar, specification of context, and cohesion (Cox, 1983, Cox & Sulzby, 1984; Sulzby, 1983a; Tinzmann, et al., 1983).

In the examples that follow, I discuss three gross ways in which the distinctions can be considered. First is an instance in which the child treats the two conditions as differing somewhat. Second is an instance in which the child takes both conditions, storytelling and dictation, as instances in which oral language should be used. In the third instance, another child also treats both conditions quite similarly; however, she imports language suited to written form into the oral form of storytelling. (I have discussed these children in terms of their progress toward being independent readers and writers elsewhere, particularly in Sulzby, 1983a, and in press-c. Here I only give a brief overview of each child's abilities as I present their examples.)

Betsy (age 6–1).   Betsy is a child who began to read independently during kindergarten; she also wrote in a mixture of advanced invented spelling and conventional spelling. She made advanced distinctions between oral and written language (although, as we shall see in the section on handwritten compositions, she is still learning more about these distinctions).

In example 2.1, Betsy tells her story and uses clearly signaled asides to the examiner. She is showing that she treats the "story" as a bracketed special piece of discourse, separate from, first, a reactive, elaborative comment to her listener and, second, a question that she addressed to the listener that referred to story content but queried the basis for that content. It appears that as children become more advanced in their literacy knowledge, they can use clearer signals about how a listener should regard pieces of discourse and they treat utterances like oral narratives as objects for discussion (see Sulzby & Otto, 1982).

Example 2.1: Betsy, Storytelling

Child: Well, um, I first picked a number
and um I looked at it
and it was number four. (2 seconds)
Funny number four, number I like. (3 s)
And um, (2 s) then, I, (2 s) um,
   picked a racer thing
and it kept, and I, (1 s) let it go
and it was, gonna, and it was racing,
and, when it was racing I let it go
and it kept twirling around and coming
   back at me. (2 s)
And I was pushing it and push–ed it, and
   I was pushing it and it wouldn't go,
so I had to, I had to carry it all the way
   to the finish line.

Adult: [Low chuckle]

Child: I mean like (pause, 3 s, child walks both hands across the table top to demonstrate) that. [The intonation here was that of an aside and Betsy shifted her posture first to look more directly at the adult, then to demonstrate, then back to her previous "storytelling" posture.]
I pushed it and pushed it and pushed it.
And it got there. (5 s)
And then, um, we all got prizes
and we decorated them, (3 s)

and, um (3 s) we only got to put one
thing on 'em. (2 s)
How come? [Aside]
Adult: [Indecipherable syllable, probably a query?]
Child: How come we only get one (pause) to put on?
[Aside]
Adult: Well, so we'll have enough for everyone.
Anything else?
Child: No.

Notice that Betsy used good control of prosodic and paralinguistic features that mark asides as being apart from her oral monologue, yet she did not decontextualize the story for a nonpresent audience. She assumed knowledge on the part of the audience, knowledge that there was a race and about who took part. In the oral monologue, she paused for brief intervals now and then, as if her purpose was simply to think about what went next. She also made "on-line" corrections, as if she were monitoring the utterances locally rather than using advance planning. (In this study, this was partially due to storytelling being first in order, but we have found this characteristic to be independent of order for more advanced emergent reader/writers; cf. Sulzby, 1981.)

In her dictation and handwritten composition, Betsy maintained the story content in basically the same form, still failing to give the audience needed information. In example 2.2, in contrast with storytelling, her intonation changed to that of dictation and she watched the adult's writing, gauging her speech speed to the scribe's writing speed. Again, she is showing characteristics typically found in children with advanced knowledge of literacy. In this example she made no asides but did let her voice drop and signal that she was repeating herself while rereading the scribe's writing. The scribe interpreted that speech as a repetition and did not write it; in the subsequent rereading, Betsy did not remark upon its absence.

Example 2.2: Betsy, Dictation

Child: Okay. Well, um, what happened (8 s)
first (5 s) was (2 s) [Speaking very
slowly and watching examiner's writing]
I (2 s) picked (4 s) a number (5 s)
and it was number four (15 s)
and that's the number I like (19 s)
And then when I started my racer up (16 s),
it twirled around and came back to me. (21 s)
So I pushed it to the end, of,
so I pushed it to the finish line. (26 s)
And, we got prizes
when we were done. (17 s)
And we got to decorate 'em.
and I (indecipherable) it. (4 s)

Like, we decorated them. [She sounded as if
    she were repeating herself and was watching
    what the examiner was writing.]
And I got to decorate mine with a butterfly. (22 s)
And, we wrote a story about. (15 s)
That's all.

Mike (age 6–0).   Mike was a child judged to be low in emergent reading ability
at the beginning of the kindergarten year. He maintained that ranking relative to the
other children throughout kindergarten and first grade. Mike was one of the most
interesting cases in the study because of the nature of his responses. While he appeared to have a limited knowledge of appropriate uses of oral and written language
characteristics in different situations, he appeared to be learning more about these
characteristics during the study sessions. In previous sessions, Mike had adapted
both storytelling and dictation toward conversation, producing both forms only with
the assistance of questions from the examiner. We characterize such performances
as aided (in contrast with unaided) storytelling and dictation.

In the examples from the April session, Mike continued to need the examiner's
questions in storytelling. However, consistent with Vygotsky's description of language as being learned through an internalization of functions experienced on the
interpsychological plane to the intrapsychological plane, he began to ask for the
questions to guide his speech in dictation. Later in the sessions in first grade, he was
able to produce the entire speech utterance without the assistance of questions from
the examiner.

In example 3.1, Mike began to tell his story as if he were taking a turn in a
conversation. Modern sociolinguistics alerts us that we have tacit understandings of
the speech signals that call for conversational exchanges or allow for interruptions
(Gumperz, 1982; Mehan, 1982; Scollon & Scollon, 1981). In this session, Mike's
examiner erroneously intervened with a question before our procedures permitted
questions. She explained later that his conversational turn-taking signals and his
previous history together were so salient that she violated her training and asked him
a question after only a long pause. (She was supposed to use a sequence consisting
of a 5-s pause; followed by a questioning look; a 3-s pause followed by "Hmm?";
and another 3-s pause followed by, "Anything else?" before asking aiding questions.) Her explanation seemed consistent with what other researchers could hear on
the audiotape.

Example 3.1: Mike, Storytelling

Child: Um (breathed in; 2 s) ah, (2 s)
         ah, (3 s) eh, (2 s)
         I liked it because, ummm (2 s)
         because I won. (6 s)
         And, uh, (16 s, then sighed slightly)
Adult: Tell me about how you won.

Child: Because I kept on making it stop from going
               off da road,
           And I got a (indecipherable, probably ''ribbon'')
Adult: Um–hmm. (pause) Did you do anything else?
Child: Uh–uh.
Adult: That's not true I know. (pause)
           Did you help anyone else?
Child: Uhhhh yes.
Adult: Well, tell me about that.
Child: Well I helped, uuh, I helped, umm, (3 s)
               Nicole by, um, getting her frog to go. (3 s)
           And how I wan—make it to go was
           I lead him with my hand. (9 s)
Adult: Anything else?
Child: No.

In dictation, example 3.2, Mike began by referring to the story he had just told. He not only asked the examiner to provide the questions which he used to reproduce his ''text'' but he also made meta-statements about her writing activity and about the written product. When he commented about the American flag flying in the school yard, he did not signal clearly whether the utterance, ''The American flag is wound up,'' should be considered to be part of the dictation or not; in fact, he continued to give the closing, ''and that's all,'' often used in oral monologues (in contrast to ''The end,'' in dictation).

Example 3.2, Mike, Dictation

Child: Uh, what did I say first?
Adult: You told me what happened.
Child: Well, I liked
           because I, ah, won the race and, ah, ahh,
           What did I say then?
           And what did I say second? (26 s)
           Are you finished writing?
Adult: Um–hmm.
Child: That's what I said?
Adult: Um–hmm.
Child: Hmm. That is a long word. (2 s; evidently
               referring to all the material the adult had written)
           Aaandd (6 s; sucked in his breath)
           what did I say next? (Made a smacking sound; 6 s)
           And they ah, (3 s) hh–aand–umm (26 s; then
               sucked in breath again, yawned long and loudly,
               then began tapping rhythmically on the microphone)
           The American flag is wound up. (3 s)
           (Mike could see the flag outside the window.)
           Hmm. (11 s; sucked in breath again) Umm, (4 s)
               and that's all.

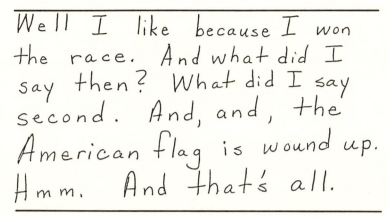

Well I like because I won the race. And what did I say then? What did I say second. And, and, the American flag is wound up. Hmm. And that's all.

Figure 1.   Mike. Scribe's copy of dictation.

The examiners were instructed to treat the child's speech as dictation, unless there were clear signals that a given portion was to be treated as an aside or a meta-statement about the task or writing. This procedure was highly dependent upon the intuitions of the examiners and we were all exploring notions about prosodic cues. In Figure 1, the scribe's copy of the dictation shows how she interpreted Mike's speech in the dictation. While we might now make different decisions about his intentions after studying the transcript, it is important to note that she interpreted, "And what did I say then? What did I say second? And, and, the American flag is wound up," as being part of his dictation. In example 3.3 when Mike reread the dictation, he omitted these statements. This is a behavior we have also found even with children reading from print.

Mike's omission of *well* and *hmm* should also be noted. Even when children are reading from print, if a scribe inserts an *um* or *hmm* which they said into a dictation, even though they can easily "sound out" such a unit, they typically omit or reject such a unit with a specific comment. Mike made such a rejection long before he was tracking the print or independently recalling the dictated speech. We would attribute this omission by Mike as being insignificant, if it were not for the growing amount of data on this phenomenon developmentally. (The words underlined were interpreted to be the words the child treated as reading.)

Example 3.3: Mike, Rereading from Dictation

Child:	Ummm. *I like because I won*
	(mumbled, but sounded as if he said *in*)
	the race. And ah, and ah, umm.
	What does dis say? (Pointing to *what*)
Adult:	*What*.
Child:	*Da, r,r,race*.
	(Indecipherable syllable, yawned loudly)
	What does dat say?

Adult: *And.*
Child: And what does this say?
Adult: *What.*
Child: Hmm. What does dat say? (Slight pause)
        What does dat say?
Adult: *Did.*
Child: *Ta—to help Ni–i–cole win da ra,race.*
        Okay, that's my whole story.

Thus, in Mike's case we can see adaptations of the storytelling and dictation tasks toward conversational situations, both those of face-to-face conversation and the interrogation techniques of interviewing. This behavior is consistent with the analysis reported in Sulzby (1982) of mode adaptations of children low in emergent reading ability. Nevertheless, Mike appeared to be using the exchanges to learn more about written language and was attentive to the scribe's writing, although he did not understand "what gets written of what is said."

Nicole (age 6–1).   I have discussed the next child, Nicole, at length in an article focusing on pauses and other prosodic features in storytelling and dictation (Sulzby, in press-a). For this chapter, I present her stories without pauses (in contrast to the examples of Betsy and Mike) for the purpose of showing the written languagelike character of the composition. Nicole performed something similar to what Scollon and Scollon (1981) have referred to as "fictionalization of self" by turning the race into a story about another group of children. Through the tasks, she made the story even more fictional. Nicole alone, of the nine children involved in this session, put in enough specification to make the story sufficiently "decontextualized," or understandable by a nonpresent audience. In example 4.1, she tells the story about an anonymous little boy and his friends, in a storytelling intonation. I have inserted interpretations drawn from the story grammar analysis of the race stimulus.

Example 4.1, Nicole, Storytelling

Once it was, um, no,	(self-correction)
once it was a very nice day out,	(setting)
and this little boy and his friend	
were outside planning a race.	(protagonist introduction and goal,
	presupposing an initiating event)
And, the race they put some	
tape down, to make the lines	(attempt, with contextualized or
	"situational reference")
And then, they raced	(attempt)
And who won was the little boy	(consequence)
He had a tie	(consequence)
and then, they made theirselves	
ribbons	(reaction)
and decorated them with crayons.	(reaction)
That's all.	(ritualized closing)

The version of the told story that I have used here is the interpretation of two transcribers who took Nicole's intonation and pausing to indicate commas and periods. Each of the above "comma pauses" were briefer than 1 s in duration. All pauses longer than 1 s were at clause boundaries and varied in length from 1 to 3 s. These pauses were judged to be appropriate to telling a story. In example 4.2, Nicole's dictation, she paused between almost every word in the first three clauses, with pauses varying from 2 to 6 s. Her intonation was clearly that of dictation, in an exaggerated word-by-word style. Here I display the story without pauses.

Example 4.2: Nicole, Dictation

One day there was a little boy and his friend	(setting with protagonists)
And they were planning a race.	(initiating event with goal)
So he put down some tape	(attempt)
and he had a race.	(attempt)
And they had a tie.	(consequence)
And they made two ribbons, otherwise it wouldn't be fair.	(reaction)
The end.	(ritualized closing)
I'm going to write the author's name.	(Meta-statement intonation of an aside, as she reached for the pencil.)

In this version, Nicole deleted the physical setting but she separated the introduction of the protagonists from the goal more clearly in the structure. The events of the race, including the function of the tape, appear to require fewer inferences from the reader; the story order proceeds to present the race outcome as a tie and the consequences to the tie more clearly than in the told version. It is important to realize that Nicole attained this clarification while she was still uttering most parts of this study a word at a time with long intervening pauses. Cognitively, this is a difficult feat, one which most of the children were observed to attain eventually during the two years of the study.

When Nicole assumed the task of writing and rereading her writing (see examples 7.1–7.5), she continued to develop the literacy qualities of the story, finally giving her protagonist a name.

Oral and Written Language Distinctions: Rereading Your Own Handwritten Compositions

First, I need to establish what I mean by children writing their own compositions. Children who are not yet writing conventionally use a number of "writing systems" when asked to write. Researchers are beginning to describe and to categorize ways that children write preconventionally, as well as to explore whether or not there is a developmental sequence to these writing systems. Some researchers seem to indicate that children are "rediscovering writing systems"—either using the idea that they rediscover writing systems that are in current usage across languages or that their rediscoveries in some ways parallel the historical development of systems of representation, including writing.

Various researchers trace the roots of writing from different ages, with an increasing number beginning to examine children's distinctions between drawing and writing. Harste, et al. (1981) found that low- and middle-income 3-year-olds made different kinds of markings, all of which looked like scribbling at first glance. These scribblings were different depending upon whether the child had been asked to write or to draw. My students and I have informally replicated their findings with 2-year-olds. Two-year-olds use "draw" and "write" interchangeably in some instances and with clearly different meanings at other times—a common developmental phenomenon in which children vacillate between conventional and "incorrect usage" of a word but remain within the same semantic domain. They also handle pencils, crayons, and markers differently, producing different kinds of markings for the two requests of "draw" and "write." Rather than drawing preceding writing developmentally, it appears that children are learning to differentiate marking into the two representation systems. Vygotsky (1978) suggested that there is increasing abstraction from real-life activity, to pretend play, to gesture, to drawing, and, finally, to writing; however, the order of appearance of the two systems in which marking is used does not appear to be linear, although control of recognizable drawing may seem to precede recognizable writing.

The children we are considering were 5 years old, in kindergarten, in a middle-class suburb of the midwestern United States. We have found that such children distinguish between drawing and writing, at some level (see Sulzby, 1981, 1983a, 1985b). Some children will draw when asked to write, but when they reread or discuss their writing attempts, they indicate distinctions, even though they convey these with a great deal of ambivalence. In the discussion that follows, I will refer to children using drawing as writing, but I do not imply that they did not know the difference between them.

Forms of Writing.   We do not yet have an exhaustive list of the writing systems used by children, nor a defensible categorization of those that are functionally equivalent. Nonetheless, we can list frequently occurring ways that children choose to write when adults ask them to write. Most of these are also seen in children's voluntary writing (cf. Bissex, 1980).

In a study done with 24 kindergarteners from whom two samples of handwritten stories were collected (Sulzby, 1985b), we found that six major categories covered the productions of all of the children: writing via drawing; writing via "scribbling"; writing via letterlike forms; writing via well-learned units; writing via "invented spelling"; and writing via conventional English orthography.[1] Two of the catego-

---

[1] In one-to-one story writing interviews, I have not yet found any child using what Clay (1975) calls the "abbreviation principle," using one letter per word element with dots used to indicate that the letter "stands for" the whole element; I have found it in group classroom storywriting sessions. In these cases abbreviation has appeared as a more advanced form of writing and was accompanied by the child's explaining how s/he used it.

ries, well-learned units and invented spelling, have subcategories, described subsequently. These categories should not be treated as a developmental ordering but as a logical division of writing system. (The reason for my caution about not overinterpreting the implied developmental ordering will be clear from the following discussion.) These categories were all found when children had been asked to write a story for an adult examiner in a one-to-one setting like the situation used in the study for this chapter.

The first subcategory of writing via well-learned units is found when a child takes a word or wordlike unit like one's own name and reorders the letters various ways in order to form different ''words.'' In the second subcategory, the child will take elements from a sequence, particularly the alphabet (as we will see with Nicole in Figures 10 and 11) and then repeat the elements in different manners. Both of these ways of writing are related to what Ferreiro and Teberosky (1982) call the variation of characters principle, that in order to read different things the print must differ. Such writing may, however, be used independently of Ferreiro and Teberosky's minimum-number principle, or that idea that a ''word'' unit must be of some minimum size in number of units else it is not writing. These two principles can be seen less easily in story writing, because children often do not use space to separate between units (again, see Nicole, Figures 10 and 11).

Writing via invented spelling can be divided into three importantly different subcategories, related to the logic of the one-to-one relationship between phonemes and graphs that the child uses. The first subcategory is shown by some children who use approximately one graph per syllable, with some variation in whether or not they fail to hear or simply lose track of a syllable occasionally.

Second, when children represent more of the phonemes than one per syllabic unit, their writing also occasionally shows a lack of one-to-one relationship between phonetic elements and graphs. This may be due to the child's treating one element as standing for more than one sound when similar sounds occur continuously or due to the child's losing track, as when the child writes a previously written unit again. This category I call ''nondiscrete or overlapping letters,'' as distinct from discrete and exclusive units.

The third subcategory is what I have called ''full invented spelling,'' in which the child indicates that all of the phonemes must be represented by a letter. Children's writing that falls into this category may have phonemes omitted, but there is an indication that beginning, medial, and final sounds all should be represented. I sometimes break down this subcategory into degrees, as have invented spelling researchers (e.g., Gentry & Henderson, 1978).

Task Differences and Within-Task Stability.   We have found that there are differences in the ways which children write under different conditions. Similar task differences have been alluded to by other researchers (Ferreiro & Teberosky, 1982; Harste et al., 1981, 1983). Here I only report differences which I have replicated. These differences are important, because they show that children do not hold a solitary conception of the nature of writing and writing systems, but that they hold different conceptions simultaneously. The Piagetian researchers Ferreiro and

Teberosky (1982) suggest that these different conceptions lead to the conceptual conflicts that bring about further development. I have offered a somewhat different interpretation, which may or may not conflict with their explanation. I argue that children build a repertoire of knowledges about written language that they can make use of selectively in order to do different things.

First, when asked to "write everything you can write," middle-class 5-year-old children write inventories in list fashion. Usually this list is arrayed in a column down the page, although the order of entering items may be bottom-to-top or mixed in top–bottom order. With very few exceptions this list will include the child's name and most children include words like *mom, dad,* and the names of other family members and friends. Some children write "common words," like *dog, cat, stop, no.* These words are written in conventional spelling with conventional letter formation. The column display serves to form word boundaries. The most infrequent responses are to use any unconventional form of writing like invented spelling, scribble, or drawing. (Also infrequent is the use of sentences or any other kind of connected discourse.)

When children are asked to add to this inventory a demonstration of "how grown-ups write," they use scribble. This indicates that they have the "less mature" writing form coded not just as a way that children write before they write conventionally, but they also have it coded as representing features of cursive writing, tied to the idea that adults use this form. Conceptually, I think this is very important, because it may indicate that they not only abstract features of performances by other people, but that they use it to help guide their own later development. This, however, is a speculation that would need careful investigation.

Second, when asked to write a story in one-to-one interviews, the same children will use what appear to be "less mature" writing systems. I have used the terms "more mature" and "less mature" in the past to describe these differences, but I am reluctant to use those terms without quotation marks. My reluctance is because I have become convinced that there is not just one developmental sequence that can be found in children's use of writing systems (as these task differences demonstrate) and, second, because I observe children appearing to use "less mature" forms to perform "more mature" tasks. That is, in order to write a "story," a piece of connected discourse, children often seem to use lower-order systems like scribbling or letter strings as means to represent a long piece of writing, even though they indicate that they are aware of conventional spelling for other items.

In writing stories, children use the abovementioned forms as well as a few others. I am not claiming that we have captured all of the forms that children would use in one-to-one settings, but that we have found a great deal of stable differences between tasks and a great deal of stability within tasks. In the current study, we focused only upon the nine case-study children for repeated samples of storywriting in one-to-one interview settings. The forms of writing that these children produced can be categorized thus: writing via invented spelling (one child each from high, moderate, and low levels); writing via well-learned units (one high child used name elements and a second used repeated letters from the alphabet); writing via random-appearing letter strings (one low child); and writing via copying (one moderate and one low child copied "environmental print" and one low child copied his own dictation). In this sample we did not find the writing via scribble nor drawing that we found in previous work, but we did find the copying which Clay (1975) has described.

In contrast with the list format for the "write everything you can write" task, children typically write stories across the page creating lines (we always use unlined paper). Wordlike elements are only rarely separated by spaces. When spaces are used between wordlike elements, they show up in children's writing in ways that appear to be conceptual rather than imitative; for example, children will use untaught devices like changing to columnar display, or drawing vertical lines between or horizontal lines beneath elements or inserting large dots or boxes between elements (also see Bissex, 1980; Harste et al. 1981, 1983).

The children in the longitudinal study of kindergarten from which these data come showed great stability of writing systems within one-to-one storywriting interviews. Only one child completely changed writing systems from January to May of kindergarten. That child was Mike, who is described in this chapter. Mike had begun with a quite small (two-letter) sample of invented spelling and changed to using copying of environmental print to stand for his story, as we later see (Figure 9).

The third set of task differences could perhaps be described as a setting difference, because the task is still that of "write a story." I have contrasted the structured individual writing sessions from the kindergarten study with group sessions from that study and with group sessions in 12 different kindergarten teachers' classrooms over a 5-year period (June Barnhart has been collecting the latter corpus with me). When children are asked to "write a story" in a group setting which they are free to talk with each other, move around the room, come and share their story, and go back and add to or change the story, they continue to use unconventional forms like children use in the one-to-one storywriting setting but with some notable differences. First, their stories become longer, often becoming multipage compositions. Second, many times they use even less-conventional writing forms. They are particularly likely to use drawing, but they typically use thematically related multiple drawings. It is difficult to get evidence of children's speech during composing by audiotaping these types of sessions. We have bits and pieces of this language from the kindergarten study, but most of the speech evidence has come from audiotapings of children's descriptions and rereadings of these stories. That speech seems to be consistent with the speech reported below for the one-to-one setting.

Composing Stories Versus "Just Writing."   When I first began to ask young children to "write your own story," in 1977, it was not clear that whatever the child did subsequently could be called "composing." What we found was that there was clear evidence that some children were composing in the sense of preplanning and that some were also monitoring what they wrote against some standard while writing. These children would later perform a "rereading attempt" that was consistent with comments made before and during composing. Other children would deny that they could write and, if urged, would produce some graphs that might not appear to have any systematic relationship with a possible intended composition. Children who wrote this way, typically using scribble, letterlike strings, or strings of well-known letters, differed in how they "reread." It was particularly surprising, however, to find that some children who wrote with these highly unconventional systems (as does Nicole, examples 7.1 and 7.2) acted as if they had composed a story, sometimes rereading with a finger moving across the letters to accompany their speech. Sometimes children used a readinglike intonation pattern and wording that was quite similar to the previously told or dictated story while looking away from the print. Other children claimed that what they had written did not "say anything," because they had not written anything. Yet another response related to this kind of writing was to claim that they did not know what they had written. This phenomenon of thinking that you might be writing something that someone else, but not you, could read has been discussed also by Clay (1975).

When we fail to find evidence of composing by young children, this does not mean that the children did not compose. It could mean that children forgot what they had been composing—or did not yet know that one should remember what one composed. Certainly even more explanations could be offered. This is a typical problem in language study involving production.

For now, I think it is important to document the convincing evidence of composition accompanying nonconventional writing systems and hold in abeyance the question of whether the other children did or did not compose. Even when the children did not show evidence of composing, we can examine what they say and do for evidence of their conceptions about writing, as we later do with Mike.

Children's Speech During Composing Task.   When children were asked to write in one-to-one sessions like the one from which these data come, they used speech in a variety of ways. Some children did not speak immediately after the directions. Some began writing immediately without pausing or speaking. Others did not speak, but paused and appeared to be thinking. Some said, "I'm thinking," while others simply looked off in space or toward a nearby wall. Then they oriented their body toward the paper and picked up a writing utensil and began writing. Some children voiced an intention at this point and others just began to write. During writing, some children said or whispered letter names and/or sounds. Other children said words and/or phrases, and still others talked about what they were writing. The last type of speech during composing appears to be quite advanced in that the child could hold in memory what was intended while writing it and still make meta-statements to the examiner about the composition. One category of speech appeared in all ability levels—the complaint category. Children would sigh, blow vigorously out through their lips, say, "This is hard," and give other indications of the effort that writing required.

Children's Speech During Rereading.   Children's rereading attempts with unconventional and nonphonetic print are very important. It might appear that children would not attempt to reread print that has no conventional cues—yet they do. Their rereadings differ widely. Of course, some deny that they can reread, because "I didn't write anything." Others attempt to read, however; intonation and wording are very important in judging these attempts, together with comparisons of how similar the story is to what was indicated about intention during the composing. Children may use a conversational intonation and actually require conversational exchanges to continue with the rereading attempt. Others use the intonation of storytelling, and others use an intonation similar to that of a beginning reader. The wording may contain elements of written language; Nicole, considered subsequently, continues to use such wording when she re-reads from her unconventional and nonphonetic writing.

I have developed a way of judging rereading attempts for handwritten as well as dictated stories. For handwritten stories, the writing system used is ignored with the exception of distinguishing whether or not the child seemed to attempt to write a piece of connected discourse. The judgments of rereading are based on whether or not the child is looking at print and whether or not the child recites a discourse unit that is the semantic equivalent of the composed discourse (see Sulzby, 1982). This instrument does not yet include more specific features of children's writing systems, but it does provide a way of describing emergent reading behaviors with children's compositions, particularly whether or not they treat the speech used in composing as a unit in memory. In the descriptions of the three children, I show how all of the issues discussed thus far can help us understand the significance of children reading from their own compositions.

The handwritten stories of all nine of the case-study children are included, in order to illustrate the range of writing systems used by these children. The children's writing samples include their code names, judged level of emergent literacy (high, moderate, or low), comments about writing systems they used, and translations or interpretations. More complete comparisons of the nine children across the 2-year study is found in Sulzby (in press-c). The stories of the three children discussed in this chapter, Betsy, Mike, and Nicole, are presented last. Nicole's writing is shown before and after she "edited" it (Figures 10 and 11, respectively).[2]

Betsy.   In Figure 8 we can see that Betsy's writing system is invented spelling along with conventional print; her invented spelling shows evidence that she thinks all phonemes are to be represented by letters. She wrote a story of eight "clauses," in one long "sentence." I inferred clauses even when there was subject ellipsis, as can be seen in the line separations in the rereading. Figure 1 seems to imply that the piece is divided into two sentences with a boundary before "We wrote a story of

---

[2] In order to project the anonymity of the children, Nicole's story had to be reconstructed since she used elements from her own name. The reconstruction here is tracing of the first draft, with a pseudonym placed in approximately the same spatial relationship to the composition as in the original. In many pieces of writing in which children use name elements, it is difficult to know whether one is reconstructing elements appropriately, so I have begun to use originals drawn from other samples and also to ask for permission to use children's first names in studies in which personal characteristics of the children are not discussed (see Sulzby, 1985b, for a nonreconstructed example).

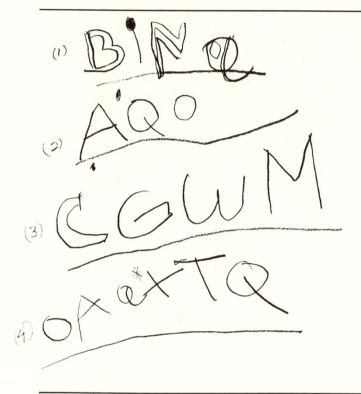

Figure 2. *Noreen. Writing system:* letter strings, origin unknown except for line 1, environmental print from crayon box. *Interpretation:* Noreen did not talk during composition. She reread twice, with the second rereading identifying parts of the physical text as "Betsy's," "Richard's," and "mine." *Rereading, without pointing:*
    Richard's (pause) Richard's spider (pause) went backwards (pause)
    and Betsy's—went front—spinning
    and mine went straight.
Rereading, with pointing (at adult's request):
    Richard's turned around and went backwards
    (pointed to line 1)
    Betsy's—this is Richard's right where that dot is
    (added a dot between lines 1 and 2)
    and (pause) Richard—and Betsy's is right here.
    (Made a dot between lines 2 and 3, then sighed)
    Betsy's went round and round
    and mine went—no—(pause)
    This is Betsy's
    and this is Richard's
    (pointing to lines 2 and 1, respectively)
    Richard (last name).
    Betsy's went—turned
    and mine went straight.

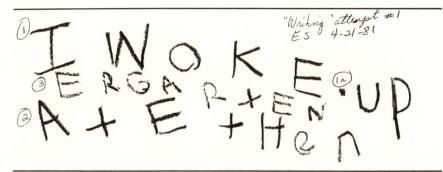

Figure 3. *Richard. Writing system:* copying environmental print (his dictation). *Interpretation:* He copied part of line 1, inserted the dot at 1a, then began copying line 2 which was further in the dictation. Line 3 was an attempt to correct his error in not copying all of the model for line 1; it consists of part of the word *kindergarten* which was elsewhere in the dictation.

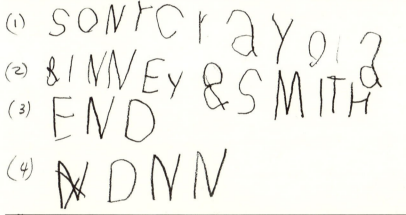

Figure 4. *Chad. Writing system:* Copying environmental print from crayon box and tape-recorder. *END* came from his dictation, but he transposed it to all uppercase manuscript. It is possible that line 4 is an invented spelling or other writing system attempt to write *end* again. *Interpretation:* Chad first "read" the story silently, pointing to each wordlike unit in the first and second lines. Then, at the examiner's request to read aloud with pointing, he pointed to one letter at a time, saying several words for each pointing. Rereading with pointing:

(Points 1–5 all went to line 1.)
(Point 1)   The starting.
(Point 2)   When we started
(Point 3)   I didn't know what we were gonna to do.
(Point 4)   And soon
(Point 5)   you told me
         and then I knew.
(Point 6, in second line)
         And then we had the race.
(Long pause, no pointing)
         The end.
The examiner asked him where it said "the end," and he pointed to the *N* in line 4, "right here."

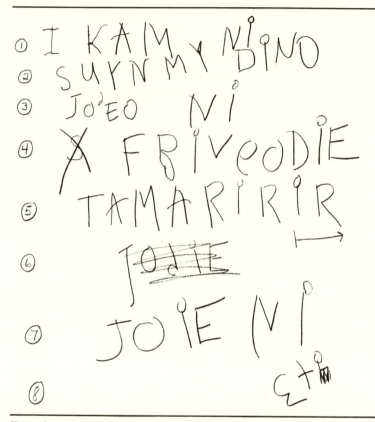

Figure 5. *Jodie. Note:* This figure was reconstructed by the author to disguise Jodie's name, because the writing systems she used included name elements. *Writing systems:* invented spelling, name elements, perhaps some conventional, and use of categorically appropriate patterns (*th* for *rd; f–ive* for first)

Translation and Interpretation:

Jodie's story, line by line:

    Line 1: I came in.

    Line 2: second Dino (her nickname for Dyson)

    Line 3: came in

    Line 4: *S* (for *second* which she self-corrected), no, first.

    Line 5: Tamara

    Line 6: came (which she scratched out and wrote again on Line 7)

    Line 7: came in

    Line 8: third.

Jodie spelled *came* as KAM, a use of invented spelling, and as JO^dEO and JOIE, explaining with each of the latter units that she spells *came* that way, even though it looks like *Jodie*. She spelled *in* consistently as *NI*, which may be a reversal of a highly visual memory, particularly since Jodie was reading independently from conventional print. She spelled *first* with what appears to be a pattern from the number word *five* and stuck a pattern from *Jodie* on the end. She spelled *Tamara* as TAMARIR and commented that it was a pattern (details of which I cannot recapture with the reconstructed pattern) and that it needed yet more, the *IR* underlined at the end. Jodie's use of patterns is even more apparent in the final unit, which consists of a backward 3 and the–*th* ending appropriate for higher ordinal words, but not for the "irregular" word *third*, usually written 3rd.

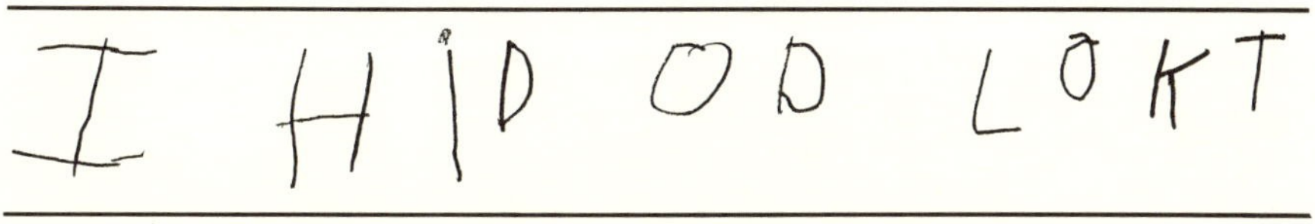

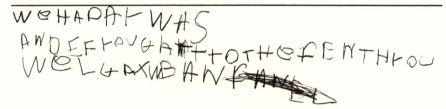

Figure 6. *Doug. Writing system:* full invented spelling. *Translation:* I had a helicopter.

WeHADAL WHS
AWDEFLOUGAHTtoTHeFENTHFOU
WeLGAXWBANGA

Figure 7. *Andrea. Writing systems:* full invented spelling, without internal spaces. Some conventional spelling (*we, had, a, and, you, the*)
Translation:
  Line 1: We had a race
  Line 2: and if you got to the finish then you
  Line 3: will get ribbon. (*End* was scratched out.)

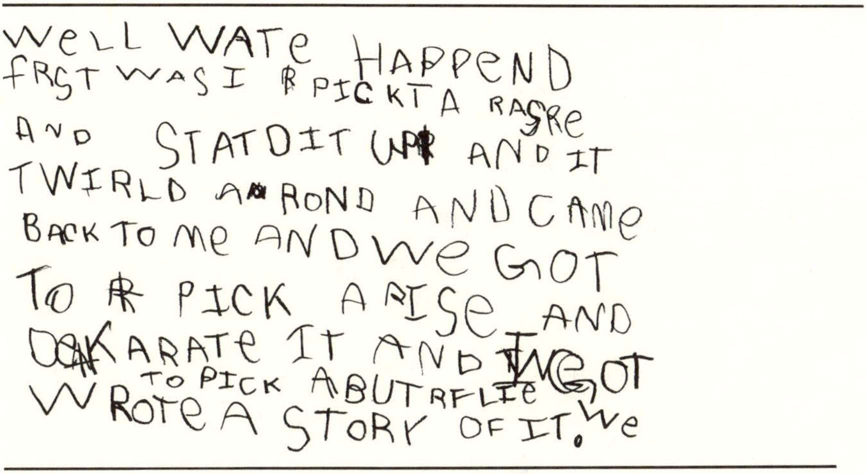

WeLL WATe HAPPeND
FRGT WAS I R PICKT A RAGRe
AND STATDIT UPP AND IT
TWIRLD AM ROND AND CAMe
BACK TO Me AND We GOT
TO R PICK A RISe AND
DeKARATe IT AND IWeGOT
W TO PICK ABUTRFLIe GOT
WRoTe A STORY OF IT. We

Figure 8. *Betsy. Writing systems:* Full invented spelling with some internal spacing and some conventional spelling.
Translation:
  Well what happened
  first was I picked a racer
  and started it up and it
  twirled around and came
  back to me and we got
  to pick a (?prize?) and
  decorate it and we (edited to I) got
  to pick a butterfly. We
  wrote a story of it.
(Explained in text).

Figure 9. *Mike*. (Explained in text)

Figure 10. *Nicole, unedited*. (Explained in text)

Figure 11. *Nicole, edited.* (Explained in text)

it,'' but this is an artifact of her editing. She made two voluntary editing changes, altering ''we'' to ''I'' and adding the ninth clause ending, ''got to pick a butterfly.'' This voluntary editing altered the plural pronoun that was the subject of the last sentence, and upon rereading, she again edited voluntarily by adding a new ''we'' to correct the final sentence. From these few details we can see that, even though Betsy did not vocalize audibly during composition, she treated her composition as an intended message which she could repair after comparison with some internal standard. She made corrections during writing but did not comment on them at the time; later she complained that her paper was messy.

Betsy's rereading was from print, accurately, thus no additional ''translation'' of her writing is necessary. She reread twice, first without pointing. Since she appeared to be reading from print and tracking that print, the examiner asked her to reread with pointing. That second rereading is given as example 5.1; it contains the asides referring to the editing changes discussed here.

Example 5.1: Betsy, Rereading with Pointing

Child: OK.
           Well, what happened first
           'as, 'as I picked a race—racer

and started it up.
And it twirled around
and came back to me.
And we got to pick a prize
and dec–o–rate it.
And we wrote a story of it.
I forgot something.
I'll change it.

Notice the sentence boundaries that the transcribers inferred from her rereading intonation. From the rereading we make a quite different estimate of characteristics that are associated with oral and written situations. In Betsy's written composition and her oral composition, we see a series of connected meaning units strung together with the simple conjunction *and*. This is a frequent feature in children's writing long after they are writing conventionally, a feature that is more typically found in oral language, in contrast with more complex, relation-cuing conjunctions used in written language. Yet in rereading, Betsy divided this piece intonationally into four "sentences," each beginning with a complete independent clause and related dependent elements, consistent with Hunt's (1965) T-unit.

Betsy used another feature that appeared to be tied to the oral context rather than to the needs of a nonpresent audience: "Well, what happened first," is her beginning rather than a beginning that orients a reader by telling that there was a race. She begins as if the audience already knows that. The "what happened first" appears to be more of an organizer for her narrating act rather than an organizer in the narrative for the reader. In a story she wrote in February, she made an even more obvious use of such organizers (see Sulzby, 1983a, p. 292, Fig. 16). She inserted phrases directly from the examiner's directions as organizers in her story. These insertions worked to create a piece that was a series of questions and answers. The questions (from the directions) were (a) "First I'll tell you when it happened," and (b) "Now I'll tell you what make her want to do it."

Cox (Cox & Sulzby, 1982) has treated these intrusions as the child's beginning to internalize (or make intrapsychological) speech engaged in interpsychologically (i.e., between people). Such a shift would be predicted from Vygotsky's (1962, 1978) theory. In Mike's sessions, in contrast, we see that he has been engaged in such interpsychological cuing and is now eliciting that cuing for his writing and rereading.

Mike.   Figure 9 shows that Mike used something that looks like a drawing and lines of letters or letterlike forms. As Goodman (1979) and Harste et al. (1981) have cautioned, we must watch composing sessions and listen to what children say during them in order to keep from drawing faulty conclusions from the finished products of those sessions. The circled numerals 1, 2, and 3 indicate that Mike wrote the bottom string of letters first, did the drawinglike form second, and wrote the middle string of letters last. What Mike said and what the examiner observed further explain the product. Mike was copying from the box of Crayola crayons on the desk. In line 1, he had left a space between the *a* and the lower-case *n;* he inserted the *y*-like form after he completed writing that line. It is the same form as the *y* used on the box, as is the *a* as well. He explained that the drawing at the top was a star.

Mike's speech during composing was affective rather than substantive. That is, he gave sounds of emotion and effort rather than naming elements he was writing. Example 6.1 is the account of what he said and did during composition, with counter numbers from Sony TCM-111 tape-recorder added to indicate time passage.

Example 6.1: Mike, Composing

101	Child:	(To adult about her observational notes) What does that say?
101	Adult:	Oh, I'm just making some notes about some of the things that we did today.
102	Child:	Umm. I don't know how to spell.
103	Adult:	Well, do the best you can, like you did before.
103	Child:	(Began writing strings of letters, copying from crayon box)
108	Child:	(Heavy sigh)
109	Child:	(Heavy sigh)
115	Child:	Hmm.
125	Child:	Ooh–wuh.
132	Child:	(Breathes out heavily)
134	Child:	Uh–uh–umm.
136	Child:	(Breathes out heavily)
139	Child:	There.

I interpret Mike's "There," to mean that the composition was finished. This statement may also provide evidence that he was composing. As we see in Example 6.2, Mike indeed claimed that he did intend for these letters to "say" something, but immediately after he finished, he asked the examiner what the paper said. Note that the counter numbers indicate an immediate beginning. Mike's question preempted the examiner's request that he reread as she indicates in her response.

Example 6.2: Mike, Rereading

140	Child:	What does dat say? (Gesturing toward page)
141	Adult:	Well, that's what I'm going to ask you.
141	Child:	I don't know what it says.
141	Adult:	(Trying to return to examiners' script) OK. Well, you really did a good job writing that down for me.
142	Child:	Well, what DOES it say?
143	Adult:	Well, I want you to read that story. Read your story to see if it says just what you want it to say.

> (The examiner made numerous deviations from allowed procedures here, due to confusion about how to interpret Mike's responses. The term "write down" should not have been used.[3])

144   Child: *I can't read.*

At this point we should note that Mike is not alone in asserting that he cannot read something he wrote that he assumes someone else can. I think this is quite different than saying that he cannot read because he cannot write. Children's understandings about the relationships between reading and writing develop from complex roots. In the remainder of this rereading session, Mike began to assert that he had "meant" the writing to "say" something. The examiner gave an encouragement request to "pretend read" to which Mike responds in Example 6.3.

Example 6.3: Mike, Rereading

150   Child: I meant it to say *army*.
151   Adult: Pardon me?
152   Child: I said I meant it to be *army*. To say *army*.
153   Adult: To say *army*? (Mike's speech was low and difficult to understand; examiner was requesting clarification and Mike responded.)
153   Child: Yeah.
154   Adult: Is that your story about what happened today?
155   Child: Yeah. I was thinking about it.
155   Adult: Uh–huh. Well, read it to me. Do the best you can.
156   Child: I think it says, (pause) um, *the army centrance.* (This might be "the army's entrance," but Mike was speaking slowly with separation so it may be a memory for words like *sentry*.) I think it says dat.
159   Adult: *The army——?* (as if asking for the final word)
160   Mike: Yeah. *The army centrance.*

While these examples indicate that the adult had great difficulty in understanding and communicating clearly with Mike, this transcript indicates a great improvement from previous sessions. In rereading dictation (example 3.4), he had seemed to expect confidently that he had "said" some things in dictation that could be retrieved from the printed version and now, in writing, he seemed to think that the adult could read what he had written. When pressed, he asserted that he had intended the piece to "say" something. Notice, however, that he was asked if the piece was about what had happened today, a reference to the race situation about which he had told and dictated a story. He said that it was and added the puzzling remark that he was

---

[3] The procedures for the interview prohibited examiners from introducing metalinguistic terms unless specifically included in the script; if children introduced them first, examiners were then instructed to use the terms to probe the children's meanings.

thinking about it. From other exchanges with Mike in which he said he had ideas in his head which he had trouble ''getting out'' (see Cox & Sulzby, 1982), I speculate that he interpreted the request to write about ''what happened today'' to include all of the events, external and internal, of the day. This is not so farfetched as it may appear; one other child wrote a relatively decontextualized account of the race, but he began it with his awakening, getting up, dressing, and eating breakfast, then all of the school-arriving events that led up to the race itself. Graves (1983) calls this the bed-to-bed story.

In summary, with Mike we observed affective language accompanying the action of writing, question/answer exchanges with the examiner in which he attempted to find out what his writing said, and, finally, a reading attempt with intonation appropriate to reading. While his performance is certainly far below that of Betsy or Nicole, he used oral and written language techniques appropriately in the first and last category and intruded an oral, interrogative exchange inappropriately only in the middle section.

Nicole.   In the section on storytelling and dictation, Nicole was used as an example of a child who used the wording of written language and reading intonation in both of those modes which are delivered orally, even though storytelling requires conventions of oral language and dictation requires written conventions. She also had read from her dictation with some tracking of print. First she had appeared to track specific words for the beginning lines, and then when asked to reread with pointing, she had matched voice and pointing for four lines, then deteriorated into sliding her finger and saying spurts of words that did not match the position, although she maintained most of the original wording. Because she was so advanced in her dictation rereading attempt, because she had begun to track some print with storybooks, and because she had edited a previous story with invented spelling, we were expecting her to use at least some invented spelling. Instead, she used writing via well-learned units and produced the two versions shown in Figures 10 and 11; from those products alone we could have inferred that she knew little about written language, yet in her rereading language we will see continued evidence of her advanced knowledge.

Nicole did not talk during composition with the exception of the following comments.

Example 7.1: Nicole, Composing

Child: Hmmm. (Pause, after writing *K* in line 4)
    I already did that.
    (She had written *K*'s in line 3, now she began line 5 with *M*'s.)

At the end of the sequences of alphabetic letters she wrote the unit that looks like

STOP, drew the line beneath it, and then wrote her complete name at the end. Figure 4 shows her "edited" version over which she wrote her first name four times. This version is discussed further in the introductions to Examples 7.4 and 7.5. The two written versions resulted in three "rereadings" which are discussed in order.

Nicole's initial rereading of her story was delivered in a word-by-word monotone, one form of reading prosody (Farr, Sulzby, & Reuning, 1985). She was not looking at the print but was instead looking out of the window. Her wording is like written language, with the exception of a rhetorical question/answer just before "the end."

Example 7.2: Nicole, Rereading Without Pointing

Child: One day there was a little boy
          and his name was Terry
          and he had a friend over
          that was named was Annad.
          And Annad wanted to plan a race.
          And they put some tape out
          that they could have a race.
          And they had a race.
          And do you know who won?
          Annad.
          The end.

In this example, she specifies the protagonists and the conditions of their planning in great detail, then collapses the actual running of the race into a summary before the consequence of the race. We have found this collapsing of what we conceived of as the "attempt" in both our "big wheel" and "race" stories even when other parts of the story are specified. Nicole's example suggests that the attempt for her is the planning and arranging of the race, rather than the race itself, with "And they had a race," becoming the consequence rather than attempt.

Nicole continued this form in the second rereading. She was asked to reread and point to where she was reading, because she maintained she was reading when the examiner asked, "Were you reading or pretend reading?" She began with the same reading prosody, sliding her finger over the line but ran out of print at the point where she maintains she "can't do it." She then began to point to individual letters or small groups of letters; this evidently led to some deterioration of the reading prosody, as she read much faster in a more conversational tone. This is reasonable, because she was now having to coordinate pointing with print and also maintain the speech. She, like many other children, did point to the print, even though in conventional terms there was no chance for her speech to match what was written.

Example 7.3: Nicole, Rereading with Pointing

Child: One day there was a little boy
          and his name was Billy.

His name was Billy.
He had a friend
and the—(notices she had run out of print)
Now I can't do it.

Adult: Why?

Child: Cause.
Oh, I have to start over.
One day there was a boy named (indecipherable)
and he had a friend o–ver
and his name was Annad
and Annad was said let's plan a race
and he put some tape down
and do you know who won?
Annad did
but they both got a rib–bon
other–wise it wouldn't be fair.

Notice that in the first part of the rereading with pointing attempt, she had signaled discrete sentences with more features of written language. In the second part,
her shift to oral prosody involved the loss of voice marking of sentence boundaries
and the insertion of more of the *and–but* conjunctions found in oral contexts.

In the example that follows, Nicole rereads during the edited part of her writing
task. In this example, she shows how children shift among choices in their repertoire. She used the repeated elements of her name as "editing," then maintained it
was "Spanish," "a real different way," "my own way."

Example 7.4: Nicole, Editing

Adult: Okay. That was really good. You did a good job rereading your story and now
you can change any part of it you want to.

Child: Okay, I wanna change this (crosses out lines 1–6). All of that.

Nicole then wrote her first name diagonally in two rows without spaces across
the previous writing sample. The adult asked her what she had changed her story to
and she recited her first name five times.

Example 7.5: Nicole, Rereading Edited Version

Child: Nicole, Nicole, Nicole, Nicole, Nicole.

Adult: That's your story about the race today?

Child: (Pause, then nodded her head yes) That's Nicole.

Adult: How is that a story about a race?

Child: Well, I wrote it a real different way.

Adult: How did you write it?

Child: I wrote it in Spanish, in my own way.

Nicole demonstrates how children with strongly developed notions of how oral
and written language are related can shift from one part of their repertoire to another. She does this both in the oral delivery form of speech and in her dealings with

the print produced through her dictation and with her own writing. She uses language to discuss language quite easily, and we probably could have found out even more from her if we had pressed. Throughout the research, we are learning to pay more attention to the explanations of children that sound odd at first and later cue us to important relationships that we have overlooked.

Conclusion

This chapter has shown examples of the speech and written products of three kindergarteners in situations that called for oral and written language. Two of the children, Betsy and Nicole, were both classified as being high in emergent literacy throughout the 2-year study, but both differed greatly in how they displayed their knowledge about how oral and written language were related. Mike, classified as being low, differed from both of them; yet he, too, displayed growing knowledge about oral and written language relationships.

All three of the children demonstrated in their speech and written products that the activities of writing and reading were sensible to them long before formal instruction, even though Mike seemed to understand them far less than did the girls. Mike showed a similar pattern in making use of the examiner's questions to one showed earlier by Betsy. All three showed us that in writing and reading tasks children use features of oral and written language as if they are related.

All three of these children demonstrated metacognitive and metalinguistic awareness about the activities and conventions of writing and reading—and they showed it about developmental patterns as well as conventional performances. That is, they commented on and inquired about their own nonconventional performances as if they are legitimate parts of literacy. From examining how children such as these treat literacy, we are coming to understand its complexity more fully.

Research in emergent literacy has advanced by looking at the child from the child's perspective rather than from adult standards. A theory of emergent literacy, however, cannot ignore adult development. Literacy develops in the child in a sociocultural context. Children learn from interaction with adults directly and from what they see adults doing in their presence. The children in my studies described how adults, particularly their parents, taught them to read and write—and described this long before they were reading and writing conventionally. So the adult as a role model is very important.

Adult development is important in another way theoretically. All development has a ''trajectory.'' I have described adult performance as something that children are aware of and can use prospectively. In a quite different way, a theory of development must describe children's current functioning in a way that allows for the development of all levels of adult proficiency. It is for this reason that the bottom-up, linear approaches fail, because they cannot explain how some adults become highly skilled, critical, and artistic writers and readers. Emergent literacy, with its assumptions that comprehension and production strategies are developing simultaneously with so-called lower-level skills and that lower-level skill acquisition is a high-level cognitive task, offers an explanation for a life-span developmental theory of literacy.

REFERENCES

Bissex, G.L. (1980). *GYNS AT WRK: A child learns to write and read.* Cambridge, MA: Cambridge University Press.

Botvin, G.J., & Sutton-Smith, B. (1977). The development of structural complexity in children's fantasy narratives. *Developmental Psychology, 13,* 377–388.

Clay, M.M. (1975). *What did I write?* Auckland, New Zealand: Heinemann Educational.

Cox, B. (1983). Tracking "it" through the woods and down the trail from emergent to independent reading. *National Reading Conference Yearbook, 32,* 243–250.

Cox, B., & Sulzby, E. (1982). Evidence of planning in dialogue and monologue by five-year-old emergent readers. *National Reading Conference Yearbook, 31,* 124–130.

Cox, B., & Sulzby, E. (1984). Children's use of reference in told, dictated, and handwritten stories. *Research in the Teaching of English, 18,* 345–356.

Farr, M., Sulzby, E., & Reuning, C. (1985). [An exploration of "reading" intonation in moving toward literacy]. Unpublished raw data.

Ferreiro, E., & Teberosky, A. (1982). *Literacy before schooling.* Exeter, NH: Heinemann Educational.

Flower, L. (1979). Writer-based prose: A cognitive basis for problems in writing. *College English, 41,* 19–37.

Genishi, C., & di Paolo, M. (1982). Learning through argument in a preschool. In L.C. Wilkinson (Ed.), *Communicating in the classroom.* New York: Academic Press.

Gentry, J.R., & Henderson, E.H. (1978). Three steps to teaching beginning readers to spell. *The Reading Teacher, 31,* 632–637.

Goodman, Y. (1979, May). *Children's knowledge about printed text.* Paper presented at the annual meeting of the International Reading Conference, Atlanta, GA.

Graves, D.H. (1983). *Writing: Teachers & children at work.* Exeter, NH: Heinemann Educational.

Green, J.L., & Wallat, C. (1981). Mapping instructional conversations—a sociolinguistic ethnography. In J.L. Green & C. Wallat (Eds.), *Ethnography and language in educational settings.* Norwood, NJ: Ablex.

Gumperz, J.L. (1982). *Discourse strategies: Studies in interactional sociolinguistics, 1.* Cambridge, England: Cambridge University Press.

Harste, J.E., Burke, C.L., & Woodward, V.A. (1981). *Children, their language and world: Initial encounters with print.* Final report to the National Institute of Education (NIE-G-79-0132). Bloomington:Indiana University.

Harste, J.E., Burke, C.L., & Woodward, V.A. (1983). *The young child as writer-reader, and informant.* Final report to the National Institute of Education (NIE-G-80-0121). Bloomington: Indiana University.

Hunt, K. (1965). *Grammatical structures at three grade levels.* Urbana, IL: National Council of Teachers of English.

King, M.L., & Rentel, V.M. (1981). *How children learn to write: A longitudinal study.* Final report to the National Institute of Education (NIE-G-79-0137 and 0039). Columbus: The Ohio State University.

King, M.L., & Rentel, V.M. (1982). *Transition to writing*. Final report to the National Institute of Education (NIE-G-79-0137 and 0039). Columbus: The Ohio State University.

Labov, W., & Waletsky, J. (1967). Narrative analysis: Oral versions of personal expression. In J. Helm (Ed.), *Essays on the verbal and visual arts*. Seattle: University of Washington Press.

Lesgold, A.M., & Perfetti, C.A. (Eds.). (1981). *Interactive processes in reading*. Hillsdale, NJ: Erlbaum.

Markowitz, J., & Moses, R. (1981). What is rugtime? In *Papers from the Parasession on Language and Behavior*. Chicago, IL: Chicago Linguistic Society.

Mehan, H. (1979). *Learning lessons*, Cambridge, MA: Harvard University Press.

Mehan, H. (1982). The structure of classroom events and their consequences for student performance. In P. Gilmore & A.A. Glatthorn (Eds.), *Children in and out of school: Ethnography and education*. Washington, DC: Center for Applied Linguistics.

Menig-Peterson, C.L., & McCabe, A. (1978). Children's orientation of a listener to the context of their narratives. *Developmental Psychology, 13*, 582–592.

Olson, D. (1977). From utterance to text: The bias of language in speech and writing. *Harvard Educational Review, 47*, 257–281.

Peterson, C.L., & McCabe, A. (1983). *Three ways of looking at a child's narratives: A psycholinguistic analysis*. New York: Plenum.

Rumelhart, D.E. (1977). Toward an interactive model of reading. In S. Dornic (Ed.), *Attention and performance VI*. London: Academic Press.

Scollon, R., & Scollon, S.B.K. (1981). *Narrative, literacy, and face in interethnic communication*. Norwood, NJ: Ablex.

Stein, N.L., & Glenn, C.B. (1979). An analysis of story comprehension in elementary school children. In R.O. Freedle (Ed.), *New directions in discourse comprehension. Vol. 2*. Norwood, NJ: Ablex.

Sulzby, E. (1981). *Kindergarteners begin to read their own compositions: Beginning readers' developing knowledges about written language*. Final report to the Research Foundation of the National Council of Teachers of English. Evanston, IL: Northwestern University. (ED 204 738).

Sulzby, E. (1982). Oral and written mode adaptations in stories by kindergarten children. *Journal of Reading Behavior, 14*, 51–59.

Sulzby, E. (1983a). *Beginning readers' developing knowledges about written language*. Final report to the National Institute of Education (NIE-G-80-0176). Evanston, IL: Northwestern University.

Sulzby, E. (1983b). *Children's emergent abilities to read favorite storybooks*. Final report to The Spencer Foundation. Evanston, IL: Northwestern University.

Sulzby, E. (1985a). Children's emergent reading of favorite storybooks: A developmental study. *Reading Research Quarterly, 20*, 458–481.

Sulzby, E. (1985b). Kindergarteners as writers and readers. In M. Farr (Ed.), *Advances in writing research, Vol. 1: Children's early writing development*. Norwood, NJ: Ablex.

Sulzby, E. (in press-a). Children's development of prosodic distinctions in telling and dictating modes. In A. Matsuhashi (Ed.), *Writing in real time: Modeling production processes*. New York: Longman.

Sulzby, E. (in press-b). Children's elicitation and use of metalinguistic knowledge about "word" during literacy acquisition. In D.B. Yaden & W.S. Templeton (Eds.), *Metalinguistic awareness and beginning literacy: Conceptualizing what it means to read and write*. Exeter, NH: Heinemann Educational.

Sulzby, E. (in press-c). *Emergent reading and writing in 5-6 year olds: A longitudinal study*. Norwood, NJ: Ablex.

Sulzby, E., & Anderson, S. (1982, April). *The teacher as adult linguistic and social model*. Paper presented at research colloquium, International Reading Association, Chicago, IL.

Sulzby, E., & Otto, B. (1982). "Text" as an object of metalinguistic knowledge: A study in literacy development. *First Language, 3*, 181–199.

Tinzmann, M., Cox, B., & Sulzby, E. (1983). Children's specification of context. *National Reading Conference Yearbook, 32,* 267–274.

Vygotsky, L.S. (1962). *Thought and language.* Cambridge, MA: MIT Press.

Vygotsky, L.S. (1978). *Mind in society: The development of higher psychological processes.* Cambridge, MA: Harvard University Press.

Wade, B. (1983). Story and intonation features in young children: A case study. *Educational Review, 35,* 175–186.

4

Intervention Procedures for Increasing Preschool Children's Interest in and Knowledge About Reading*

Christine E. McCormick
Eastern Illinois University

Jana M. Mason
University of Illinois at Urbana-Champaign

In this chapter Christine McCormick and Jana Mason provide a rare example of an intervention study that takes an emergent literacy perspective. The authors have built on Mason's print awareness research to design a kindergarten reading program that promotes children's interactions with meaningful text and emphasizes the functions of print prior to the forms of print. Children from different socioeconomic backgrounds participated in the program, and their achievement in various aspects of literacy development was found to be higher than that of a control group. Particularly important across studies that employed different degrees of intervention was giving children their own copies of "small books." Another important contribution of this chapter is the authors' discussion of the role which parents played in the experimental children's progress in the literacy program.

Questions of the value and appropriateness of reading instruction for children who have not yet entered first grade have been debated for most of this century. The maturationist view emphasizes delaying instruction until children are 'ready'' for formal reading instruction, traditionally in first grade (Morphett & Washburne, 1931, among others, cited in Coltheart, 1979) even though descriptive studies (Bissex, 1980; Clay, 1972; Ferreiro & Teberosky, 1982; Mason, 1980) show that young children learn concepts about reading before going to school.

The debate regarding reading instruction is part of the broader context of intervention in the motor and cognitive skill domains. Hunt (1982, 1983), citing his own research and that of others, rejects the long-held contention that early training of preschool children has "no marked effect upon ultimate skills" as the widely

* The research reported herein was supported in part by the National Institute of Education under Contract No. NIE 400-81-0030, and portions were presented at the American Educational Research Association Convention in Montreal, Canada.

quoted work of Gesell purports to show. Reanalysis of identical twin studies by Dennis (1941), Gesell and Thompson (1929), and McGraw (1935) which seemed to indicate that the untrained twin caught up with the trained twin actually showed the contrary effect, namely, that the trained twin continued to retain an advantage. Also, early intervention studies by Hunt and associates and by Heber (1978) have shown that dramatic increases in intelligence test scores are possible through early intervention. Hence, the evidence does not support the argument for an overriding influence of maturational readiness. Rather the issues seem to focus on what type of instruction is most appropriate at a given time in a child's life. Early reading, which is our area of concern, still lacks a clear description of what should be taught and in what manner.

Our view is that the meaningfulness of print must be emphasized before engaging children in word analysis. That is, we propose that there exists a hierarchy of prereading concepts. First, children must learn that particular and meaningful words and messages have printed counterparts (functional knowledge). When they have understood this concept (or set of concepts), they will be able to learn the letter-sound characteristics of the language (form and conventional rules). Further, we suggest that this hierarchy is not closely related to traditional views about maturational readiness for school instruction and is partially acquired by many children prior to formal reading instruction in first grade.

This position is derived from evidence by Bissex (1980), Clay (1972), Clark (1976), Ferreiro and Teberosky (1982), Mason (1980), Mason and Au (1981), Mason and McCormick (1979), Mason and McCormick (1981), and McCormick and Mason (1981). Children often acquire considerable knowledge of what and how to read as a function of informal experience in recognizing and reading words, spelling, printing, and being read to. An important aspect to this knowledge is an initial emphasis on meaningfulness of printed words and messages rather than on letter-sound characteristics. The following description of the proposed hierarchy from Mason and McCormick (1981) clarifies this point.

LEVEL 1: THE FUNCTIONS OF PRINT

In the first level, reading is highly contextualized; in a sense, it is similar to looking at and remembering pictures. Consequently, as children learn to recognize words that appear on traffic signs, packages, labels, billboards, and signs, attending mostly to the meaning, they do not realize that words need not be context-specific. Hence they may not recognize a familiar word in a new context, knowing, for example, STOP on a stop sign but not elsewhere. Also, even though they can learn words, they may not report their knowledge as we would expect. For example, several 4-year-olds in one of our studies learned the word rabbit, but later called it "bunny." Finally, although they frequently learn to name letters, they do not know how to use them for remembering words. For example, when asked to spell short words (with magnetic letters), they typically lay out in a random order all the letters we have provided. Thus, at this level of development, children are learning how to relate their oral language to print. However, the strategies for recognizing printed words are relatively ineffective and often tied to inappropriate clues.

LEVEL 2: THE FORM OF PRINT

As children become better acquainted with printed forms of words and letters, by, for example, learning the alphabet, having books and signs read to them, and attempting to print letters, they pay closer attention to print. This gives them opportunities to notice structural characteristics of print, for example, the same word can appear in different places and some letters have particular sounds that are repeated in words. This suggests that children's attempts to write, spell, and read familiar words (Bissex, 1980; Chomsky, 1977; Paul, 1976; Read, 1971) foster a change in viewpoint initiating a level 2 understanding of reading. Children can reorganize their conceptual representation of how to learn and remember printed words by beginning to use letter-sound relationships. With this more accurate understanding about print, they are able to learn a large number of words, they can make quite reasonable guesses about spelling short words, and they will try to sound out some words they have never seen. However, as documented by Biemiller (1970), Bissex (1980), and Söderbergh (1977), their orientation at this level of development to letters and sounds may lead them to ignore or pay insufficient attention to context. Also, they have not learned that many individual letters have more than one sound and that clusters of letters provide more accurate cues to sounds than do single letters. We think this explains their attempts to map each letter to a unique sound (e.g., "we are" for *wear*, "bigit" for *bight*), use the more familiar patterns for some letters or letter clusters (e.g., "rech" for *reach*, "blod" for *blood*, "word" for *weird*, "mote" for *moot*), or become completely confused by words which violate the letter-sound patterns they have learned (e.g., "kanol" for *knoll*, "waff" for *wharf*, "brush" for *bush;* (Mason, 1976; examples by first-grade children).

LEVEL 3: COORDINATION OF THE FORM AND FUNCTION OF PRINT

A third level of development is needed that appears to occur through extensive experiences in reading. We have found that children eventually notice the repetition of sounds for letter clusters in words (e.g., *seed, need, feed*) and realize the possibility of manipulating letter sounds in words. Bissex (1980), for example, describes a child's observation that to write *look,* replace the *b* in *book* with *l;* and Söderbergh (1977) pointed out games her child played with the morphophonemic characteristics of our language. Since a heightened awareness of orthographic redundancy and phonological patterns must reduce the burden of recognizing words, we suppose that this allows attention to be fixed once again on meaning. That is, because children now have efficient means to recognize letter patterns and letter sounds, we propose that level 3 readers can feature again the meaningfulness of print. This suggests that they hold a more flexible view toward letter-sound relationships, being better able to recognize words that have unique patterns, and, making good guesses about the pronunciation of new words, they can skip unknown words in order to attend to text meaning. Thus, level 3 readers have acquired a sufficiently precise conceptualization of reading that they can progress rapidly in reading and can read and learn from more complex texts.

This hierarchical model of beginning reading skill was partly verified with data collected on children tested at the end of kindergarten and retested at the beginning of first grade (McCormick & Mason, 1981). Over the summer, a substantial change of knowledge of letter names characterized children who were at level 1, a developing awareness of consonant sounds in words and simple spelling skill, in part, characterized children at level 2, and a developing understanding of vowel sounds described children at level 3. Similarly, monthly testing over a school year of preschool children who were provided with advantaged schooling and home experiences (Mason, 1980), showed a progression through level 1 into level 2 or progress in level 2, well ahead of most children their age. While predictable changes in knowledge about early reading was apparent among these children of middle-income families, we had not studied or tried to intervene with children from low-income families. We believed we had effective early reading materials and procedures but needed to test them with children who were more likely to be at risk academically.

In this chapter, we will draw on aspects of our earlier work which led us to construct materials and procedures for our intervention studies. We will first describe how parents differ in providing an atmosphere that favors learning to read. Second, we will document how their children differ in knowledge of letter names and sounds. Third, we will provide evidence of successful informal intervention strategies appropriate for children just beginning to understand the communicative value of the printed word. We will suggest that such an intervention may be most beneficial to those children least likely to ''get off to a good start'' in reading.

SUPPORT FOR READING AT HOME

Three groups of parents from two of our earlier studies (Mason, 1980; Mason & McCormick, 1981) were given questionnaires regarding their support for activities related to reading. Responses were obtained from professional parents in a university community, parents who were primarily secretaries, students, and clerks in a small college community, and parents receiving public aid. Parents from the higher-income groups reported a higher level of support than did the public-aid parents, confirming our supposition that parent income or education is correlated with parents' attention to preparing their children for reading. Table 1 shows the percent of responses for each group.

On nearly every question the public-aid parents responded in the mid- or low-support categories more often than did either other group. Two items with extreme group differences regard the number of alphabet books owned by the children and the frequency of discussion with parents concerning educational television. Many

Table 1. Parents' Estimates of Support for Reading (Percent in Each Response Category)

	Public-aid Parental Response (N = 19)			Mid-level Parental Response (N = 15)			Professional Parental Response (N = 38)		
	Very Often	Occasionally	Seldom	Very Often	Occasionally	Seldom	Very Often	Occasionally	Seldom
Hears story records	0	16	84	13	27	60	26	50	24
Watches *Sesame Street*	37	47	16	40	47	13	79	16	5
Discusses *Sesame Street*	11	47	41	7	80	13	42	42	16
Ask for books reread	53	26	21	67	27	7	68	24	8
Ask to be read to	68	32	0	80	20	0	84	16	0
	6x week	4x week	2x week	6x week	4x week	2x week	6x week	4x week	2x week
Outings with parent	26	21	53	47	53	0	37	52	11
	each week	1,2× month	seldom	each week	1,2× month	seldom	each week	1,2× month	seldom
Goes to library	5	26	68	7	53	40	8	26	66
	2 hr/week	1 hr/week	½ hr/week	2 hr/week	1 hr/week	½ hr/week	2 hr/week	1 hr/week	½ hr/week
Time read to	42	47	11	40	27	33	45	42	13
	several	1	none	several	1	none	several	1	none
N alphabet books	53	5	42	67	20	13	68	29	3

more of the mothers on public aid indicated little or no support on these items.

We later learned that some items on our questionnaire had underestimated the range of some items. For example, comments by some parents and later interviews with others revealed that many professional parents read not just 2 hours a week but every day, provided, not just 1 alphabet book but up to 20 (median = 3), and owned up to 200 children's books (median = about 20). Thus, the questionnaire and our augmented survey point to considerable variation among parents in their support for reading or learning about how to read at home.

CHILDREN'S PRINT KNOWLEDGE

The children of the parents in the three groups and children in four additional groups were given several tasks of print knowledge. Two tasks of print knowledge, letter-naming and consonant-sound identification, were given to all the groups, so they can be compared here. The children's responses to these tasks show discrepancies among social class groups similar to those noted previously from parent question-naire responses. In Table 2 are data we collected from three groups of 4-year-old children of professional parents (groups 1, 2, and 3), 4-year-old children of secre-taries, students, and clerks in a small college community (group 4), 4- and 5-year-old children from a rural area (groups 5 and 6), and 5- and 6-year-old children of parents who were on public aid (group 7). Keeping in mind that letter naming is the single best predictor of achievement in beginning reading from among those skills commonly measured on currently available reading readiness tests (Bond & Dykstra, 1967; Lowell, 1971; Silvaroli, 1965, as cited in Muehl & DiNello, 1976), the children were approaching first grade with very different skills in letter naming and consonant-sound identification. Children of professional parents named more letters than any other group and were matched only by the year-older rural children in consonant sounds. Group 5 rural children's scores were depressed in comparison to their age mates living in urban areas (groups 1–4). The children in the public-aid group (7) were similar to the older group of rural children (6) in letter naming but had not transferred that knowledge to consonant sounds. Thus, the children were entering first grade with large differences in letter naming and consonant-sound identification skills.

To test our supposition that substantial differences among the children remained when they entered school and that those with the least knowledge of beginning read-ing skills (group 7) were at academic risk, we searched for and found the first-grade school records of 15 of the 19 children from the public-aid group. Nine (60%) had been placed in a remedial reading program, and 4 of these 9 also repeated kindergar-ten or first grade. A similar search for the group 4 children (lower middle class) indicated that none of the 11 children for whom a follow-up was possible had re-peated first grade; however, 1 child had received remedial reading instruction and 1 child was receiving extra instruction from a learning disabilities teacher.

In addition to the fact that the public-aid children were less skilled in letter naming, their mothers appeared to be less aware of the specific skills their children

Table 2. Preschool Children's Letter Knowledge

| Parent Description | University Professionals | | | Students, Secretaries | Farmers, Factory Workers | | Public-Aid Recipients |
	Gr.1	Gr.2	Gr.3	Gr.4	Gr.5	Gr.6	Gr.7
Sample size	38	25	40	15	66	53	19
M age in months	53.2	51.5	50.5	52.0	49.0	63.0	67.0
Upper-case letter naming (%)	94	88	78	71	28	53	58
Lower-case letter naming (%)	77	—	—	44	14	34	38
Identifying consonant sounds (%)	20	24	30	07	03	28	09

had acquired. Mothers in the public-aid group (7) overestimated how many letters their children could identify in 32% of the cases, whereas mothers in the lower-middle income group (4) overestimated the number of letters their children could identify in 13% of the cases.

Other of our studies showed substantial differences among children in the same classrooms. For example, in McCormick and Mason (1981), children were asked to read 2- and 3-letter high-frequency words. From among 50 children entering first grade, the 6 with the least knowledge of letters could read on average 1 out of 28 words; the 38 in the middle knew about 11 words, whereas the 6 most advanced children knew 26 of the 28 tested words. The low-scoring group could identify only 4 of 52 letter sounds, whereas the top group identified 45 letter sounds. Similarly, in an unpublished analysis of 203 entering-first-graders' reading, 94 could read none of the 20 common words showed to them, but 6 could read them all. Nineteen could not identify any consonant-sounds, whereas 27 could identify all 32 they were shown.

The evidence indicates that children who enter first grade at the bottom of the class usually continue to be behind their classmates in reading (Calfee & Piontkowski, 1981). Hence, an intervention which fosters interest in and understanding of the printed word before children enter first grade may be very important for those children entering first grade who have little familiarity with printed letters and words and so are likely to be less successful in acquiring reading skills.

INSTRUCTIONAL INTERVENTION

A year-long training study in a university community of preschool children's (groups, 1, 2, and 3) acquisition of print knowledge (Mason, 1980) compared the effects of an orientation to the meanings of printed words to the effects of an emphasis on letter names and sounds. A higher recall of printed words that had been taught and higher scores on a task of reading new 3-letter, common words supported the hypothesis that the meaning treatment was more effective. We supposed, but had no proof then, that the children made more progress because the word meaning treatment had featured the use of very easy-to-read little books. Observations of the children during the fall semester revealed that the meaning-oriented group spent more playtime reading, writing, or involved in reading-related activities than did the letter-oriented group (23% and 15%). Tests given at the end of the school year showed that, whereas both groups knew letter names, the group oriented to the meaning of print had somewhat higher scores on tasks of word reading, spelling, and printing than did the other group. However, because other materials also varied and the same teachers did not teach both groups, there was no way to measure the effects of the book materials alone. The next year a careful record of the number of easy-to-read little books borrowed for home use determined that children borrowed from 1 to 29 books during the year, an average of 9 books. Interviews with the teachers indicated that they believed the books were leading children to become more interested in reading at an earlier age and to make more rapid progress in their knowledge of printed words and letters. We were thus encouraged to study the intervention of reading activity for preschool children more systematically and with children who were obtaining less support at home for reading.

At this point we believed that learning to read the little books had significant impact on preschool children's interest in reading, because reading or reciting the books encouraged them to be more attentive to or aware of print in their environment. The next studies began a series which focused on the little books as a means of fostering children's interest in and knowledge about beginning reading.

We constructed books with very simple story lines (often a single sentence separated into short phrases, one phrase to a page) and our own simple line drawings. We evolved an instructional procedure that relied on rereading. Children were encouraged to read or recite the words from each page after a demonstration by the teacher. Each story had a punch line ending which we thought would delight the children, and we aimed for a text that would foster accurate recitation by the children. Throughout this report when we refer to a book reading, we are describing the children's responses to one of our stories. (See the Appendix for examples.)

A training study was conceived for Group 4 children (children of college students, secretaries, and clerks). As reported in Mason and McCormick (1981), children were trained for a 2-week period using the little books and emphasizing either the print meaning or the letters and their sounds and shapes. Analyses of the children's responses in the videotaped lessons suggested that they profited more from instruction that helped them think about the meaning of printed words than from instruction that emphasized letter names and letter sounds. It was argued, not that these young children should never receive letter instruction, but, because they had had so little acquaintance with print, as a first step they needed to understand the relationship of printed words to meaning and to their own language.

In this study all but one of the children could recognize no letter sounds or words but most could name a few letters. As expected, analyses of their videotaped lessons showed that they responded with greater frequency and accuracy to level 1 training tasks which emphasized the meaning of printed words and reading words in context (book reading) than they did to the level 2 training tasks which focused on initial consonant sounds. This finding was confirmed by comments from preschool teachers and parents that the little books provided a format in which the children could successfully participate; the task was compatible with their conceptual understanding and skills.

A favorable short-term impact of learning to read these stories was then extended by giving each child several favorite little books to take home. Even though the parents were not alerted to the use of the books, a follow-up questionnaire 3 weeks after the intervention indicated that 13 of the 14 children still living in the area were very interested in the books (the other child forgot to take his books home from school) and that 12 of these 13 were "reading" the books either occasionally or frequently.

The comments by the parents were uniformly positive and enthusiastic. Two immediate effects were apparent. First, according to parents, their children began to "act like readers" because of these books and for the first time wanted to read (these) stories over and over to parents, siblings, and even stuffed animals. Second, these materials made the parents more aware of the children's interest in letters and words. Not only did the parents report that their preschoolers were more interested in reading other words after the intervention, but they became more involved in responding to the child's questions concerning letters and words.

The long-term effect of our little books was surprising considering the relatively short intervention and the fact that any impetus for using the little books came solely from the children. Six months after the intervention the parents responded again to our questionnaire concerning their children's knowledge and parental support. The estimates of children's knowledge of and interest in letters and words significantly increased, even though estimates of parental support did not change (Mason & McCormick, 1981). As a further test of the impact of our materials, the following year a matched group of parents whose children had not received the materials was given the questionnaire. The estimates of child knowledge and parental support were nearly identical to the experimental group prior to the intervention. Thus, we could say with confidence that our materials and intervention had a significant impact on these 3-and 4-year-old children's knowledge of and interest in letters and words.

Our work thus far allowed us to make several general conclusions. First, children of low socioeconomic status (SES) are entering school with less knowledge of letters, letter sounds, or words than are children of higher SES, and the parents of these children are not fostering or supporting acquisition of prereading skills to the same degree that parents in higher-SES levels are doing. Second, easy-to-read books are especially appealing to preschool children and can make a significant impact on children's interest in prereading and knowledge of letters and words. Third, parents respond extremely favorably and take a more active interest in their child's early reading skills when easy-to-read books are available.

Because even a 2-week intervention is an expensive undertaking and not likely to be implemented in many preschool centers, and because of the outstanding popularity of the little books with all children who used them, we decided to try out a low-cost procedure that could be duplicated by any school or preschool center. We devised and tested two minimal intervention procedures. One was directed to a Head Start class in a small city in central Illinois. We visited the classroom on three occasions, videotaping lessons to the children for the purpose of demonstrating to the teacher how to help the children learn to read the little books and to document change in reading by the children themselves. The results were reported by Mason, McCormick, and Bhavnagri (1983) showing that the children eventually did make substantial gains in their reading interest and ability to participate in the reading lesson. The other minimal intervention procedure involved giving low- and middle income parents a packet of several little books and guidelines for their use as they brought their preschool child for the preschool screening provided by the school districts in the spring of the year. This was carried out for two consecutive years. Wave 1 children, on two occasions during the next months, received another packet of books by mail. Parents met us only once—at the screening—and the child saw us only when tested, and never realized we had sent them the books. Wave 2 children received only the packet of books at the preschool screening. The children who came to kindergarten the following fall were then tested and compared with classmates who had not received the materials. This experiment, which was reported by Mason and McCormick (1983), is presented next.

METHOD

Procedure

The Wave 1 experimental group consisted of all the prekindergarten children that came on 2 days of the 5 that were open for the preschool screening. Children were free to come on any of the 5 days, and we included in the experimental group all the children registering for kindergarten on the 2 days we were available for pretesting. They were given the Developmental Indicators for the Assessment of Learning (DIAL), the screening instrument used by the school district to identify those children in need of further evaluation by special education personnel, and measures of letter identification, spelling, and book reading, in which children were asked to read our "Stop" story before and after a demonstration by the examiner. The parent that accompanied them filled out a questionnaire assessing parental support for early reading and was asked for an estimate of the child's interest in and knowledge about print. Following the testing, the child was given a copy of the little book s/he had been shown how to "read," and the parent was given a packet of three more books and a 3-page guideline for their use. We were pleased that all parents were interested in participating. During the summer, we sent by mail another packet of little books and another questionnaire to fill out which asked about their child's interest in the books, possible gains in knowledge, and the parent's estimate of usefulness. A third packet of several little books was sent to their homes in the fall. At the beginning of kindergarten, these children, along with classmates who served as matched controls using the Peabody Picture Vocabulary Test (PPVT), were measured on a revised version of the Letter and Word Reading Test (Mason & McCormick, 1979). The subtests were: naming signs and labels in and out of context, naming 10 uppercase letters, printing a letter, a word, and the child's name, spelling four 3-letter words, reading 20 common 2- or 3-letter words, identifying consonant sounds, and reading 3 little books, one of which the experimental children had been given to take home. The subtests were repeated in May with another set of little books, and the following year first-grade teachers were asked to rank all their children by reading ability.

Wave 2 children (those who were registering for kindergarten on 2 of 4 days of preschool screening) were similarly tested during the preschool screening and introduced to a little book. Parents were again given guidelines and the children were given a packet of little books. These children, however, did not receive other packets of books later and were not retested at the end of the school year. Wave 2 children were also matched with a control group using the Peabody Picture Vocabulary Test-Revised (PPVT-R). Both groups were tested in early reading: naming 10 upper-case letters, spelling four 3-letter words, reading 20 common 2-or 3-letter words, and reading 3 little books. One book was familiar to the experimental group, and the other two were new to both groups. With one of the new stories, the children were asked to identify specific words after hearing it read to them (a procedure similar to that described by Morris, 1981, as a measure of the young child's concept of word). With the other two, the children were asked to read or try to read the story.

Subjects

Twenty-three Wave 1 children entered kindergarten (scattered among three class-rooms in the school district) and were present in school at the beginning and the end of the year for our follow-up tests. They were compared with 22 children who had not received the early reading materials but were in the same 3 classrooms in 3 schools. The following year, 27 Wave 2 children from another small, rural school district then were tested during the preschool screening using the same selection procedure. These children were compared with 26 classmates from the same two classrooms. Their posttest was administered in November of the children's kinder-garten year. Both posttests were given by experimenters who did not know which children were experimental and which were control group subjects.

RESULTS

Wave 1

A stepwise multiple regression program (SPSS) was used in order to predict children's end-of-kindergarten reading test scores. The first predictors were the child's gender and PPVT score. The next predictor was treatment (experimental vs. control). The child's age, information from parents about their support for reading, and parents' estimate of their child's letter knowledge and word knowledge were omitted from the final analysis since an earlier analysis showed that they did not add to the prediction. Thus, a 3-variable model (gender, PPVT score, and treatment) was used to predict May scores on *word knowledge* (sum of subtests of common words, sign and label words, and identification of consonant sounds in nonsense words), *letter knowledge* (the sum of uppercase letter naming and printing), *spelling knowledge* (the number of letters correctly positioned to spell four words), *story knowledge* (the sum of the number of words read from the three little books), and the *whole test* (sum of all subtests). Table 3 presents a summary of the 5 regression analyses; Tables 4 and 5 display information about each test variable.

Analyses of Wave 1 children's reading knowledge indicate reliable and longlasting effects of the treatment. Word knowledge and spelling scores at the end of kindergarten (May testing) were predicted by treatment and entering vocabulary (PPVT). Story reading was predicted by treatment only and letter knowledge by the

Table 3.   Multiple Regression Results, Wave 1 Children ($N = 45$)

Variable	Unstandardized beta	F value	Sig.	R^2	R^2 Change
Word Knowledge					
Sex	5.49	1.60	.21	.09	.09
PPVT	.65	8.36	.01	.22	.13
Treatment	7.73	3.64	.06	.28	.06
Letter Knowledge					
Sex	.16	.08	.78	.02	.02
PPVT	.10	11.62	.00	.23	.21
Treatment	.16	.09	.77	.23	.00
Spelling Knowledge					
Sex	.65	.10	.76	.03	.03
PPVT	.31	8.13	.01	.16	.13
Treatment	3.98	4.07	.05	.24	.07
Story Knowledge					
Sex	3.82	1.73	.20	.03	.03
PPVT	.17	1.22	.28	.04	.01
Treatment	11.95	19.41	.00	.35	.30
Whole Test					
Sex	9.80	1.60	.21	.08	.08
PPVT	1.23	9.36	.00	.20	.12
Treatment	23.82	10.82	.00	.36	.16

Table 4.   Wave 1 Test Descriptions by Treatment, November Testing

Variable	Possible	Experimental ($N = 23$)		Control ($N = 22$)	
		M	SD	M	SD
1. Age in months		65.09	3.12	64.91	3.96
2. PPVT		106.61	10.81	108.91	8.92
3. Sign & label identification	24	18.41	3.22	16.76	3.21
4. Sign & label reading	24	4.86	4.81	3.52	3.54
5. Letter naming	10	7.14	3.31	5.81	3.78
6. Spelling	24	2.05	3.46	0.43	1.07
7. Printing	3	1.95	1.00	2.10	0.77
8. Word reading	20	0.68	1.99	0.10	0.30
9. Consonant identification	32	0.64	2.98	0.29	1.31
10. Town story	11	2.55	1.99	2.24	1.79
11. Stop story	13	7.45	4.01	1.76	1.84
12. Lunch story	11	3.82	3.71	1.67	1.46

Table 5.   Wave 1 Test Descriptions by Treatment, May Testing

Variable	Possible Score	Experimental (N = 23)		Control (N = 22)	
		M	SD	M	SD
1. Sign & label identification	24	19.13	2.87	18.82	2.15
2. Sign & label reading	24	7.91	5.66	5.55	3.96
3. Letter naming	10	9.43	1.83	9.36	1.40
4. Spelling (3-letter words)	12	5.74	4.18	3.91	4.06
5. Spelling (4-letter words)	12	3.52	3.75	2.36	2.98
6. Printing	3	2.35	0.88	2.41	0.85
7. Word reading	20	2.83	5.42	1.00	1.80
8. Consonant identification	32	7.22	10.94	5.91	9.47
9. Stop story	13	10.35	2.59	6.00	3.16
10. Farm story	25	10.70	9.19	4.09	3.82
11. Bed story	19	15.65	2.14	15.45	2.42
12. WRDKNWL (2 + 7 + 8)	76	17.96	18.54	12.45	11.70
13. LTRKNWL (3 + 6)	13	11.78	2.13	11.77	1.90
14. SPLKNWL (4 + 5)	24	9.26	7.74	6.27	6.72
15. STYKNWL (9 + 10 + 11)	57	36.70	12.23	25.55	5.30
16. WHLTEST (all)	170	75.70	33.67	56.05	20.93

PPVT only. Information from the parent questionnaire did not predict children's reading knowledge because, entered after accounting for vocabulary (PPVT) differences, it was not sensitive enough to pick up subtle differences in parental support for reading.

The treatment affected not only story reading but also word reading and spelling. Because the words on the word reading and spelling subtests were new (in the sense that the words were not in the little books) and two of the three stories in the story subtest were new, the results showed that the treatment influenced not only children's reading of the story that was given to them but transferred to reading new stories and reading and spelling new words. Moreover, the lack of a vocabulary effect when story reading was the dependent measure suggests that the treatment helped to overcome incoming language-ability differences among the children. The lack of effect of treatment when letter knowledge was the dependent variable is not surprising, since letter naming and name printing had been taught to most of the children while in kindergarten.

Finally, longer-term effects of the treatment were assessed at the conclusion of first grade. The control and experimental children had been distributed among five first-grade classrooms in this small school district, and all classrooms used the same basal reading series. The first-grade teachers in the school district were asked to rank the children in their classrooms according to reading skill and to give the reading group classification for each child. The teachers, who were unaware of the minimal intervention study, ranked a total of 111 children, 21 of whom had been in the control group and 18 in the experimental group.

Table 6. Multiple Regression Results, Wave 2 Children (N = 53)
Total Story Score

Variable	F Value	Sig.	R^2	R^2 Change
Sex	3.76	.058	.07	.07
Age	2.41	.100	.09	.02
PPVT-R	2.78	.050	.15	.06
Treatment	6.30	.000	.34	.19

To compare the groups a proportional ranking for each child was calculated and then averaged for each group. The average ranking for the control group was the 41st percentile and the average ranking for the experimental group was the 46th percentile, although the children had originally been matched on PPVT scores early in their kindergarten year. During the calculation of the proportional rankings it appeared that very few of the experimental children were in low reading groups. When the number of experimental and control children in the low reading group for each class was counted, there was only 1 (6%)[1] from the experimental group but 6 (29%) from the control group. (For the entire first grade, 32 of 111 (29%) children were in low reading groups.) While the proportional rankings of the experimental and control groups show a small difference, the striking disparity in the number of children placed in low reading groups indicates that the impact of our intervention appeared most notably among those children likely to get off to a slow start in beginning reading instruction.

Wave 2

Wave 2 children, who had been given fewer books and were tested at an earlier time, showed a smaller instructional effect. Children's story reading (Table 6) but not word reading or spelling was affected by treatment and the PPVT-R. The effect was reliable for an old story ("Stop") and a new story ("Ghosts"). However, the word identification task using a new story ("Apples") was in the expected direction only and did not reach statistical significance (Table 7). The diminished treatment effect for Wave 2 children could be explained either by an earlier posttesting date or to the provision to parents and children of fewer materials. Either way, the main finding of enhanced book reading for old and new stories was replicated.

A FURTHER EXAMINATION OF INDIVIDUALS

For many years our society has focused on reading acquisition within the perspective of schooled instruction. Only recently have we realized how much information young children acquire about print before beginning formal reading instruction and

---

[1] The single experimental child in a low reading group during first grade was a little girl who had the lowest standard score (85) on the PPVT for the experimental group. Her match (on PPVT) in the control group was ranked *below* the low reading group in first grade, and the teacher added the comment that this child was not yet reading.

Table 7.   Wave 2 Test Descriptions and Group Comparison, October Testing

Variable	Control (N = 26)		Experimental (N = 27)		M diff.	Sig. Level
	M	SD	M	SD		
PPVT-R	100.04	10.92	100.07	9.14		
Age in months	65.85	4.99	63.39	3.20		
Upper-case letters	5.86	4.13	4.71	3.99		
Spelling	3.93	6.16	2.86	5.50		
Common word identification	.50	.96	.43	.88		
Stop story	3.25	3.18	7.73	4.44	− 4.20	.000
Ghost story	1.88	2.60	4.03	3.07	− 2.74	.009
Apple story	3.74	2.68	4.80	2.87	− 1.40	.169
Story score (all 3 stories)	8.88	6.92	16.57	7.29	− 3.93	.001

how this knowledge affects the success of instruction they receive. The change in viewpoint has already influenced attitudes about failure to read, and it has fostered kindergarten instruction in reading and parental support for reading before children start school. The results here impinge most directly on the third change. A few simple reading materials and a brief set of guidelines to parents can influence children's attention to print, their knowledge about how to read stories, and their later performance in first grade.

Up to this point in the analysis, we have not addressed an important issue which must follow from a finding of a successful intervention. That is, why did it succeed? In the hopes of understanding why the minimal intervention had an impact, we compared 4 Wave 1 children, a boy and a girl each from the experimental and control groups. Since our intervention affected children who were less well-prepared to participate in first-grade instruction (and thus likely to be placed in the low reading group), we chose to exemplify children with entering test scores among the lowest in their group. The 2 experimental children had correctly named only a few of the letters presented at the initial testing at the preschool screening. We compared them with 2 control children whose initial testing in November of the kindergarten year was very similar to that of the two experimental children. All used the same reading readiness workbook (prescribed by the school district) in kindergarten, and all 4 children received special reading instruction, in addition to their regular classroom instruction, through Chapter 1 programs in the first grade.

The mothers of the 4 children were interviewed at the conclusion of their child's year in first grade, using an interview being developed by Mason and Bhavnagri to examine home influences on reading acquisition. All 4 children were from two-parent, lower-middle-class homes. All mothers reported that their child brought school papers home several times a week and that they would review the papers with their child. All said that the children had homework (usually reading or math workbook pages or dittoed sheets) several times a week and that they would give help if needed—usually helping with directions. All the children watched several hours of television a night (although less in warm weather) and cartoons all Saturday morning. The 4 mothers reported encouraging certain types of decisions by their children such as choosing a restaurant for dinner or how to spend their birthday money, and all mothers had expectations of their child for home responsibilities, the most common being keeping the child's bedroom "picked up."

Our testing of the children's knowledge about reading revealed differences in their progress as a function of the treatment. A member of the experimental group, Wendi, at the initial testing during the preschool screening readily attempted our "Stop" story and gave a verbal description of the illustrations. She tried letter names and numbers for the 10 upper-case letters she was asked to identify but did not correctly identify any. When asked to spell 3-letter words using movable letters, she did not respond.

Her mother reported in the questionnaire at the preschool screening that Wendi could recite a few letters of the alphabet, that she was read to about 2 times a week, that she would once in a while make alphabet letters while drawing or painting, and that she had more than 20 children's books at home, including an alphabet book.

In the follow-up questionnaire (accompanying the second set of books sent to the child's home about 6 weeks after the first set were given at the screening), the mother reported that Wendi was still very interested in the books, frequently reading them to herself and occasionally asking someone else to read them to her. She reported that Wendi seemed more interested in naming and printing letters, was more interested in reading and writing words, and was more interested in reading or looking at books since receiving the books at the screening.

When tested in November of her kindergarten year, Wendi recognized 1 word out of 12 sign and label words. These words were presented first in the context of a sign or label, such as a box of crayons, a stop sign, or a Kool-Aid package (to assure familiarity), and then were presented out of context, but using the script appearing in the sign or label. She correctly named 4 of 10 upper-case letters and attempted the spelling task, but chose incorrect letters for each word. When asked to read the familiar "Stop" story, she correctly read all 13 words exactly as printed and gave adequate descriptions of the illustrations in a new little book.

In May of the kindergarten year, Wendi recognized 2 printed words from the sign and label task: STOP and M&M. She correctly named all 10 upper-case letters and correctly spelled all 4 words requested: *cat, top, sat* and *pot*. She identified 28 of 32 consonant sounds in 3-letter nonword strings, e.g., *pab, dak, lam*. Again, she correctly read the 13 words in the "Stop" story, read (or recited) 23 of 25 words in the "Farm" story (a book she had received in the mail), and reported 15 of 19 words in a new story about bedtime. (See the Appendix for the text of these books.)

At the conclusion of first grade, Wendi was ranked sixth in a class of 22 and in the upper-middle reading group. During the interview with her mother in the first weeks of summer following first grade, her mother stated that Wendi loved to play school with her 4-year-old sister and that this included frequently reading to her sister and writing on a little chalkboard, although the mother was not sure about what was written and guessed it was probably names and short words from school. When asked if she remembered the little books, the mother said Wendi still had them, although they were worn out. The mother said that Wendi would read ("had memorized them really") the books to whoever would come to the house and that Wendi would always take the stories on visits to her grandmother. The mother stated that she thought the stories were helpful; they "were a good idea for (Wendi) . . . They helped her know that reading was more than one word, that words went together."

The second child from the experimental group, Jason, in the initial testing attempted to read several pages of the "Stop" story but did not turn the first page without the additional cue of "What comes next?" After the book was read to him, he correctly repeated 12 of 13 words in the story without reminders to turn the page. He correctly named 3 of 10 upper-case letters and gave incorrect letter names for the other 7. When asked to spell the 3-letter words with movable letters, he lined up all 7 available letters, with none in the correct position.

In the parent questionnaire given at the preschool screening, Jason's mother reported that he would recite a few letters of the alphabet in order, that he was read to about two times a week, that he occasionally made letters in his drawing or painting and that he had about 10 books at home, including an alphabet book.

When the follow-up questionnaire was sent about 6 weeks later, his mother stated that Jason "looked at the books at least once a day," occasionally reading them to himself or other family members, and occasionally asking someone to read the books to him. Mother reported increased interest in naming and printing letters, reading and writing words, and reading or looking at books since the first books had been given to him.

Jason was absent during the testing in November. In May of his kindergarten year, Jason recognized the following 4 sign and label words: crayons, STOP, EXIT, and M&M. He correctly named all 10 upper-case letters and on the spelling task gave the correct initial consonant for the 4 words, then adding the rest of the available letters. On the consonant sound task, Jason did not blend the 3-letter strings but correctly produced 10 of 32 consonant sounds. When asked to read the "Stop" story, he correctly identified 9 of 13 words and when asked to read the farm story (received in the mail), he mentioned that he had this book at home, but that his mom had not read it to him. He did correctly identify 5 of 23 words in the book. He also correctly repeated the 19-word bedtime story which was first read to him by the examiner.

At the conclusion of first grade, Jason ranked twelfth of 23 and was in the middle reading group. In the interview with Jason's mother in the first weeks of summer vacation, his mother reported that Jason listened to stories read to his 4-year-old brother about twice a week and occasionally read a story to the brother himself. The mother reported that Jason frequently wrote at home, mostly lists of names and words copied from books. He also played school occasionally on weekends when his 5- and 7-year-old stepsiblings visit. His mother reported that he usually read something every day such as stories by Dr. Seuss or Smurf comics. When asked about the little books, his mother stated that she thought they gave him a "good start'' and that he still had them in his drawer. She explained that they were his books, and this made him more interested in reading. She remembered that he knew ''some of the words from the pictures.''

Carla was in the control group, and at her first testing in November of her kindergarten year, she recognized 2 sign and label words: STOP and EXIT. She correctly named 5 of 10 upper-case letters (with no response to the unknown letters), and gave no response on either the spelling or consonant identification tasks. She readily attempted the ''Stop'' story and correctly identified 2 words. On a second story she also identified 2 words correctly. In May she identified 3 sign and label words: crayons, STOP, and EXIT, and correctly named all 10 upper-case letters. She still did not respond to the spelling or consonant tasks. When asked to read the little books, she correctly identified 5 words in the ''Stop'' story and 7 words in the ''Farm'' story. She reported 11 of 19 words in the ''Bedtime'' story.

At the conclusion of first grade, Carla was ranked eighteenth in a class of 24 for reading skill and was in the low reading group. In the interview her mother reported that a 10-year-old sister read to Carla about twice a month and that Carla read library books such as Dr. Seuss stories, although she preferred playing games with her sister. When asked about writing at home, her mother stated that Carla usually wrote, names mostly, during church on Sundays but did not write at home. During the discussion, her mother stated that Carla had not been as interested in learning to read as her sister had been and that the parents had been concerned about her progress all year. The mother reported that she had asked the teacher for a conference several times in order to get suggestions for helping Carla with her reading, but that the teacher had not responded. Her mother said that any suggestions that could be given to parents would have been helpful to them.

The second child from the control group, Billy, was first tested in November of his kindergarten year. He recognized none of the sign and label words, correctly named 1 letter and did not attempt the spelling or consonant tasks. He readily attempted the ''Stop'' story, correctly identifying 3 words, and read 2 words in another story. In May, he recognized 1 sign and label word, EXIT, named all 10 upper-case letters, spelled *cat*, but would not attempt the other words, and could not identify any consonant sounds. On the ''Stop'' story, he identified 3 words and gave 6 words on the ''Farm'' story. He correctly repeated 14 of 19 words from the ''Bedtime'' story.

At the conclusion of first grade, Billy was ranked nineteenth in a class of 24 and was in the low reading group. In the interview his mother explained that no one read to Billy now because school was out. He tried to read from his story book when school was in session but not in the summer. She also stated that at the first-grade teacher's suggestion, they began to limit his TV watching. Billy was not interested in the alphabet or books before kindergarten.

Despite the similarities among the 4 children at the beginning of kindergarten, the control children scored lower on the spelling, consonant, and story-reading tasks at the end of kindergarten, and were ranked well below the 2 experimental children at the end of first grade. This may be explained by differences noted in the interview. The control children, but not the experimental children, were reported by parents as having been not interested in printed letters and words prior to first grade. The parents of Billy were not displeased with his limited progress, and although they appeared to ensure that he completed his school work, their responses suggest that they were not very involved in monitoring his progress in reading or felt that it was entirely the responsibility of the teacher. Even though Carla's mother appeared distressed over her daughter's slow progress in reading and frustrated that she did not know what to do to facilitate the acquisition of reading skill, she felt helpless to intervene in a positive manner without direction from the teacher. Our impression is that the parents of these control children either did not know how to encourage their child's interest in printed letters or words or did not spontaneously respond to child-initiated opportunities to talk about printed letters and words. The experimental children, however, were reported to have responded with enthusiasm to the books and to have involved other family members in their use of the books.

All 4 children had very low letter-naming scores on the initial testing. By May of the kindergarten year, all had mastered upper-case letter naming and were able to print their names, both skills emphasized in the kindergarten program. However, the two children from the experimental group showed dramatic improvement on consonant-sound identification, whereas the children from the control group were still unable to identify any consonant sounds at the end of kindergarten. These differences reflect the larger group differences. For both the experimental and control groups, only one child in each identified any consonant sounds on our task in the November testing. In May, only 45% of the control group but 64% of the experimental group identified at least one consonant (with mean scores of 5.9 and 7.2, respectively).

DISCUSSION

As frequently happens, answering one question, namely, how an intervention can affect young children's early reading, has now raised other questions. How should future interventions be implemented, and what are theoretical and instructional implications of this work? Concerning implementation procedures, our results (and the personal response from a kindergarten teacher who had begun to use the little books to supplement her regular prereading activities) suggest that easy-to-read books are especially helpful to children entering school who are less well prepared for reading, the most obvious effect being that the children like the stories and can readily behave like readers with books that they can read or recite and which belong to them. Should these materials be provided only to those children with limited knowledge and interest in reading at the beginning of kindergarten? Since all the parents of Wave 1 children who responded to our questionnaire 6 weeks after receiving the initial packet of books reported that their child was still interested in the books and all reported increased interest in printed words, we think everyone should be given these materials, but we cannot be sure of this position.

The study also does not determine when or how many books should be sent home. We chose to send them before and at the beginning of kindergarten, because our other studies had determined that they could be read by such young children. If they had been sent during or after kindergarten, would they have been as effective? We do not know. We also cannot compare the effect of these materials to others, though we certainly do not suppose that these are uniquely effective.[2] We can only recommend that some materials that children can easily read and enjoy reading be provided to parents.

How to advise parents about the use of early reading materials was not studied. Although the experimental children accurately recognized significantly more words in the books, in the specific cases described earlier, Jason recognized as few words in the "Farm" story as the two children from the control group. He said "I have this one at home" when he first saw the book, but added that no one had read it to him. Although his responses were short, appropriate phrases, they did not match the exact words of the text. This raises the question of how to encourage parent involvement. Beyond that is the issue of whether memorizing the specific words printed in each story is essential. Must we stress that a parent read the book several times to the child before allowing the child to read it independently? The ease with which children remembered a story from only one reading can be seen in the high scores on the "Bedtime" story which suggests that one reading might be enough. Furthermore, although parental responses have been uniformly positive, we know the extent to which they read our guidelines for using the books varied. In the initial followup of a larger group of 67 families from the Wave 1 study, 78% of the parents reported reading the guidelines, but of that group, only 46% read them carefully. Twenty-two percent said they did not read the guidelines at all. If we had found some way of assuring or encouraging all the parents to read the guidelines, the outcomes for the children might have been even greater.

Theoretical Implications

Although not the focus of the intervention studies, several questions of a theoretical nature were raised. The hierarchical model of early reading provided a basis for construction of materials and techniques. Their appeal and success is explained by the level 1 focus on the function of print. That is, recognizing words in a meaningful format provides children with an easy mapping of spoken word to printed word which matches their level of understanding of how to read. Nevertheless, this has not explained the apparent generalizability to other early reading skills. Why and how does a recitation of meaning-laden print foster an attention to the sound–symbol relationship of print? Does it occur because learning to recognize a

---

[2] For example, the *Caption Books* described in Clay (1972) use complete sentences, a matching illustration, and often a repetitive theme. A second example, Bill Martin's *Instant Readers*, (Holt, Rinehart, & Winston, 1970) use a much longer text (with rhyming or sentence pattern repetitions) and have more complex illustrations and varying print formats. Our books, as can be noted in the Appendix, have a very brief text with only several words or a phrase per page. The illustrations are likewise simple and uncluttered. We have recently published our books and information is available by writing to the author(s).

set of printed words and to name letters leads children to hear the sound of letter names in words? Did these books facilitate the move into level 2 because they repeated easy-to-remember words so that children began to associate the presence of particular letters with particular phonemes? Or is there an over-arching conceptual shift, a change in children's approach to learning about complex information, that is fostered by the use of easy-to-read materials? The Wave 1 experimental group not only could read old and new stories more accurately, but made a greater improvement on consonant-sound identification, spelling, and word recognition during the second semester of kindergarten. While this suggests that allowing the child to behave like a reader facilitates the acquisition of beginning phonetic awareness of words, it does not explain why. These questions need to be examined in future work by analyzing changes in children's understanding of print meaning in conjunction with changes in their phonological awareness.

A second question of theoretical importance concerns the development of the concept of a word. Morris (1981) suggests that a conceptual knowledge of "wordness" underlies both spelling and reading. To what extent does story reading, rereading, and reciting help in the development of the concept of the word? Possibly, sign, label, and simple story reading help the child to understand how spoken story words correspond to printed words. Our research suggests but does not prove that reading in context is very important.

A third question regards the role of parents in introducing reading to their children. We have survey evidence that rural and lower-SES parents do not provide enough support for reading activity; we have anecdotal evidence from our two examples from the Wave 1 control group that the parents were either uninterested or unsure about how to introduce their child to print. Does a child's enthusiasm for easy-to-read books lead the parent to initiate print-related interactions with the child? Or does a child, given materials that require little help from parents, keep plying the parent with questions? Our self-report data from parents whose children used the little books is unclear on this point, but it could be objectively documented. We need to learn whether these informal parent–child reading-related interactions are important, because the parents are encouraged to be more involved or because the children, finding pleasure in reading or reciting stories, initiate questions to parents about print.

In conclusion, over several years of studying the development of print knowledge with preschool children, we have learned that there are more and less effective orders of early informal reading instruction. We have shown that our minimal intervention with the little books can have a significant impact, particularly for children who are entering school less well prepared for reading instruction. We believe that one critical factor in their success may be parental involvement which is fostered by the child's interest in reading. The use of easy-to-read books exemplifies one way of encouraging positive parent—child interaction regarding printed words. However, we still lack a satisfactory explanation of how children derive meaning from print and whether children's search for the meaning in printed information causes or merely coincides with their development of phonological awareness.

Instructional Implications

As a practicing school psychologist, McCormick has been encouraged about the potential applicability of the little books with children at the first level of early reading. The appeal and usefulness of the books have been apparent to her since she first used them with a group of preschoolers.

Many times, as a school psychologist McCormick was asked to test a child who was not progressing satisfactorily in kindergarten or first grade on beginning reading skills. The working assumptions of the teachers who made the referrals were that if a child did not acquire letter-sound correspondences or blending skills at the prescribed rate, then the child was immature, "slow," or had a learning disability. The recent theoretical work by Mason and others has suggested a more appropriate interpretation for viewing a slow start in reading. This view offers a breakthrough for teachers and school psychologists not only in how to describe the child but also what to do about the slow progress. The model has suggested that children progress first through a context-dependent level of acquaintance with print before moving into the second level in which they begin to apply phonetic analysis. A personal observation by McCormick of kindergarten and first-grade instruction in rural areas of the Midwest suggests that most school instruction begins with a primary emphasis on this second level of development and makes little provision for those children not conceptually prepared to integrate this beginning phonetic analysis training into their understanding of and acquaintance with printed words. The activities which focus upon letter-sound correspondences often ignore children's need for conceptual understanding of the meaningfulness of print. A hierarchical explanation of early reading development can encourage teachers to distinguish between those children conceptually prepared to begin with letter-sound correspondences and those needing a program in which meaningfulness of print is emphasized before moving on to letter-sound correspondences. Our work with the little books gives an example of the type of activity appropriate for the child at the first level of early reading.

Closely related to this issue is the possibility of using these materials as a focus for parents of children getting off to a slow start in reading. Our work has shown that as a group rural and lower-SES children are not entering school with the letter-naming and word and book-reading knowledge of urban and higher-SES groups and that the parents of these children are not as effectively involved with encouraging their child's interest in print as are higher-SES parents. Furthermore, our questionnaire responses indicated that most of these parents are willing to help, if given clear suggestions. One of the appealing features of the little books is the involvement of both children and parents in activity which is easy for everyone to carry out. The little books appear to provide a successful initiation into reading activity and to help parents focus on meaningful aspects of reading when working with young children.

The conceptual framework for our work is readily accepted by the teachers and administrators in the small rural school districts in which McCormick worked. Many believe in a developmental model of learning, although they also espouse the notion of a maturational readiness for reading. Working with them has meant explaining that, while the maturational component may be relevant to being able to sit still and listen to and carry out teacher directions, it does not address adequately the conceptual demands of reading tasks. Teachers and administrators need to learn that a low score on a school readiness test need not be interpreted to mean that a child is "not ready" for any instruction in reading. It has been important to explain that, even if the decision is made to delay formal instruction, the parent or preschool teacher should be given appropriate informal teaching strategies for the child, and the little books can be viewed as a prototype of the type of suggestions helpful in such cases. The little books can illustrate to parents that readiness for school does not just happen with increasing age. These books show the parent how the child's interest in reading can be fostered and offer an easy way to interact with the child regarding print.

The importance of our work also has application to other beginning reading instruction. In McCormick's work with Educable Mentally Handicapped (EMH) students, the classes often focused on letter-sound correspondence drills or sight-word recognition drills. The letter-sound drills may be inappropriate, if the children can be shown to be at the first level of early reading development, and even the sight-word approach may be poor because it often focuses on words not personally meaningful to the children, such as color words, number words, and words that do not match a familiar referent (e.g., *the, you, is, here, that*). Teachers can be coached to allow these children more time with level 1 activities such as recognizing words in the meaningful context of signs and labels, constructing spoken-word-to-print contexts, and reciting easy-to-read little books before moving into phonetic analysis and sight-word recognition.

Thus, an understanding of the theoretical justification for meaning-related materials is an important addition to teachers' and school psychologists' knowledge of the acquisition of beginning reading skills. And, most importantly, for these school personnel who need daily to make decisions about their hard-to-teach children, the notion of levels of early reading development offers useful insights for the construction of appropriate reading materials and about how to begin teaching children who enter school with skills and conceptualizations characteristic of our level 1 reader.

REFERENCES

Biemiller, A. (1970). The development of the use of graphic and contextual information as children learn to read. *Reading Research Quarterly, 6,* 75–96.

Bissex, G. (1980). *GNYS AT WRK: A child learns to write and read.* Cambridge, MA: Harvard University Press.

Bond, G.L., & Dykstra, R. (1967). *Coordinating center for first grade reading instruction programs* (Final report, HEW Project No. X-001). Minneapolis: University of Minnesota.

Calfee, R., & Piontkowski, D. (1981). The reading diary: Acquisition of decoding. *Reading Research Quarterly, 16,* 346–373.

Chomsky, C. (1977). Approaching reading through invented spelling. In L. Resnick & P. Weaver (Eds.), *Theory and practice of early reading.* Hillsdale, NJ: Erlbaum.

Clark, M. (1976). *Young fluent readers: What can they teach us.* London: Heinemann.

Clay, M. (1972). *Reading: The patterning of complex behaviour*. Auckland, New Zealand: Heinemann.

Coltheart, M. (1979). When can children learn to read—and when should they be taught? In T. Waller & G. MacKinnon (Eds.), *Reading research: Advances in theory and practice* (Vol. 1). New York: Academic Press.

Dennis, W. (1941). Infant development under conditions of restricted practice and of minimal social stimulation. *Genetic Psychology Monographs, 23,* 143–189.

Ferreiro, E., & Teberosky, A. (1982). *Literacy before schooling*. London: Heinemann.

Gesell, A., & Thompson, H. (1929). Learning and growth in identical twin infants. *Genetic Psychology Monographs, 24,* 3–121.

Heber, R. (1978). Sociocultural mental retardation: A longitudinal study. In D. Forgays (Eds.), *Primary prevention of psychopathology: Vol. 2, Environmental influences*. Hanover, NH: University Press of New England.

Hunt, J. (1982). *Toward equalizing the developmental opportunities of infants and preschool children: The 1982 Kurt Lewin Address*. Champaign: University of Illinois.

Hunt, J. (1983). *The role of early experience in the development of intelligence and personality*. Champaign: University of Illinois.

Lowell, R.E. (1971). Reading readiness factors as predictors of first grade reading. *Journal of Learning Disabilities, 4,* 563–567.

Mason, J. (1976). Overgeneralization in learning to read. *Journal of Reading Behavior, 8,* 173–182.

Mason, J. (1980). When do children begin to read: An exploration of four year old children's letter and word reading competencies. *Reading Research Quarterly, 15,* 203–227.

Mason, J., & Au, K. (1981). Learning social context characteristics in prereading lessons. In J. Flood (Ed.), *Understanding reading comprehension*. Newark, DE: International Reading Association.

Mason, J., & McCormick, C. (1979). *Testing the development of reading and linguistic awareness* (Tech. Rep. No. 126). Urbana: University of Illinois, Center for the Study of Reading. (ERIC Document Reproduction Service No. ED 170 735)

Mason, J., & McCormick, C. (1981). *An investigation of prereading instruction from a developmental perspective: Foundations for literacy* (Tech. Rep. No. 224). Urbana: University of Illinois, Center for the Study of Reading. (ERIC Document Reproduction Service No. ED 212 988)

Mason, J., & McCormick, C. (1983). *Intervention procedures for increasing preschool children's interest in and knowledge about reading*. Paper presented at the meeting of the American Educational Research Association, Montreal.

Mason, J., & McCormick, C. (1985). *Little books for early readers*. Charleston, IL: Pintsize Prints.

Mason, J., McCormick, C., & Bhavnagri, N. (1983). *How are you going to help me learn? Issues in providing reading instruction to preschool children*. Paper presented at the meeting of the Society for Research in Child Development, Detroit, MI.

McCormick, C., & Mason, J. (1981). What happens to kindergarten children's knowledge about reading after a summer vacation? *Reading Teacher, 35,* 164–172.

McGraw, A. (1935). *Growth: A study of Johnny and Jimmy*. New York: Appleton-Century.

Morphett, V., & Washburne, C. (1931). When should children begin to read? *Elementary School Journal, 31,* 495–503.

Morris, D. (1981). Concept of word: A developmental phenomenon in the beginning reading and writing processes. *Language Arts, 58,* 659–668.

Muehl, S., & DiNello, M.C. (1976). Early first-grade skills related to subsequent reading performance: A seven year followup study. *Journal of Reading Behavior, 8,* 67–81.

Paul, R. (1976). Invented spelling in kindergarten. *Young Children, 31,* 195–200.

Read, C. (1971). Preschool children's knowledge of English phonology. *Harvard Educational Review, 41,* 1–34.

Silvaroli, N.J. (1965). Factors in predicting children's success in first grade reading. In J.A. Figurel (Ed.), *International Reading Association Conference Proceedings, 10,* 296–298.

Söderbergh, R. (1977). *Reading in early childhood: A linguistic study of a preschool child's gradual acquisition of reading ability*. Washington, DC: Georgetown University Press.

APPENDIX

EXAMPLES OF TEXT FROM *LITTLE BOOKS FOR EARLY READERS* (MASON & McCORMICK, 1985)

Stop

stop car
stop bus
stop truck
stop, stop, stop
stop for the cat

Ghosts

a happy ghost
a sad ghost
a little ghost
a scary ghost
boo!

Funny Farm Family

one baby chick, peep
two baby chicks, peep
three baby chicks, peep
four baby chicks, peep
five baby chicks, peep
a–a–and
one big baby duck, quack

Apples

red apples
yellow apples
green apples
blue apples
red apples, mmm
yellow apples, mmm
green apples, mmm
blue apples, yuk

Time for Bed

brush your teeth
read a story
get a hug
climb in bed
nighty-night, sleep tight

5

The Contracts of Literacy: What Children Learn from Learning to Read Books*

Catherine E. Snow
Harvard University Graduate School of Education

Anat Ninio
Department of Psychology The Hebrew University, Jerusalem, Israel

Two researchers with complementary lines of research merge their perspectives in this chapter. Catherine Snow's studies have focused on language acquisition, especially on the role of routines in the process. Anat Ninio, working in Jerome Bruner's lab on mother–child interaction, found picture-book reading to be a highly routinized activity. Both Snow and Ninio independently have continued to investigate parent–child reading practices, focusing especially upon their effects on language acquisition. In this chapter they turn their attention completely to the contributions of book reading to the child's literacy development and discuss how children learn the "contracts of literacy," the basic rules related to the use of books and the meaning of texts.

A child's development is, of course, the product of multiple forces; biologically programmed growth and change, changes induced by the child's observation of and interaction with the environment, spontaneous internal reorganization designed to help deal with the increasing complexity of the information to be stored, and the effects of structured interactions planned by that most potent source of development, the "knowledgeable adult." Both of us have focused on the role of the knowledgeable adult in children's development. The similarity of our views on that role provided the common ground that led to collaboration on this chapter. Our personal interests and research histories parallel one another in a surprising number of ways, but we never worked together until 1983, when both of us were at the Insti-

---

* The authors would like to express their appreciation to the Institute for Advanced Studies, The Hebrew University of Jerusalem, for the hospitality which made this collaboration possible; to the Spencer Foundation which funded some of C. Snow's research on book reading; and to the Social Science Research Council and the Human Development Center, The Hebrew University, which funded some of A. Ninio's research. Thanks are due to Renira Huxley and the Edinburgh Language Acquisition Project for permission to quote from their corpora.

tute of Advanced Studies of Hebrew University. Accordingly, we present our research separately in the next two sections.

Both of us had (and have) a primary research interest in language development, both have looked at the transition from early communicative forms to language, both have analyzed mother–child interaction as it contributed to language development, and both have an interest in cultural sources of parent–child interaction patterns. Because we have both observed mother–child interaction in western, literate societies, we have been confronted with the situation of book reading—a frequent and powerful source, we feel, of learning about language. Our previous work has concentrated on the effects of book reading on children's developing communicative skills, on vocabulary, and on linguistic forms. In this chapter, we celebrated our common interests and our short-term proximity by reconsidering the interactions we had studied so often for evidence of parental effects on children's language acquisition with a new question in mind: What does participation in such interactions teach children about literacy? We turn to that question in the final section, after a brief review of our earlier research.

SNOW'S RESEARCH

In 1974, my second study of mothers' speech to children produced a finding which, at the time, was noted in the report (Snow, Arlman-Rupp, Hassing, Jobse, Joosten, & Vorster, 1976) as intriguing but minor. The finding, that mothers' speech to children during book reading was more complex than during free play with toys, was explained as a likely consequence of the role of the book in setting a topic. Since the book constrained the topic, it was hypothesized, the mother was free to devote a higher percentage of her utterances to making comments, which are typically longer and more elaborate than topic-introducing utterances. Now, with the benefit of Ninio and Bruner's (1978) article showing that book reading is a remarkably routinized activity, together with more recent findings of my own showing that maternal speech during routines is more complex than during interactions in which the child is being introduced to novel objects and activities (Snow, Perlmann, & Nathan, 1984), that 1976 finding seems both more interpretable and more interesting.

The notion that book reading is a routine had been introduced to the research literature by the Ninio and Bruner article, but the degree of routinization of book reading became clear to me only after several months of taping my own son, Nathaniel, during the period of his early language acquisition. Book-reading events occurred often during those tapes, not just because it was a favorite activity, but also because it was a quiet activity—one ideally suited to easy transcription. Furthermore, the same books tended to recur—most frequently, the Richard Scarry *Storybook Dictionary* and Richard Scarry's *Best Word Book Ever*. During the sessions of reading those books with Nathaniel, and even more strongly while transcribing the book-reading tapes, I was struck by how predictable the event was, yet how much development was occurring in his language within that situation. These observations convinced me that book reading may be, in fact, the ideal routine for language learning. Opening a book to a particular page allows the situation of that page to recur with a clarity and a totality that does not characterize other recurrent situations such as breakfast or bath time, which are always different in detail. Furthermore, although the event pictured on a particular page constrains the talk that occurs, there is room for considerable development in the talk and elaboration of the information presented as well: a shift from labeling the people and objects involved to discussing the event that is pictured, then to discussing the precursors and consequences of that event. The experience of reading a particular book again and again enabled Nathaniel slowly to assume aspects of the adult role—to ask in later sessions the questions that I had asked during earlier ones, to provide himself the labels, descriptions, and explanations that he had earlier demanded from me. The analyses of these recurrent book reading sessions were presented in three papers which documented: (a) the degree to which routinization of the book-reading event was imposed on it by Nathaniel (Snow, 1983); (b) the contribution of the recurrent picture discussions to Nathaniel's acquisition of particular linguistic forms (Snow & Goldfield, 1983); and (c) the contribution of the recurrent picture discussions to his understanding of narrative events (Snow & Goldfield, 1982). I have now begun to analyze transcripts of the routinized book-reading interactions of 4 additional mothers and children, replicating the finding that control of topic introduction and of information provision shifts from mother during the early sessions with an unfamiliar book to the child after 6 to 10 readings (Snow, Nathan, & Perlmann, 1985).

The various studies of book reading were all undertaken with the aim of studying language acquisition, but of course it became quite clear that, in addition to vocabulary, syntax, and story grammars, books provide the opportunity for children to learn a good deal about the skills subsumed under "literacy"—recognizing letters, distinguishing between print and other marks on the page, understanding that print represents spoken words, learning how to hold books, to turn pages, to start at the front, to wait for the ending, and myriad other skills that serve a first-grader well. I have documented how parent-child interaction contributes to the acquisition of some of these literacy skills (Snow, 1983), but maintain, nonetheless, that the acquisition of such skills through book reading cannot by itself explain why children whose parents read books to them end up as better readers (Goldfield & Snow, 1984). Nor does it explain social class differences in reading achievement; in fact, recent studies of low-income, low-SES families suggest that such families may provide books for their preschool and older children just as middle-income educated parents do (Chall, Snow, Barnes, Chandler, Hemphill, Goodman, & Jacobs, 1983; Miller, 1982). I do believe that early parent–child interaction around books contributes to literacy as well as to language, and that the quality of such interaction might explain social class differences, but through its influence on skills much harder to acquire, much more subtle and elaborate, than book handling or letter recognition. Reading a book for the sixth or tenth or twentieth time provides a child with exposure to more complex, more elaborate and more decontextualized language than almost any other kind of interaction, and the ability to understand and to produce decontextualized language may be the most difficult and most crucial prerequisite to literacy. Furthermore, reading books with a parent provides a child with an opportunity to learn the rules for reading—what we refer to in the third section of this paper as the "contracts of literacy"—rules which go far beyond prescriptions for decoding sounds and recognizing words and which are, accordingly, much harder to learn.

NINIO'S RESEARCH

My interest in picture-book reading began in 1975, while I was spending a year in J.S. Bruner's lab in Oxford, studying the beginnings of language in young children. At a certain point, we were looking at videotaped home observations of mother–infant dyads which had been collected over the previous year in order to trace the development of labeling in naturalistic circumstances. We were struck by the high concentration of labeling, both by mothers and by babies, when mother-child dyads were jointly looking at picture books, and decided to concentrate on describing the development of referential speech within this one context. The high concentration of labeling in the context of picture-book reading did not seem to us to be an accident; rather, picture books, because they offer little opportunity for grasping and manipulation, free the child's attention to be directed to their symbolic, rather than concrete, characteristics. In Werner and Kaplan's (1963) terminology, picture books help the child to establish a new mode of treating the world as "objects-of-contemplation" rather than "things-of-action."

Although there were videotapes available of several infants, we decided to concentrate on just one child, tracking his development over a span of 11 months, from 8 to 18 months of age. We limited our sample to one dyad, not because there was a great deal of variability among the different dyads who had been videotaped, but precisely because there was such an amazing similarity in their behavior that it seemed unimportant to describe more than one.

We found (Ninio & Bruner, 1978) that the book-reading behavior was to a high degree routinized; that is, it was made up of a small number of steps that followed a predictable sequence. The routine was organized in small units, "cycles," extending over no more than a few utterances, centering on one picture which the dyad was engaged in labeling. The very simple steps in such a cycle involved (a) one participant getting the other to focus his or her attention on a picture; (b) attempting to get the other participant to label the picture; (c) if this is done, providing positive or negative feedback on his or her performance; (4) if this is not done, the first participant providing a label for the picture.

We were struck by the stability of this routine over the 11 month period, although in the meantime the child had progressed from attempts to eat the page to being able to participate fully in the verbal dialogue. It was evident that the mother was the source of the stability: She accepted the child's contributions as attempts to take his turns, even if they amounted to no more than an excited scream, and if no child response was forthcoming, she supplied the child's turns for him. She kept the dialogue going, but also continually adjusted her demands on the child to his developing ability. Within this constant frame, the words the child eventually produced could be regarded simply as a more adultlike substitute for the communicative forms that he had utilized earlier in the dialogue—smiling, reaching, pointing, and babbling vocalizations. All these early forms had been consistently interpreted by the mother as expression of the child's intention either to request a label or to provide one. Thus, participation in a ritualized dialogue, rather than imitation, was found to be the major mechanism through which labeling was achieved.

When at the close of my year in Oxford I got to read a preprint of Catherine Snow's just-completed paper on the development of conversation between mothers and babies (1977), I could not help marveling at the similarity of the conceptual framework within which we were working. Our subsequent book-reading studies, although done independently, belong very much to the same paradigm and are continuing evidence of the affinity of our viewpoints.

Before leaving Oxford, I decided that there were further aspects of the book-reading context that I wanted to explore. I collected transcriptions of all occurrences of book reading by mothers and infants from all the tapes in Bruner's lab. Renira Huxley, who was also on Bruner's research team, was at the time preparing typed transcriptions of the observations at the Edinburgh Language Acquisition Project in which she had participated before moving to Oxford. When she heard that I was collecting further English book-reading data, she offered me the opportunity to make copies of the Edinburgh transcripts, in accordance with the policy of that group to make their data available to all interested investigators. Samples from these transcripts are incorporated in the present chapter.

After returning to Israel, I carried out new observations of picture-book reading, this time with 40 Hebrew-speaking mother–child dyads (Ninio, 1980a, 1980b, 1983). The Israeli children were about 19 months old, and were observed once looking at 3 picture books, which we brought to their homes for that purpose. One of the aims of this study was to investigate the effect of maternal education and socioeconomic status (SES) on the book-reading behavior. Half the mothers were from low-SES families of Asian and North African origin, and the other half were of high-SES families and European origin. All the mothers were Israeli Jews.

The most important finding was the similarities in the mothers' behavior across the two groups, which were much more pronounced than the differences, despite the large cultural differences between the subsamples. In all major respects, this study replicated the findings with the single middle-class English dyad reported by Ninio and Bruner; i.e., all the mothers established a routinized dialogue around the activity of picture labeling. Nevertheless, infants whose mothers had little education were already at some disadvantage in comparison to infants whose mothers had higher levels of schooling. Low-SES mothers seemed adequate as teachers of vocabulary for their infants' concurrent level of development, but their teaching style was not future-oriented, not sensitive to changes in the infants' needs, and therefore probably inadequate to enhance rapid progression to more complex levels of language use. The low-SES mothers' relative lack of skill in eliciting active labeling from their infants had probably resulted in the latter, already at 19 months, having a less firmly established productive vocabulary than high-SES infants of the same age.

Although my major interest in picture-book reading has been its contribution to language acquisition, I believe, with Catherine Snow, that participating in joint picture-book reading helps young children to internalize some basic skills and concepts important for true literacy. In the following, we describe some of these. But I am afraid that one thing to be learned from picture-book reading got short shift in our discussion—and that is that books are a source of enchantment and wonder. This message might, after all, turn out to be the most important contribution of picture-book reading to the acquisition of literacy.

THE CONTRACTS OF LITERACY

Communication has been described as the act of creating a bridge between two social worlds which are quite separate from one another until the communicative act is accomplished (Rommetveit, 1974). Viewing communication in this light reveals what an enormous and risky undertaking literate communication is, because it constitutes attempting to create that bridge under the least propitious of circumstances, without knowledge of the intended recipient's social world, without opportunity for repair or correction of incorrectly interpreted messages, or for amplification of inadequate messages.

The contrast between face-to-face communication and literate communication is especially sharp for the young child for whom face to face communication typically requires bridging only the distance between two very close and similar social worlds. By virtue of knowing a great deal about the child's life, recent activities, control of language, and likes and dislikes, and by virtue of great willingness to compensate in comprehension for the child's shortcomings in production, the adult caretaker typically merges his/her own social world or viewpoint with that of the child, thus ensuring effective communication. No such ''scaffolding'' is available for the child when he faces a written text.

Reading books is an act of communication with an object: a book. Literate persons are able to perform this feat because they have been taught a complex set of rules for the use of books as communicative partners.

Very few of the rules of literacy are explicit or can be taught explicitly. Reading and comprehending texts depend on many tacit ''contracts'' and ''metacontracts'' (cf. Rommetveit, 1974) between literate persons concerning the use of books and the meaning of texts—contracts which have very little to do with the ability to decipher a written word.

Most young children in western middle-class families are inducted into the contracts of literacy at an early age within the context of joint picture-book ''reading'' with their caretakers. It is our purpose to reanalyze our own past research on the interaction between parents and their preschool children during book reading in order to reveal how children are inducted into literacy and especially how they are tutored in the special rules that hold for literate, but not for face-to-face, encounters.

In two respects, picture-book "reading" is different from the true literary encounter in which a person confronts the book and the text as the sole communicant. In the first place, the literary "text" in picture-book reading is the picture and not the written word (cf. Ninio and Bruner, 1978). Reading the text does come into parent–child discussions at some point (e.g., Snow & Goldfield, 1983), but this occurs many months after book reading has been established as a picture-discussion activity. Indeed, during those early stages, if children pay attention to the text, parents respond in a way that does not differentiate text from picture. In the following exchange, for example, the text is simply labeled "writing," as if it were a picture of writing rather than writing itself:

1. (Nathaniel, 2;5.17)
    N: This?
    Adult: It's all writing.
    N: Lots . . . lots of writing.
    Adult: Yeah, lots of writing.

In the second place, picture-book reading is a joint activity, whereas true reading is solitary. As a result of these differences between the two contexts, there are many things which children learn from picture-book reading which are irrelevant or only indirectly related to literacy: for instance, new vocabulary items; rules for carrying on a conversation; rules for interpreting pictures (see Friedman & Stevenson, 1980, for a discussion of picture-reading rules). However, the terms of the basic meta-contract concerning the nature of books and book-input are identical in solitary and in social reading, if we take pictures as the direct analogues of written text. In other words, the metacontract established for picture-book reading is directly transferable to true reading.

In the following, we shall present these basic rules of literacy and follow their establishment in sessions of joint picture-book reading between preschool children and their mothers.

Books Are for Reading, Not for Manipulating

The very first period of joint picture-book reading is devoted to teaching young children that books are different from other objects (Ninio & Bruner, 1978). Children have to learn that books are for reading, not for eating, throwing, chewing, or for building towers. Books are the prototypical members of a category just being discovered by the child, "objects of contemplation" as differentiated from "things of action" (Werner & Kaplan, 1963). Considerable direct teaching goes on about the "correct" use of books, that they are for looking at, not for handling like other objects:

2. (Richard, 11.7)
    Mother: (Restrains R) No, it's not for eating.
        No.
        Sing a song of sixpence (sings).

R: (Vocalizes)
Mother: Yes.
R: (Grabs book)
Mother: No! (Pulls away book)
    I'll take it away if you start eating it.

3. (Stephen, 8.7)
S: (Grabs book and mouths it)
Mother: Oh, dear, no.
    (Tries to take book from child's mouth)
    Is it better to eat?
S: (Lowers book from mouth)
Mother: That's it.
S: (Mouths book)
Mother: Oh, don't eat it.

Careful handling is also encouraged:

4. (Richard, 12.21)
R: (Tries to turn page)
Mother: Steady on.
    Don't be so rough.

Specific instruction is given on holding books the right way:

5. (Richard, 1;1.7)
Mother: You've got it all upside down and the wrong way around.

on starting at the front:

6. (Richard, 1;1.7)
Mother: Look, let's start at the beginning.

7. (Richard, 1;1.7)
Mother: No, come on, we are going through this way.
    That's the way we read a book.
    Not backwards.

and on reading them from the beginning to the end:

8. (Richard, 1;1.21)
Mother: Ah–ah (Restraining child from turning pages wildly).
    You'll have to learn to turn the pages properly.

9.(Richard, 1;1.21)
R: (Turns several pages at once)
Mother: Don't be so greedy (Laughs).
    Come one, one at a time.
    You hold on to it with the right hand and you can't turn it over with your left.
    It doesn't work.

      R: (Changes grasp on book)
Mother: That's it.
          That's two pages instead of three.
          Look Richard.
          One at a time.

10. (Richard, 1;2.7)
Mother: Let me turn the pages.
          Steady on!
          You have to go past the kitten first, come on!
          You can't just go on to your good ones.

In Book Reading, the Book Is in Control; the Reader is Led

This rule establishes the respective roles of the book and the reader in the literary communicative encounter. The book is the dominant partner in this kind of encounter: Its role is to control what the reader is to think about while reading. The proper role for the reader is to be led by the book. In joint picture-book reading, children are taught that the book is in control of the current conversation between the child and the adult. Specifically, the rule is that the topic of the conversation is determined by a picture under joint attention. Indeed, if joint attention does not exist, the adult (or later the child) goes to great effort to establish it, precisely as a way of establishing a topic for discussion (see Ninio & Bruner, 1978).

11. (Richard, 8.14)
Mother: Look, look, look.
      R: (Looking at page)
Mother: See them, dolls.
      R: (Grabs cloth book and mouths)
Mother: You're much more interested in that, aren't you?
          Yes.
          Now, look.

12. (Richard, 1;1.21)
Mother: Look, there is a little boy with a camera.
          Look.
          Richard! (Touching him)

13. (Jacqueline, 1;9.23)
      J: Oh, see, Mummy!
Mother: What is it?
      J: (Points to picture of crane) X mum, X mum.
          Oh, see.
Mother: It's a crane.

The existence of a contract like "the picture is the topic" dictates that talk should be about a picture under discussion. Mothers know and follow this rule, of course, but children are still learning it. They deviate from it in a number of ways: For example,

by discussing real world (or, in example 14, television) topics, which mothers deal
with, if possible, by establishing connections to a picture:

14. (Josh, 1; 6.1)
    J: (Turning to watch TV screen)
              Mommy a tree a me.
    Mother: Is that a little boy?
              Can you say boy?
              Boy?
              Boy is climbing the tree.
              With all the leaves in it.
              Like the book here.
              (Turns back to find page discussed earlier)
              Look, see the leaves.
              Those are leaves.
              And this tree has all those leaves.
              (M continues to talk about picture in book.)

If the child's real-world topic cannot be made relevant to the picture, the mother
either prohibits it or terminates the book-reading session:

15. (Josh, 1;5.16)
    Mother: You know what?
              His hat just looks like Paddington's hat.
              Does that look like the yellow Paddington's hat?
              Remember?
    J: (Tries to get up to find his Paddington bear)
    Mother: No, you don't have to go get it.
              You don't have to go get it.
              I was just trying to make you realize that it's the same hat.
              The same hat as Paddington's.
              But Paddington is sleeping so leave Paddington alone for now.
              Can you leave Paddington alone?
              Show me Paddington's hat.
              Show me the bear's hat.

Sometime's the child's utterance is relevant to a different picture, in which case the
mother ensures the validity of the rule by finding the picture the child is talking
about:

16. (Jim, 1;11.6)
    J: Broked broked (Pointing to picture of car).
    Mother: That car isn't broken yet.
              That's the car that gets broken later on.
              You have quite a good memory.
              Later on this car gets broken.
              (Finds page with broken car) See, all the wheels fall off.
              It gets broken in the last picture.

See, it's broken now.
But over here where we see it (turning back) . . .
Where were we?
Over here (pointing to original picture) it's not broken yet.
Not broken yet.
It's okay now.
It gets broken later.

The work done by Jim's mother to find the picture Jim was talking about and to explain the connection makes clear how inviolable is the rule that the talk must be about the picture.

Pictures Are Not Things but Representatives of Things

Probably the most important ''contract'' concerning the nature of book input is that it is to be interpreted as symbolic. In the context of picture-book reading, children are taught that pictures are symbolic representations. The teaching involves both aspects of the nature of symbolization: (a) that the symbol is not itself the real thing; (b) while at the same time it represents the real thing. Thus parents discourage their children's attempts to treat the picture as real but continually draw relations between pictured objects or events and real-life objects and events.

At the onset of book reading, children seem puzzled by the two-dimensionality of pictures and spend much time touching and scratching the pictures or attempting to grasp or pick them up. Consider the following examples:

17. (Richard, 11.7)
        R: (Looks at picture, vocalizes)
Mother: That's that, yes.
        R: (Touches page, middle finger scratches picture)
Mother: Yes, rabbits.
        R: (Touches picture)
Mother: Lots of rabbits.

18. (Jonathan, 11.14)
Mother: What have we got here, oh lots of nice things to eat (points).
        J: (Looks at picture)
Mother: (Points to a picture) Peas.
        J: (Touches picture)
Mother: Peas.
                What are they, peas?
        J: (Leans close to picture, touches it and scratches it, pulls pointed finger across picture)
Mother: Yes, you like peas, don't you?

Children have to learn that although pictures show three-dimensional objects, these visual objects cannot be picked up, smelled, or heard. That is, children have to learn the *limits* of representation. In the next example, Richard learns that pictures are objects only visually:

19. (Richard, 1;3.14)
      R: Tick tock (opens book to picture of clock).
            Tick tock (buries head in book to hear clock).
  Mother: (Laughs) What are you doing?

This lesson is learned only gradually, and the tension caused by the partial
"objecthood" of symbols is in evidence for some time.

Consider the following series of exchanges between Jim and his mother:

20. (Jim, 1;10.8)
  Mother: Look at all those bananas.
            Wanta eat those bananas?
      J: Eat dem.
            Bananas (Pretends to pick up and eat).
  Mother: Eat dem bananas.
            Eat dem.
            Look, here's mustard.
            That's mustard.
      J: Eat dem too.
            Eat dem.
            Eat dem (Tries to eat the page).

                        .   .   .

  Mother: That car fell in the water.
      J: Eh pick up (2×).
  Mother: You want to pick it up?
      J: Nope.
  Mother: Nope.
      J: Heavy.
            Heavy car.
  Mother: That's a heavy car, too heavy to pick up?
      J: Mama pick up.
  Mother: Umhum, fell off the boat.
      J: You fix.
            Fix em.
  Mother: I don't know how to fix them once it falls in the water.

                        .   .   .

      J: (Insistently) Em pick.
            Em pick up fire truck.
  Mother: Pick it up?
            I can't pick up that truck (2×).
            Anyway, it's just a picture.
      J: Not picture.
  Mother: It's a picture (2×).

Although adults expend considerable effort to discourage young children from
treating pictures as real, nonsymbolic things, their major concern is to establish the

real-life relevance of the symbol. Often, such reference is explicitly pointed out by the adult. In the following examples, the pictured object is related to an object owned by the child:

21. (Robert, 10.10)
Mother: Look, some bricks?
           Bricks.
           Like at home.

22. (Robert, 10.10)
Mother: Look, that's like your ball.

23. (Jonathan, 11.14)
Mother: What have we got, the cups.
           Cups and plates.
     J: (Points)
Mother: Yes, they're cups, aren't they?
           They're a lot like Jonathan's mugs.

24. (Jonathan, 11.14)
Mother: It's a ball, isn't it?
           Where's your ball?
           Where's Jonathan's ball?

25. (Jonathan, 1;3.16)
Mother: Oh, now, what are they?
           Are they shells?
           Are they shells?
           They are shells.
           They are the same like you got upstairs in mummy's bag.
           Aren't they?

26. (Jacqueline, 1;6.6)
Mother: What's that, your pram?

27. (Jacqueline, 1;8.23)
Mother: There's bricks like what you've got.

28. (Christopher, 2;1.0)
Mother: What's that?
     C: A chair.
Mother: Uh uh.
           Do you have a chair like that?

Alternately, the pictured object might be identified with one owned by a family member.

29. (Jonathan, 11.14)
Mother: A red car, like Daddy's.

30. (Jeremy, 1;11.1)
Mother: Like Phillippa's (his sister's) doll.

or seen recently:

31. (Jonathan, 1;2.0)
Mother: That's a steamroller, isn't it.
           We saw one of those yesterday.

32. (Jacqueline, 2;0.13)
Mother: Oh look—there's a milkman like ours.

More complex relationships between the object pictured and the real world are explicated by mothers who point out how the object is used in a familiar activity.

33. (Richard, 1;2.7)
Mother: A toothbrush.
           You use one of those now, don't you?
           Sort of.

34. (Jacqueline, 1;7.12)
Mother: It's a comb for combing your hair with.

35. (Jeremy, 2;1.17)
Mother: What's this?
     J: Brush.
Mother: What do you do with the brush?
     J: Cleaning.
Mother: Cleaning?
           Do you clean your teeth?
     J: Yes.

or how it is responded to in the real world:

36. (Richard, 1;2.7)
Mother: Milk.
     R: (Smiles)
Mother: What's that?
     R: (Looks at mother, smiles)
Mother: Yes? (Laughs)
           Good, isn't it?

Finally, relating pictured events or activities specifically to the child's own activities is frequent:

37. (Stephen, 8.7)
Mother: A little boy asleep.
           That's what you look like in bed.
           That's what you look like when you're good and asleep.

38. (Jacqueline, 2;0.20)
Mother: (On picture of letter coming through letter box)
           What's that come through the door, see, Jacqueline?
           What's come through the door?
           What did you go and get from the letter box this morning?

39. (Jim, 1;10.8)
     J: Piggies.
           . . . .
           Reading a book (2×).
Mother: Um hum.
           Just like we're doing.
           That doggie's reading a book.
           Just like we are.
     J: Uh read a book too.
Mother: Yeah, we read a book too.

Within a short while, children learn to comment on the relation between pictures
and objects, pictured events and real-life events, themselves.

40. (Jonathan, 1;2.0)
Mother: (Points to picture of clock)
           What's that?
           That's a clock.
     J: (Grabs mother's wrist and explores it, vocalizing)
Mother: No, the clock is . . . where's the clock?

41. (Jonathan, 1;3.16)
Mother: Where's the watch?
           Jonathan, where's the watch?
     J: (Points at picture of watch)
Mother: That's right.
           Yes.
     J: (Points at experimenter's watch).

42. (Jim, 1;10.23)
Mother: He's operating this crane thing that has hoses on it.
           The water's coming out.
     J: Jim water.
Mother: Jim water.
           You were spraying water yesterday with your pretend hose.

           . . . .

     J: Jim hose.

Mother: Yeah, Jim has a hose.
           You were playing with it, pretend hose.

In the following example, Nathaniel works very hard to get his mother to understand the connection between a picture of an apple tree and his own experience picking apples. His language during this exchange was labored, hesitant, and revealed
considerable frustration:

43. (Nathaniel, 2;6.24)
      N: Tree.
Mother: What kind of a . . . ?
      N: Tree apples.
           Under the tree apples all picked up these . . . in these.
Mother: What . . . ?
      N: Pick up these put in these.
 Mother   What's in the trees?
      N: Who's this there?
Mother: Who's this where?
      N: Dada da pick up da apples like Nathaniel like Liz.
Mother: Pick up apples like Nathaniel and Liz did under the trees, that's right.
           Long time ago, that was.
      N: Dit dit out to eat apples an . . . and anne anne jam.

The problems Nathaniel overcame to make this real-world connection explicit reveal clearly that he has learned the contract that pictures are symbols, meant to be
related to real world experiences.

In learning about the nature of pictorial representation, young children are introduced to the domain of symbolic representation in general. Just as two-dimensional
pictures can represent three-dimensional objects, so can any jointly agreed-on
signifier, whether an arbitrary combination of sounds or a piece of writing. Thus,
exposure to representational materials might be an important mediator in the establishment of the tacit "contracts" underlying symbolic representation in oral and
written language.

Pictures Are for Naming

Another basic "contract" established during picture-book reading is that book input
(i.e., pictures and words) is to be *read;* that is, the appropriate behavior at seeing a
picture is to say a word that goes with it. With young children in the early stages of
joint picture-book reading, words are not used to help the child to interpret a picture. Rather, it is taken for granted that the picture is directly interpretable by the
child as representing some familiar object, and words are used to fit a name to the
interpreted meaning of the picture. In the future, the same behavior will be the appropriate one with respect to the printed word: It is meant to elicit a spoken word.

It should be emphasized that the emission of conventional sounds on seeing an
object is a highly artificial behavior as far as the young human primate is concerned.
At the age range we are discussing, children are in the sensorimotor period of their
development, and their habitual mode of interaction with objects is to act on them

physically. Emitting sounds at objects (i.e., labeling them) is a meaningless behavior, functionally speaking. Picture-book reading is the context *par excellence* where this behavior is modeled for children: In the dyad studied by Ninio and Bruner (1978), 75.6% of all labeling utterances emitted by the mother in nine observational sessions over a period of eight months referred to pictures. Within the picture-book reading situation itself, labeling utterances are by far the most frequent type of utterance emitted by either adult or child, especially when the children are at the 1- or 2-word stage (Ninio & Bruner, 1978; Snow & Goldfield, 1982). Picture-book reading, in this early form, is nothing but a continuous effort to achieve "ostensive definition" of words by one of the participants or the other (Ninio, 1980a, 1980b, 1983; Moerk, 1972).

Pictures, Though Static, Can Represent Events

Book input (i.e., pictures as well as words), though by itself static, can represent dynamic actions, events, sequences, relations, motives, and consequences. Whereas a single picture is a symbol for a three-dimensional object, just as each word refers to a single referent, organized complexes of pictures (or words) can portray higher-order aspects of reality. Children are taught to relate several pictorial components to each other in order to see the emergent whole:

44. (Jonathan, 1;1.0)
Mother: Oh, look, there is a cat (pointing) catching mice.

45. (Richard, 1;4.14)
Mother: That's mummy.
           And that's daddy.
           Look.
           What are they doing?
     R: Teeth.
Mother: They're doing their teeth, aren't they?
           They're going to bed.
           There's the basin and there're the taps.
           They're in their dressing gowns.
           They're going to bed, aren't they?

Many pictures in children's books present more than objects for labeling; they often portray actions or events. A rule known to mothers and taught to children during sessions of book reading is that an event is the central, but not sufficient, element in a narrative. Pictured events are not treated like pictured objects, simply as an opportunity for labeling. A picture of a banana elicits "banana" and a picture of a cow "cow," but a picture of a collision elicits a whole story about who did it, to whom, how, and why, as does a pictured fire, fall, collapse, or surprise.

Narratives propped by a pictured event are a series of miniature self-contained descriptions of some selected aspect of the whole. The basic problem posed by events is that of segmenting, categorizing, and selecting aspects of them for discussion. Adults, because they are party to the contracts that also govern the author's behavior, know what is important in a given picture, what "the point is." Children do not know; indeed, the most potent effect of book-reading sessions such as we have analyzed may be that they learn how to "see the point" of pictured events in books.

How is the topic selection organized? Typically, during the early discussions of any given pictured event, the adult selects aspects of it for discussion, either by asking questions or by providing information about them. Children, when looking at those same pictured events on subsequent occasions, seem to operate in accordance with a rule of the form: Previously identified topics should be specifically mentioned or presupposed. It is as if the children have no rule of their own for topic selection and fall back on a very general strategy of modeling their behavior on adults' previous behavior in the situation.

The fact that, in looking at a complex pictured event, the child follows the adult indications in topic selection, suggests that the convergence on strategies of segmentation and categorization which makes communication between two separate individuals possible is a product of "training." Children can eventually select and segment the topics that make sense to adults, because they have been taught, for the events in question, what those categories are. Only after several years of requiring picture-by-picture explicitation of the right categories do children abstract the rules that generate those categories.

The difficulty of the task of selecting the right topics for discussion, i.e., of getting the point, is revealed in a series of discussions between Jim, aged 22 to 23 months, and his mother about a picture of several fire engines converging on a tiny fire. The point of the picture for Jim's mother (and, we presume, for any adult) is the imbalance between the tininess of the fire and the large number of engines, the multitude of firefighters, and the hectic level of firefighting activity portrayed. Jim, in the course of six discussions of the picture, took over from his mother eight different topics originally introduced by her, including: (a) the fire engines; (b) the fire; (c) a dog tripping; (d) a misdirected fire hose; (e) the resultant mess; (f) a firefighter falling off a truck; (g) the fire chief talking on the telephone; and (h) spraying the fire with water. The one topic she introduced more than once (in fact, at every reading of the page) which he did not adopt, was the tininess of the fire (Snow et al., 1985).

Discussing events as central elements in narratives places certain demands on the conversational partners to produce complete, satisfactory narrative structures. These demands are revealed during book-reading sessions by the kinds of questions mothers require answers to—not just *what* and *where* questions, typical of discussions of pictured objects, but also *how, what then,* and *why* questions designed to elicit a full understanding of event sequences, motives, and consequences. Such a full explicitation of narratives cannot be demanded, of course, until the child is at least familiar with the names of objects and characters involved in the event. It is, accordingly, something that develops after repeated discussion of a picture and probably more readily with somewhat older children (Snow & Goldfield, 1982).

Book Events Occur Outside Real Time

Successive discussions of one pictured event can build on one another in a way which demonstrates that book time is continuous and is not affected by intervening segments of real time. Consider the following example:

46. (Nathaniel, 3;4.15)
         N: Read this one.
  Mother: This says "about."
             "Pickles and the piglets are
             about to have suppper."
             "The piglets are running about."
             "Sit down at your places, piglets."
         N: What de dey're doing?
  Mother: What are they doing?
         N: Running around because . . . he's . . .
             There's only one seat.
  Mother: Well that's true.
             There is only one seat.
             How are they supposed to sit down if there's only one seat?
         N: Uh, why is there only one seat?
  Mother: I don't know.
             And Pa Pig . . . no, this is Pickles . . .
             Pickles Pig grabbed the only seat.
             That wasn't very nice, was it?
         N: They're supposed to be eat . . . they're sitting down . . . at the floor.

Looking at the same picture 3 days later, Nathaniel initiates the picture discussion at a point that presupposes much of the information brought out in the above conversation, taking it as shared knowledge:

47. (Nathaniel, 3;4.18)
         N: Oh why they don't have why they just have one seat?
  Mother: I don't know.
             Maybe maybe Pickles knows that the piglets are so lively that they never sit down anyway.
         N: He's sitting down.

In the following example, Nathaniel presupposes the shared availability of information from discussions of the picture which had occurred several weeks earlier to ask first, where the event is pictured and second, for an explanation of it:

48. (Nathaniel, 3;4.8)
         N: (Turning page) Where's de piglets
             are are crying?
  Father: Where's the piglets are crying?
         N: Where is dem two dey're crying?
             Why they're crying?
  Father: Why are they crying?
         N: Why they were crying?

Finally, he recalls in the next example the extensive previous discussions about the "point" of the picture, that the back of Mr. Fixit's lorry had been smashed, so there was no place for him to put the oven he was carrying:

49. (Nathaniel, 3;4.8)
       N: What he doing?
  Mother: What's he carrying on his back?
       N: Has a oven.
             Why nowhere to where to put the oven?
             Why?

Nathaniel's willingness in these examples to ignore real time intervals of several days or weeks between successive readings and treat the discussion of a given picture as a continuous event shows that he has learned the contract distinguishing book time from real time. His parents' willingness to accept his presumption of shared knowledge in these cases confirms for him the correctness of this contract. Snow and Goldfield (1982) hypothesize that children's growing ability to deal with elaborated narrative structures depends precisely on their knowing this contract, since the full story structure gets built up only over a series of book-reading sessions. The presupposition of previously established information enables the dyad to elaborate the event structure more than could otherwise happen.

Books Constitute an Autonomous Fictional World

The separateness of "book time" from "real time" (see contract 6) is a product of the autonomous fictional worlds created by books. In the next example, we see many of the contracts discussed above at work: The picture is discussed as an event; the *point* of the story, first missed by Nathaniel, is made explicit; a connection is made between pictured entities and the real world, now not with real-world objects or places but with real-world social conventions But in addition, this example reveals the existence of a contract to accord characters in the fictional world their own existence independent of the author. Readers can share characters' food preferences (bones are declared yummy by Nathaniel), can approve or disapprove of their behavior, and can even exhort them to act differently (in Nathaniel's case, evidently without yet fully understanding why). This contract concerning the autonomy of the fictional world is, of course, the source of the power of fiction to entrance. The contract means that *Little Women* or *Black Beauty* can never be dismissed as "just stories" and therefore justifies the reader's emotional reaction to Beth's death or to Beauty's trials:

50. (Nathaniel, 3;4.9)
       N: Read this one.
  Mother: Which one.
       N: This one.
  Mother: "Bone.
             Dingo went into a restaurant.
             The waiter served him a bone for lunch."
             Do you think that was funny?

N: Yeah!
Mother: Look what Dingo did.
         What'd he take into the restaurant with him?
N: His hat.
Mother: And what else?
N: And what else?
         His car.
Mother: His car.
         Are you allowed to take your car into a restaurant?
N: No (emphatically).
Mother: Dingo, get that car out of there.
N: You drive it out, Dingo.
Mother: You drive it right out and you put it in the parking lot and you walk back in,
         please.
N: Why?
Mother: Cuz that's what you do in restaurants.

Nathaniel has not yet fully learned the contract about the autonomy of fictional worlds—he still needs encouragement to treat the fictional characters as independent agents.

    51. (Nathaniel, 3;4.10)
    Mother: Tell Squeaky to get off there, and then let's turn the page.
    N: Squeaky get off there.
             Get off there Squeaky.
             Squeaky, Squeaky.
             Get off there.
             Get off there.

Here, he is just starting to be able to collaborate with the author of the book to create a fictional world in which characters have feelings, intentions, needs, and obligations. This is the first step toward entering into the very elaborate set of contracts and metacontracts which a full control of literacy will eventually constitute for the child.

   Full literacy skill involves the ability to create and to comprehend realities that depend for their existence entirely on language. The problems children have with learning to read may derive more from the difficulty of dealing with decontextualized language than from the difficulty of dealing with print (Snow, 1983). Dealing with a fictional world, in books as Nathaniel does in the above example, or in verbal play, may provide valuable practice in the decontextualization skills necessary to read nonfictional autonomous texts as well.

CONCLUSION

We have identified seven contracts which govern adult behavior during bookreading with preschool children and which children have to learn, if they are to participate successfully in such book-reading interactions. There are undoubtedly additional contracts and perhaps somewhat different ones for different parent-child dyads, different social classes, or different cultures.

The learning that goes on during book-reading sessions consists most importantly, in our view, of learning about the kinds of contracts we have identified rather than the learning which might also occur about letter recognition, grapheme–phoneme correspondences, or sight–word reading. The most important difference between literate and face-to-face communication is not that the first is visual and the second auditory, but that different rules are in effect. Analyzing the nature of the rules or contracts governing various sorts of communicative encounters and the contexts in which such rules can be learned by preschoolers may help us to analyze the difficulties children have in meeting the demands of literacy during their school years.

REFERENCES

Chall, J.C., Snow, C.E., Barnes, W., Chandler, J, Hemphill, L., Goodman, I., and Jacobs, V. (1983). *Families and literacy.* Final Report to N.I.E., Harvard Graduate School of Education, Cambridge, MA.

Friedman, S., & Stevenson, M. (1980). Perception of movement in pictures. In M.A. Hagen (Ed.), *The perception of pictures.* New York: Academic Press.

Goldfield, B., & Snow, C.E. (1984). Reading books with children: The mechanics of parental influence on children's reading achievement. In J. Flood (Ed.), *Promoting reading comprehension.* Newark, DE: International Reading Association.

Miller, P. (1982). *Amy, Wendy, and Beth: Learning language in South Baltimore.* Austin: University of Texas Press.

Moerk, E.L. (1972). Principles of dyadic interaction in language learning. *Merrill-Palmer Quarterly, 18,* 229–257.

Ninio, A. (1980a). Ostensive definition in vocabulary teaching. *Journal of Child Language, 7,* 565–573.

Ninio, A. (1980b). Picture-book reading in mother–infant dyads belonging to two subgroups in Israel. *Child Development, 51,* 587–590.

Ninio, A. (1983). Joint book-reading as a multiple vocabulary acquisition device. *Developmental Psychology, 19,* 445–451.

Ninio, A., & Bruner, J. (1978). The achievement and antecedents of labelling. *Journal of Child Language, 5,* 1–14.

Rommetveit, R. (1974). *On message structure: A framework for the study of language and communication.* London: Wiley.

Snow, C.E. (1977). Development of conversation between mothers and babies. *Journal of Child Language, 4,* 1–22.

Snow, C.E. (1983). Language and literacy: Relationships during the preschool years. *Harvard Educational Review, 53,* 165–189.

Snow, C.E., Arlman-Rupp, A., Hassing, Y., Jobse, J., Joosten, J., & Vorster, J. (1976). Mothers' speech in three social classes. *Journal of Psycholinguistic Research, 5,* 1–20.

Snow, C.E., & Goldfield, B. (1982). Building stories: The emergence of information structures from conversation. In D. Tannen (Ed.), *Analyzing discourse: Text and talk.* Washington, DC: Georgetown University Press.

Snow, C.E., & Goldfield, B. (1983). Turn the page please: Situation specific language learning. *Journal of Child Language, 10,* 551–570.

Snow, C.E., Nathan, D., & Perlmann, R. (1985). Assessing children's knowledge about book reading. In L. Galda & A. Pellegrini (Eds.), *Language in play*. Norwood, NJ: Ablex.

Snow, C.E., Perlmann, R., & Nathan, D. (1984). *Why routines are different: Situational effects on children's and mothers' speech*. Paper presented at the Third International Congress for the Study of Child Language, Austin, TX.

Werner, H. & Kaplan, B. (1963). *Symbol formation*. New York: Wiley.

6

Creating Family Story: "Matthew! We're Going to Have a Ride!"*

Denny Taylor
Teachers College, Columbia University

Denny Taylor's work in emergent literacy has always been concerned with family as much as with children's writing and reading development. In this chapter she offers an example of a "prose home movie," a means of understanding what happens during family storybook reading that is essentially a narrative account created jointly by researcher and parent. The prose home movie is a departure from more traditional means of reporting research on this topic such as was just presented in the Snow and Ninio chapter. Taylor's chapter offers an intriguing means for understanding how parents and children jointly construct both family and story when they share books. She ends her discussion by posing 10 significant questions for future research on family storybook reading.

For the child, all language is doing something; in other words it is meaning. (Halliday, (1973)

Hunting through my early writings for the beginnings of this chapter, I came across a dusty paper that I had written some years ago for a course on ''The Family as Educator.'' Laid out in traditional fashion, the introduction is followed by the statement of the problem and then come the questions, numbered and presented one after another:

1. How is literacy woven into the daily life of the family?
2. What learning opportunities within the home environment have been instrumental in the acquisition of literacy by individual members of the family?
3. How are the experiences of learning to read in school mediated by individual members of the family?

These were the questions that hastened my departure from traditional educational research and pushed me into field studies of unknown dimensions and worrisome forms.

Since writing that paper, I have spent much of my time visiting families, talking with parents and children, and watching them as they go about their daily lives. I

---

* To Cullen, Jessica, Sarah, and Matthew. With thanks.

have visited middle-class families and families living below the poverty level, two-parent families and single-parent families, families in which the mother works outside the home and families in which the mother stays home. It is this experience that has enabled me to develop descriptions which provide some insights into the many complex and interrelated ways that children's literate activities are mediated and affected by multigenerational family patterns and by their personal experiences of everyday life both within and outside the family (Taylor, 1981, 1982a, 1982b, 1983a, 1983b). Among the perspectives that I have tried to develop are descriptions of the ways in which rituals and routines of written language usage appear to conserve family traditions of literacy whereas others appear to change the patterns of the past. Building upon this multigenerational perspective, I have tried to describe the ways in which patterns of family literacy are constantly evolving to accommodate the everyday experiences of both parents and children, with the introduction of a younger sibling leading to the systematic restructuring of any given routine. This eventually led to the descriptions of the ways in which the children themselves, as integral members of a social organization, use print as one medium through which they master their surroundings, build new social connections, and establish new environmental relationships.

When I contemplate the early questions that I asked and then think about some of the perspectives that I subsequently tried to develop, what strikes me most is the static quality of the literacy that I initially envisioned and the fluidity of the literacy that I eventually attempted to describe. In the questions literacy is still and unmoving, a reified concept to be examined and studied. But in the family, no such literacy exists. Literacy is a dynamic process of immeasurable complexity that moves imperceptibly with the family, accommodating to the personal experiences of individual family members, and taking shape in the enduring events (Whitehead, 1925) of their combined life histories. Each family member's experience of print is personally constructed as well as socially owned, so that what is literacy to one may not be literacy to another. I believe that it is within this context, in the unremarkable daily events of family life, that children learn of print as a social enterprise as well as a solitary endeavor, and that it is from this perspective that we can begin to appreciate the plurality of literacies that are a part of a child's world.

This somewhat idiosyncratic perspective has evolved, as I have, in the field, working with families who have young children who are learning to read and write. As I have watched and waited, listened and talked, I came to appreciate how little of their lives we really understand. The more time I spend in the field, the more urgent my desire to capture on paper some fleeting moment of everyday life, to glimpse the world as it appears to the family. It is this overwhelming need to preserve what Bateson has referred to as the "integrity of the data" (Lipset, 1982) which has led me to search for new ways of developing natural histories of family literacy. In this chapter I want to share with you one of the attempts that I have made in this direction.

Since 1977, when my family literacy research began, I have been trying to gain a better understanding of what happens when families share storybooks. At the beginning, it seemed such a straightforward task. Such naiveté! How simple it sounds and how difficult it becomes. The world is complex and very frustrating. In the early phases of the research, I was particularly concerned with finding ways of obtaining data which would not "lift" the sharing of stories out of context. And, as the research progressed, this has become increasingly important, for the sharing of storybooks is an intimate occasion which does not easily lend itself to "naturalistic" observation. The intrusion of a researcher at such times would undoubtedly impose restraints on the family's experience of storybook reading. Video recordings create similar difficulties; for although much remains the same, somethings at least are changed, and we are stuck with our inventions of investigating the world. Using an audio recorder is somewhat less intrusive, for it is easily forgotten as it quietly records the sounds. But that is, of course, the major disadvantage of using audio recordings, for you do indeed capture the sounds of voices and not the people. One of the ways that I have tried to overcome this difficulty is by sharing the tapes with the families that have recorded them for me. When a mother agrees to record stories for me, I give her a tape and ask her to put the tape recorder in the location in which they usually share storybooks and to switch it on as they get ready to read. The request is casual, deliberately so; it is my intent to gain access without intrusion and by so doing, to change as little as possible. The taping of the stories can take as little time as a few days or as much as several months. Family matters take precedence. To give you an example, a tape recently arrived with the following note:

Dear Denny

At last—a recorded tape! Thanks for your patience and your recorder. The tape would have been in your hands sooner had it not been for several colds and ear infections; then I let it sit in the recorder for two or three weeks trying to outwait a recent teething/ear infection spell, only to discover (when I went to record) that there was less than one minute on the tape!!

The mother who wrote the note had the tape for 3 months before it was returned.

Once I receive a tape, I spend time listening to it myself, and then I invite the mother to come and listen to it with me. Such occasions are audio-recorded and, as we listen, I become privy to at least some of the ways in which the mothers themselves see the storybook occasions that they share with their children. But it is still a very imperfect way of working, for although I still believe that using a tape-recorder is the least intrusive of the data collection procedures, I am very much dissatisfied with the ways in which I have tried to "capture the world" through the use of this medium. My dissatisfaction is less with the taping procedure than it is with what to do with the tape once I have received it. To describe the talk leaves me with nothing more than inert scripts which send me back to the analytic constructs of the research literature. Talking with the mothers does indeed enable me to gain some understanding of the social contexts in which the stories were shared, but I would be the first to admit that the information is fragmented and open to misinterpretation.

As I have mused about the problem that I have created for myself, I have returned to the writings of a number of scholars, but to two scholars in particular. It is in statements that have been made by Hymes (1980) and Bateson (1936/1958) that I have found at least a partial solution to my difficulties. To recap, the task is to develop texts which come as close as possible to the ways in which the families themselves see the activity of storybook reading. Hymes (1980) calls such writings narrative accounts, and he states:

> Instead of thinking of narrative accounts as an early stage that in principle will be replaced, we may need to think of them as permanent, whose principles are little understood, and whose role may increase. (p. 98)

It was such narration that I wanted to explore, for it seemed to me that the humanizing and sensitizing effects of these accounts had value above and beyond their scientific validity. These thoughts sent me back further to the introduction to Bateson's (1936/1958) classical text *Naven*. Echoing his father's concern for the interrelationships between art and science, Bateson states:

> The artist . . . can leave a great many of the most fundamental aspects of culture to be picked up not from his actual words, but from his emphasis. He can choose words whose very sound is more significant than their dictionary meaning and he can group and stress them so that the reader almost unconsciously receives information which is not explicit in the sentences and which the artist would find it hard—almost impossible—to express in analytic terms. (pp. 1–2)

As the readings merged with the practical problem of recreating a family storybook occasion, I began to appreciate the dimensions of the task. It seemed to me that I needed what Salinger (1955) referred to as "a prose home movie," a collaborative venture in which the text becomes the common ground that the writer and the participants share. What is essential is a narrative account that realistically recreates the storybook occasion in such a way that the family can see themselves in the writing; an account that can then be explored in light of other, more traditional, research findings on families and storybook reading.

At about this time, one of the mothers, Cullen, who has been recording stories for me, arrived with a new tape. Cullen also brought some of the books that she had read with her 3 children. And, as she took them out of her bag, she explained, "Okay, these are some of what is on this tape and not everything is from beginning to end or exact text. It's a real hodgepodge, very representative of our family and how we are right now." For a researcher intent on capturing a fleeting glimpse of some other's world, this was an exciting moment, but more was to come. As we listened to the first few minutes of the tape, Cullen told me that the story "epitomized" what she thought was "almost perfection in sitting down with a group of 3 children and reading." Cullen went on to explain that "although there were lots of interruptions and everybody was going in different directions," she felt it had "really worked." The story was *Chester Cricket's Pigeon Ride* by George Selden (1981), selected by the mother for the researcher to study.

The task had now become to develop a text which comes as close as possible to the ways in which one mother sees the activity of storybook reading with her 3 children. It was my hunch that through the process of interpreting the story, Cullen would be able to achieve what Erickson (1982) described as an "overall contextual perspective" that can "only come through intimate and continuous personal acquaintance" (p. 162). The approach to the development of the narrative owes much to a piece in the *Times Literary Supplement* (London) by Paul de Man (1982). In the article "The Return to Philology," de Man focuses upon the teaching of literature and problems of "modern" approaches. It is within this context that he speaks of a course that he attended at Harvard which was taught by Reuben Brower. De Man states that in Brower's classes:

> Students, as they began to write on the writings of others, were not to say anything that was not derived from the text they were considering. They were not to make any statements that they could not support by a specific use of language that actually occurred in the text. (p. 1355)

And so, the process began. Cullen worked with me to develop a transcript of the sharing of *Chester Cricket's Pigeon Ride*. We sat each morning in her kitchen listening to the audiotape of the storybook occasion, writing down the words and talking about each moment as it occurred. All this we audio-recorded, and after each session, I would return to my office with the original recording, the transcript, and the audio recordings of the transcription process. Then, using all three, I tried to construct a "prose home movie" so that Cullen could "see" herself in the inferential description that I was developing. I played with the ways in which the words came together and the imagery that I was creating, but nothing is included in the narrative that does not occur in the audiotapes or transcript. Each sentence is supported by the descriptions and interpretations that Cullen provided during the many hours that we listened to the original tape. Cullen became the interpreter of their lives (Frake, 1980). Each day, as I returned to continue developing the prose home movie of the storybook occasion, I would read to Cullen from the messy pages of the emerging narration, and she would comment on their "authenticity." Occasionally, we would change a word or a phrase that jarred with the imagery of the piece, but for the most part, Cullen was pleased with the way the narrative was progressing. We continued each day, until we had finished describing the family storybook occasion that revolved around the first eight pages of text in *Chester Cricket's Pigeon Ride*.

My first impulse in using the narrative was to relegate it to an appendix and to present to you, the reader, an analysis of the text. But this, of course, runs counter to my belief that narrative is more than an early stage of research (Hymes, 1980) to be replaced upon production by some more involved and analytic construction. Thus, with some trepidation, I am going to present the entire narrative; a prose home movie for you to study. But first a little preparation. Suspend judgment. Put aside your knowledge of the importance of storybooks for young children who are learning to read. Try to forget what you have read in the literature of mother and child dyads reading together. Instead, take yourself into the storybook occasion, and imagine the ways in which Cullen and her children create a story for themselves and for Matthew, the baby, as they work together in becoming (Wolcott, 1982) a family.

"MATTHEW! WE'RE GOING TO HAVE A RIDE!"

The story is read in the bedroom that Sarah, 5, shares with her 7-year-old sister, Jessica. Cullen, their mom, is sitting on the floor in the middle of the room. The tape begins as Matthew, who is heading for the recorder, says, "What's that?" Cullen repeats "What's that?" as she moves the tape recorder out of the way. Sarah comes over to where her mother is sitting and says, "What?" Cullen quickly asks, "Do you want to hear *Chester Cricket's Pigeon Ride?*" Jessica says, "Yeh! Yeh! Yeh!", enticing Sarah and Matthew into sharing the storybook; and then in a hushed voice, she tells them, "You have to be quiet." Cullen says, "No," and makes some throaty noises as she stops Jessica from telling Sarah that the tape-recorder is on. Cullen diverts Sarah's attention by asking her, "Where's Matthew?" Sarah responds by calling, "Matthew! We're going to have a ride!" Jessica says, "I love Chester books," and Matthew runs over to his mom. Cullen says, "Whoa!" as he plops into her lap, and Sarah gets her puppet to say in a squeaky voice, "Hi Jessica! Hi Jessa!" Cullen draws Matthew into the book by asking, "Matthew, do you see the cricket?" Matthew repeats, "Cricket." "Right," says his mom, "there's the cricket." Sarah, who is experimenting with words, adds, "Cricket, pigget." Cullen, pointing at the cricket, continues talking with Matthew. "That's Chester," she says. Sarah adds, "Look at his feet. That's where—" but Cullen is still in tune with Matthew, and she ignores Sarah's comments as she tells Matthew that "Chester is going to take a ride on a pigeon." Cullen begins the book: *"Chester Cricket's Pigeon Ride* by George Selden." Sarah says, "He does good things." Cullen, still focused upon Matthew, asks him, "Matthew, can you see the cricket?" Matthew says, "Cricket," and his mom continues by asking him, "Where's the pigeon?" Matthew makes sounds for "Where's the pigeon?" while Sarah keeps going with "He does good drawings," and then she adds, "Did he draw this?" Matthew points to the pigeon, and Jessica responds by saying, "Good boy!" As Jessica keeps Matthew interested in the book, Cullen picks up on Sarah's question about the drawings. She says, "Well, let's see, 'Pictures by Garth Williams.' Garth Williams did the pictures, Sarah." Sarah repeats, "Garth Willums," and her mom says the name again, emphasizing the ending, "Garth Will*iams*." Sarah asks, "With crayons?" Cullen questions, "Well, what do you think he used? Does that look like crayon to you?" Matthew is singing, and Sarah continues, "Did he copy from a machine?" Matthew is still singing as Cullen responds to Sarah's latest question. "No, I think he probably drew them himself and the machine reproduced them in the book." Matthew is turning pages and has found a picture of Harry Cat and shouts, "A cat! A cat!" Jessica, joining in the conversation about the drawings, says, "I think he used a pen." Matthew continues, "A cat! A cat! A cat! A cat!" Jessica adds, "A special kind of pen." "A cat! A cat! A cat! A cat!" Cullen says, "Pen and ink this is called." "A cat!" shouts Matthew. "Pen and ink and a special machine," says Sarah. "And then a special machine," adds her mother. "A cat," sighs Matthew. Cullen turns the pages back to the beginning of the story and says, "Let's start at the beginning again." "A cat." Cullen begins, "Okay":

Life in New York is very exciting. It especially was thrilling for a Cricket named Chester from Connecticut, who just two weeks ago had found himself in the Times Square subway station. It was there that he'd managed finally to free himself from a picnic basket. And then had been more or less adopted by two families: the Bellinis, who ran a newsstand, and a mouse and a cat named Tucker and Harry, who lived in an old abandoned drain[1]

Cullen hesitates, reading around Matthew's fingers as they try to turn the pages. Matthew takes a breath. Cullen continues:

drainpipe. So much happened to Chester during these first two weeks in the city that he could hardly believe he was the

Matthew says, "Pussycat."

same country cricket who used to spend his days eating and sleeping and sunning himself on his stump in the country.

Cullen stops near the bottom of the page. She looks at the busy black and white drawing and asks Sarah, "Do you see the stump in this picture Sarah?" Sarah points and asks, "This?" "Mm Mm," responds her mom, "where would he sun himself, do you think?" "In the sun" is Sarah's straightforward answer. Cullen says, "Right" and then adds a ponderous "Mmm" as she thinks about Sarah's response. Matthew adds another "A cat." Cullen pursues her questions, "What is a stump Sarah?" "A cat." "A stump?" asks Sarah. "Like this?" She points at the stump in the picture. Cullen wonders if Sarah knows that the stump is the remainder of a tree, and so she continues, "Well, what is a stump?" Matthew shouts his own words. Sarah answers her mother, "The tree was starting to grow and then somebody says, 'I want to find things to chop' and he chops the tree." Cullen goes on, "And what is left?" Matthew holds his mom's face trying to get her to look at him, and says, "Ma." Sarah says, "A stump!" Matthew says, "Mama, Mama" with his hands on Cullen's cheeks. Cullen finishes talking with Sarah, "And that's where Chester Cricket used to have to sun." Matthew doesn't give up. He goes on, "Mama, Mama." Cullen says, "Yes Matthew," and he says his own special words for "I turn the page." Cullen tells him, "Well it's not time to turn yet, just a few more words. You listen Matthew."

For a few days Mario Bellini, the boy who had found Ches——

Matthew gets off his mom's lap. "Look Matthew, look!" calls Sarah, and anticipating the end of the page, she tries to bring Matthew back to the book. Jessica says, "Shhh."

Chester his first night in New York, took him around [turns page] and introduced him to everyone who worked in the Times Square subway station.

---

[1] Excerpts reprinted by permission of Farrar, Straus, and Giroux, Inc. from *Chester Cricket's Pigeon Ride* by George Selden. Pictures by Garth Williams. Text copyright © 1981 by George Selden. Pictures copyright © 1981 by Garth Williams.

Matthew goes to the closet and opens the door. He goes through the books on the shelf and comes out with *I am a Mouse,* a "Golden Study Book" which has stiff cardboard pages. He opens the book and says, "Dee Dee," and then as he turns the pages, he says, "Mouse," "Ah chickadee," "Owl," "Dee Dee," and "Birdie," filling the rest of the story with his own "reading" words. Cullen does not stop. She continues to read as Matthew reads his book:

> He met all the countermen from lunch stands, the conductors on the Shuttle, the clean-ing men who swept the station and the three girls who worked in the Loft's candy store. And they all liked Chester. It somehow made them happy to think that there was a little insect from the countryside living right there in the heart of New York.

Sarah asks a question, "Can we read the girls one again? Girls one." Jessica says, "Sh, Sh, Sh." Cullen stops reading. "From Loft's Candy Store?" she asks Sarah. She paraphrases the story, "Err, he was meeting all the people from the subway station, all right?" "Yeh," responds Sarah. Cullen reads, "And the three girls that worked in the Loft's candy store." Sarah is insistent, "And gave him? And gave him?" she asks. Her mom goes back to the book, "Well it says, 'And they all liked Chester. It somehow . . .'" Sarah interrupts, she has heard this part of the story before. "But they're supposed to. But you said, you said when you read it the first time, you said the girls gave him candy each morn day." Cullen pauses for a mo-ment and says, "Well, maybe it says that somewhere." Matthew is still turning the pages of his book. "Owl," "Duck," and other words are said as he looks at the pictures. Cullen returns to the story:

> It somehow made them happy to think that there was a little insect from the country-side living right there in the heart of New York. He became the pet of the whole sta-tion.

Cullen stops reading and speaks to Sarah, "Here comes the part that you remember, I think":

> The countermen fed him, the conductors gave him free rides back and forth on the Shuttle, and the three girls saved him a chocolate cream candy every now and then.

Sarah is pleased. "That's the one," she says. "Is that what you remember?" asks her mom. "Yeh," says Sarah. "Now tell me," Cullen pauses and then continues, "if you worked in the subway station and one of the Bellini family came and intro-duced you to a cricket, what would you think?" "I would say it's very nice," re-sponds Sarah, and then she repeats her reply, "I would say it's very nice." Sarah continues with her own agenda, asking her mother to help her with her valentine necklace. "Can you put this on me?" she says. But Cullen is attending to Jessica who is still talking about crickets. "We had two crickets in the classroom," she tells her mother. Sarah interjects, "I love putting necklaces on me." Cullen is speaking with Jessica, "So you've experienced meeting a cricket then." "Yeh," says Jessica, "but we've never heard it sing." Cullen adds a ponderous "Mmm," and then Jessica adds, "And I've experienced that they die very quickly." "Mm, Mm," agrees her mother. Sarah is still playing with the necklace, and she offers to read the words on the heart-shaped pendant to her mother. "I'll read this to you," she says. "I'll read this to you." Cullen tells her "to go ahead." Sarah reads, "BIG KISS." Her mom asks her, "What does the BIG begin with?" Matthew is singing his way through his book. Cullen adds, "What letter?" Sarah says, "B." "And what does Kiss begin with?" "K," says Sarah. Cullen tells Sarah that she is surprised that she knows the answers to her questions. Jessica says, "Now keep going," bringing her mom back to the book. "All right." Cullen returns to the story:

> But Chester didn't only stay in the subway station. One Sunday afternoon Mario took him to the Planetarium.

Jessica asks, "Where's the Planetarium?" Cullen tells her "The Planetarium is in the Museum of Natural History." "It is?" says Jessica in surprise. "Mm, mm," confirms her mom. Jessica continues, "So the Bellini's could be a real family?" "Sure," says her mom. And Jessica goes on, "They could be poor. They could own a newsstand and find a cricket and," she takes a thinking pause, "And–an–an that," Jessica says, holding on to her turn. "Mmm," says her mom. Jessica continues, "But I'm not sure about the mouse and the cat." Cullen begins, "I don't know the whole story," but she is interrupted by Sarah who begins to cry because Matthew shuts the book. Cullen speaks to him, "Matthew when you close the book it upsets Sarah. Let's open it so we can hear the words." Sarah shows Matthew her valentine necklace. "Look Matthew, look. I'll put it on you. I'll put it on you. I'll put it on Matthew, Mom." But Matthew does not want to wear the necklace, so Sarah puts it on the chest. Cullen goes back to the book, recapping the story before she starts to read. "All right, so Mario took him, took the cricket, Sarah, to the Planetarium." Matthew says, "Mommy" goes over to the chest and grabs Sarah's necklace. Cullen reads:

> Chester thought that was *awfully* interesting! Back home, his favorite pastime had been stargazing.

Sarah gets her mom's attention. "Mom, Matthew's got my necklace." Cullen says, "You know, that might be just the thing to distract him while we read about Chester." Sarah disagrees, "I think it's going to get torn." Jessica says, "No." Cullen tells Sarah, "The string is very strong. That string I wouldn't be concerned about." Sarah considers this information and says, "Oh yeh. That heart is very heavy." "Heavy," echoes Matthew. "Mm, Mm, exactly," agrees Cullen, as she returns to the story. "Well, here we are in the Planetarium with Chester, Sarah." "I see Chester," says Sarah. "Where?" asks her mom. Sarah points to the little cricket on Mario's shoulder and says, "Right there." "Oh, you're absolutely right," agrees Cullen, pleased that Sarah is still in tune with the story. Cullen returns to the Planetarium, "And in the Planetarium they have a special room. The planetarium. Where the lights go out and they project all the stars." "Oh, yeh!" Jessica chimes. "We've been there." Cullen says, "That's right. Uh-huh. So this is what he's doing. He's stargazing in a room and they're telling us that's one of his favorite things to do at home." Cullen is back to the story:

> The top of his stump made an excellent observation platform, and he loved to come out and watch the slow drift of stars across the night sky. And in the Planetarium Chester recognized the same stars. They were showing a program called "Summer Nights." But all the changes that took place in a whole summer in Connecticut, the rising and falling of the constellations, happened in just a few hours in the Planetarium.

Cullen stops and speaks to Sarah. "Now Sarah, what is an observation platform?" Sarah says, "I don't know." Her mom continues, "Well what do you think? Well let's see here." Sarah leaves and goes over to the closet with Matthew. He puts his book on the shelf and says, "All gone, all gone." Cullen pursues the question, "The top of his stump. Chester's stump made an excellent observation platform." Jessica knows the answer; she sucks in her breath and raises her hand. Cullen raises her eyebrows to signal that she wants Jessica to wait and then adds, "Remember he's looking at the night sky." Cullen returns to the picture of the stump and continues, "If Chester was observing the sky, what part of his body is he using?" Matthew makes his own sounds to join in the conversation. Sarah sits as Chester sits and says, "He could be like this." "Sure," agrees her mom, "he could be sitting there. Well, what is he using to observe?" Jessica opens her eyes wide and says, "Like that. What am I, what do you use when you try to, kinda." Jessica thinks for a second and says, "*See*," then she quickly adds, "no that's not right." Sarah responds, "When you look at something." At the same time, Cullen gives another hint, "When you observe the sky." Sarah has another go as Matthew adds some more words to the conversation, "You, you, you look with your eyes." "Yeh," says Jessica, pleased and relieved that her sister has got it. "Yeh that's it!" agreed Cullen and she adds, "So an observation deck or platform would be a place you would choose to see something. And Chester was looking at the sky." Jessica looks at the picture and laughs at the drawing of one man who is looking up and seems to be all hair and nose. "With the nose!" she laughs. Cullen chuckles and says, "He was looking up, he was observing." Matthew makes some complaining noises, and Cullen continues, "Now there's another word here, 'constellation,' do you know what that is, Jessica?" "Oh, oh, um," says Jessica. Matthew tickles Sarah, "Ticka-ticka, ticka." Sarah laughs, and then they giggle together. Jessica has been thinking about her mom's question, and she asks, "Is it something for the stars and the moon?" "Yes," says Cullen, and then she asks, "Is it one star?" "No," is Jessica's quick response. Cullen agrees, "No, it's a whole group of stars, right?" Jessica continues talking about stars while Sarah, who is still being tickled, tells Matthew, "You have long nails!' and then she adds, "No! No!" as he continues to tickle. Matthew stops and picks up Sarah's necklace and starts to swing it around. Cullen steps in, "Matthew, no Matthew, Matthew." Sarah begins, "Don't use," but Cullen continues trying to divert Matthew's attention, "Where's your book, Matthew?" Sarah finishes her sentence, "Don't use my necklace as a weapon." "A weapon," echoes Matthew. Cullen tells Matthew, "Necklaces are for decoration." Sarah asks her mom, "Can you put it on him?" "Well, no," says Cullen, "I think he just wants it around his wrist." She returns to the book:

At one point, when he saw a shooting star, Chester got so excited he began to chirp.

Cullen calls Sarah back to the book, "Sarah come and see this illustration." It is the end of the page, and she is about to turn it. Cullen goes on:

The sound went very well with the theme of "Summer Nights."

Sarah stops playing with Matthew and goes over to see the pictures. Matthew is disappointed. "Sarah," he scolds. Cullen reads, "The only trouble was," as Sarah searches the picture for Chester; "I see Chester Cricket," she cheers. "Where is he?" Cullen asks. "Here," says Sarah. "No I don't think so, Sarah," says her mom. Sarah persists, "Let me see Chester Cricket." Jessica has joined in the hunt and has found the cricket, "No, here he is. He's in Mario's hand." "Oh yes," says Cullen "Mm, mm." Sarah goes back to her game with Matthew, and he continues tickling her. Cullen reads:

The only trouble was, after the show was over, Chester found that he had a very stiff neck from looking upward so long.

Matthew says, "Sarah." "On the same day," begins Cullen. "Mama, Mama, Mama, Mama," chimes Matthew. Sarah is putting barrettes in her hair. "On me, ah Sarah," says Matthew. "Sarah's barrettes," Cullen responds, but the barrette is caught in Sarah's hair and she wants it out. "Oh we have it here," Cullen comments, as she sees the barrette. "Ah," says Matthew, grabbing for it. "Oh gently, gently," urges his mom. "Mommy," complains Sarah, as Cullen tries to untangle the barrette from her hair. Cullen is back to the story:

Chester was very interested in the dinosaur skeleton and the meteorite—he was really a very curious sort of person—and he loved the room with the diamond and ruby and all the other beautiful jewels! Mario asked a guard if they had any insects in the museum, and the guard said they used to, but that room was now closed. Chester Cricket really was glad to hear that. He didn't much want to hop along a glass case, looking down, and see some of his own ancestors pinned on little pieces of cardboard, with their names printed neatly under them.

Cullen stops, "Why do you think he'd feel that way?" she asks. Jessica answers, "He wouldn't like it too much to see his ancestors killed." Mm, mm," agrees Cullen, and then Jessica adds, "He would like to see them alive." "Well," Cullen is back to the story:

One afternoon, Mario took Chester to his first movie. They sat

Cullen says, "*on* the balcony" and then corrects herself and says, "*in* the balcony." Matthew has distracted her as he grumbles at her and says, "other side." Matthew wants to breast-feed and "other side" is his word for such occasions. Cullen continues reading, and Matthew gives up the idea of nursing and sits singing his own words as he participates in his mom's reading.

and the boy put the cricket up on his shoulder so he'd have a clear view of the picture.

> The air conditioning in the theater was so cold Chester had to wrap himself in Mario's collar to keep from shivering. And the movie itself made him very sad.

Sarah interrupts and asks Cullen, "Why?" There are no clues in the text, so Cullen reads ahead to see if there was an answer to Sarah's question. "Well, let's see," she says and then begins to read, "It took place in the country, which looked for all the world like Connecticut." Matthew has Sarah's necklace and laughs, "On me," he says. Sarah looks at her mom and asks, "Can you put it on Matt?" "No," says Matthew, and Sarah then asks, "Well, will you put it on me?" It is a quick exchange, and as Cullen puts the necklace on Sarah, she pursues the question of why Chester is sad. "He was sad because it reminded him," she begins. "Of Connecticut," adds Jessica, finishing the sentence. "Right," replies her mom, "which is where he used to live." Jessica says, "Like you get homesick." "Right," agrees Cullen, and again she is back to the story:

> It took place in the country, which looked for all the world like Connecticut. Chester was looking so hard at the fields and trees that he forgot to follow the plot. By the end of the show, he could almost have cried for homesickness.

Cullen turns the page and calls Matthew back to the book. "Matthew, come see the cat. This is the cat you saw." "Meeow, meeow," purrs Jessica, as she encourages Matthew to come and see the pictures. Matthew comes, looks at the cat and says, "A cat, a cat!" Jessica begins to read, "The night after the movies," she stops. Her mom says, "Go ahead, you can read," and Matthew says, "A cat!" Jessica continues as Matthew adds a word or two here and there in the story:

> The Bellinis, Mario and his mother and father, went home early. Tucker Mouse and Harry Cat came over to the newsstand, as they did every night, to listen to Chester's adventures of the day. Of course, going to the movies was nothing new to them. They would sneak out into Times Square and dart into a theater two or three times a week. Tucker knew more secret entrances—hidden holes and loose boards—than any other mouse in New York.

Cullen says, "Humm," as if pondering a question, and then she says, "That mouse sure looks comfortable. What's unusual about a friendship between a cat and a mouse?" Jessica answers her mom, "Because they're together," she says, "and usually cats chase mice." "A cat" says Matthew. Cullen responds, "There's the cat, Matthew." "And there's Chester Cricket," Jessica says, joining in the conversation her mom is having with Matthew. "CRICKET," Sarah pronounces the word carefully for Matthew to say, "I teach, I teached." "Cricket," chirps Matthew. "Mm, right, Matthew," says his mom. "I I I taught him!" shouts a gleeful Sarah. Matthew is holding something in his mouth, and his mom tries to find out what it is. As she turns the page of the book, she questions Matthew. "What have you got in your mouth there, fiddle diddle?" "What's that?" she asks again. "A marble," says Sarah, answering her mom's question. "Marbles are for rolling, Matthew," explains Cullen. Sarah begins, "I'll show you, give me——." Cullen continues, "Let Sarah show you how a marble will roll." Sarah pretends to roll the marble across the floor. "Go like this," she tells Matthew, and she pretends to roll a marble and makes the sound of a marble hitting the floor. "Dap, dap, dap." she says, roll-ing a pretend marble. When this does not work, Sarah opens her mouth wide and makes a good long "Ahhhh." "Take it out, honey," Cullen tells Matthew. "Go like this," continues Sarah, "Ahhhhhhhhhh." Jessica sucks in her breath; she is worried that her brother might choke. Sarah frowns, "He's holding onto the mar-ble," she says, and then another word of encouragement. "I'll give you a piggy," she croons. Matthew ignores the tiny, pink pottery pig that his sister is offering to him, and he runs down the hall. Sarah is about to get up. Cullen stops her, "No. Stay here, Sarah," and she pursues Matthew down the hall, removes the marble from his mouth, and puts it into his hand. While their mom is out of the room, Jessica and Sarah pick up the jack-in-the-box. "Get him in," says Sarah, as Jessica pushes the jack down into the box. Matthew is back, and Sarah is trying to get him to trade the marble for the jack. Sarah laughs as the jack pops up. "Give me the marble; this is what you want," she says to Matthew in a singsong voice. "Give me the marble." Matthew grabs the jack-in-the-box. "I'll hold the book," says Sarah. "I'll read it to you," Jessica tells Sarah. Matthew plays with the jack-in-the box as Jessica reads. He bangs on the lid, until the jack appears. Jessica is untroubled by his noise and reads along, contented that Sarah and her mom are listening to the story:

> "Naturally I enjoy the films," Harry Cat said, and flicked his long tail around his forelegs. "But I really prefer the . . .

Jessica stumbles over the pronunciation of "legitimate," and Cullen says the word for her. "Then, after a little help with "theater," she continues to read:

> For the past five years I've been the most eager theater goer in New York. I've stood in the balcony, I've hidden backstage—why, once I even hung on a chandelier. There's nothing I wouldn't do to see a good play. Ah, the glamour—the romance of the thea-ter!

"Sarah," Matthew calls Sarah away to play with the music box. Jessica goes on:

> "I love it!"
> "That's nice," said Chester. "Have you been to many plays, Tucker?" He was still feeling blue, and didn't want to talk much.
> "A few," the mouse answered indifferently.

Matthew is back and holding his mom's face to get her attention. "Mommy, Mommy," he says getting her to look at him. Sarah winds up his musical jack-in-the-box and calls, "Come here, Matthew!" enticing Matthew away, so that Jessica can read. She plays a peek-a-boo game with Matthew and the jack. "Look Mat-thew, look, look," she says, as she pushes the jack back into the box. "Where'd go," Matthew says and laughs as the Jack reappears. As Jessica reads, Matthew and Sarah play nearby. They play with the jack-in-the-box, then a vehicle, and then a ball. There are no more "disturbances," as Sarah and Matthew play; Jessica reads with her mom. And so it goes:

> "I like musical comedies more."

"What's a boor!" said Harry Cat.

"So I'm not a highbrow," said Tucker.

"So what of it? Chester, you would probably like musicals, being a musician your-self."

"Maybe I would," said the cricket. But even the thought of music, which usually made him . . .

Jessica hesitates. Cullen, in tune with her daughter, says, "very happy." "Very happy," repeats Jessica and continues reading:

couldn't cheer Chester up now.

"We could go tonight," said Harry.

"There's time to catch the second act of that new show that opened last week. It's just a little light review, but very enjoyable, I hear."

"Do you want to, Chester?" asked Tucker Mouse.

"Oh, I don't think so," said Chester.

"Why don't you two go?"

"Is anything wrong?" asked the mouse. He suspected from the way Chester spoke that there was something bothering him.

"Not really," said the cricket. "But I don't feel like going out again today."

And so it ends, as Jessica reads to her mother, Sarah and Matthew play nearby. It is bedtime and each of the children have once again taken part in the family story. "We should end here," says Cullen as Jessica closes the book.

DISCUSSION

The story that surrounds *Chester Cricket* is complexly structured, deeply embedded in the life history of the family and in the personal biographies of the individual family members. To me, it is a celebration of family, an encounter (Goffman, 1961), with distinct foci of attention and meanings that serves to emphasize what Erickson (1982) has referred to as "the profound influence of social participation structure in shaping the individual's opportunity to learn" (p. 170). As the threads of multiple conversations are woven together into family talk, the children are ac-tive participants in the web-making process that creates the family story. As the children listen, talk, read, and play, they learn how to deal with one another in the intimacy of the family storybook occasion. Each child learns the importance of so-cial flexibility, a commodity which Bateson (1972) states "is a resource as precious as oil or titanium" (p. 497). They are learning of themselves, of each other, and the social world in which they live. Speaking of earlier times, Dubos (1981) writes:

Having to study, read and play in contact with adults for several hours around the fam-ily lamp imposed restraints on one's behavior, but constituted a training for the ines-capable difficulties of later social contacts. (p. 53)

Today, in some families at least, the storybook has become the family lamp, for as Cullen says, "It's a good way to pull all the loose ends together." It enables the children to integrate their experiences of everyday life in readiness for their negotiations of tomorrow. This, I believe, is the meaning of the opening quotation in which Dewey (1938/1976) speaks of extracting the full meaning of present experience as "the only preparation which in the long run amounts to anything."

It is from this perspective that I want to extend the discussion to focus specifically upon the images of family storybook reading that fill the academic literature. In an excellent review of the literature on parents reading to their children, Teale (1981) examines the various ways in which we have explored this process. We have measured "the extent to which reading to children is associated with their development in language and literacy"; tried "to elucidate on a theoretical level certain general consequences of storybook reading events"; examined "the relationship between 'parental style' in reading and the child's performance on certain prereading related tasks"; studied "the organization and significance of storybook reading events"; and looked at the "processes and consequences of reading to children." And yet, it would seem that for all this study, we have yet to look at the familial signification of reading stories to young children. We need to know more not only of the ways in which storybook reading helps children to read, but also of the ways in which such occasions gain significance in family settings. Here are a few questions that we need to ask:

1. How and under what circumstances do parents read stories to their children?
2. How is the occasion perceived by individual family members?
3. How do families use storybooks in the mediation of their experiences of one another?
4. How do families use storybooks in the interplay of their social and cultural worlds?
5. How are the nuances of familial relationships expressed and explored within the storybook occasion?
6. How do families use storybook occasions to balance family unity with individual diversity?
7. How do families use storybooks to gain access to the conceptual worlds of individual family members?
8. How do rituals and routines of storybook reading evolve in familial settings?
9. How do families impart to their children appropriate strategies and procedures for the story to ultimately make sense?
10. How and in what ways do the children themselves participate in the storybook occasion?

In the present chapter I have tried to take an artist's step back to allow the narrative to carry the message of the family, but clearly this is only a beginning, for we need to know much more of family storybook occasions if we are to understand their functions and uses in the lives of the children that we study and teach. We need to know more of how the occasion appears to those who engage in it and of how they interpret the nuances of such intimate settings. Our most compelling task is to balance our studies of the development of language, literacy, and learning with natural histories of the social and cultural circumstances of family literacy and such occasions as family storybook reading, so that we might eventually learn more of the ways in which children gain access to the social world of their literate heritage.

In *Thank You, Fog,* Auden's (1974) last book of poems, there is a section called "Shorts." Among these last thoughts of the poet laureate, there are three deceptively simple lines which have always struck me as important to keep in mind when studying family literacy and storybook reading. Auden writes:

> Bound to ourselves for life
> we must learn how to
> put up with each other.

Literacy, it seems to me, has as much to do with this as it has to do with the language of the mind. Literacy draws meaning from the lives of children and not from the analytic constructs that we create. It is from this perspective that I want to take you back to the quotation from Bateson, in which he speaks of the interrelationships between art and science, and forward to Updike (1983) who writes fiercely of the need to "maintain allegiance to the world and a fervent relation with it" (p. xviii). If this is the maxim of the artist, it is also the axiom of the scientist, for to get close to the children that we care so much about we must peel away misplaced abstractions and maintain allegiance to their world and a fervent, even fierce, relation with it.

REFERENCES

Auden, W.H. (1974). *Thank you, fog.* New York: Random House.

Bateson, G. (1958). *Naven* (2nd ed.). Stanford, CA: Stanford University Press. (Original work published by Stanford University Press, 1936)

Bateson, G. (1972). *Steps to an ecology of mind.* New York: Chandler.

de Man, P. (1982, December 10). *The return to philology. Times Literary Supplement* (London), 1355–1356.

Dewey, J. (1976). *Experience and education.* New York: Collier Books. (Original work published by Kappa Delta Pi, 1938)

Dubos, R. (1981). *Celebrations of life.* New York: McGraw-Hill.

Erikson, F. (1982). Taught cognitive learning in its immediate environments: A neglected topic in the anthropology of education. *Anthropology and Education Quarterly, 13,* 149–180.

Frake, C. O. (1980). Plying frames can be dangerous: Some reflections on methodology in cognitive anthropology. In A.S.D. 1 (Ed.), *Language and cultural description: Essays by Charles O. Frake.* Stanford, CA: Stanford University Press.

Goffman, E. (1961). *Encounters: Two studies in the sociology of interaction.* Indianapolis, IN: Bobbs-Merrill.

Halliday, M.A.K. (1973). *Explorations in the functions of language.* London: Edward Arnold.

Hymes, D. (1980). *Language in education: Ethnolinguistic essays.* Washington, DC: Center for Applied Linguistics.

Lipset, D. (1982). *Gregory Bateson: The legacy of a scientist.* Boston, MA: Beacon Press.

Salinger, J.D. (1955). *Franny and Zooey.* Boston, MA: Little, Brown.

Selden, G. (1981). *Chester Cricket's pigeon ride.* New York: Farrar, Straus, and Giroux.

Taylor, D. (1981). The family and the development of reading skills and values. *Journal of Research in Reading, 4,* 92–103.

Taylor, D. (1982a). Children's social use of print. *The Reading Teacher, 36,* 144–148.

Taylor, D. (1982b). Translating children's everyday uses of print into classroom practices. *Language Arts, 59,* 546–549.

Taylor, D. (1983a). *Family literacy: Young children learning to read and write.* Exeter, NH: Heinemann.

Taylor, D. (1983b). Reflections on parenting. *Family Process, 22,* 341–346.

Teale, W.H. (1981). Parents reading to their children: What we know and need to know. *Language Arts, 58,* 902–912.

Updike, J. (1983). *Hugging the shore: Essays and criticism.* New York: Knopf.

Whitehead, A.N. (1925). *Science in the modern world.* New York: Free Press.

Wolcott, H.F. (1982). The anthropology of becoming. *Anthropology and Education Quarterly, 13,* 83–108.

7

Separating "Things of the Imagination" from Life: Learning to Read and Write

Shirley Brice Heath
Stanford University

Shirley Brice Heath has conducted extensive enthnographic research in working-class white and black and mainstream communities in the Piedmont Carolinas. In this chapter she focuses upon the language and social interactional characteristics of sustained, face-to-face adult–child talk typical of each of the communities. The examples she presents illustrate how both the opportunities for preschool children to participate in such events and the actual structure and content of the event as it develops in interaction are intertwined with the culture of the family and community. Heath concludes that such factors have significant effects on children's developing orientations to literacy.

One of the oldest and most frequently debated notions among literary authors is imagination. In the western tradition, debates over the role and power of imagination have continued since the earliest Greek writings. Samuel Coleridge's treatment of imagination in *Biographia Literaria* (1817) stimulated European and American writers of the past century to question whether imagination is a synthesizer or a multiplier of images. The image-making power of language has in recent decades been as debated for the reader as for the writer. Both use imagination to separate themselves from the natural world; every work of imagination is an analogue made up of only the fragments of life available to the imagination of the cocreators of text—reader and writer.

An American literary figure whose writings on imagination foreshadowed key issues that social scientists of the 1980s have taken up in their study of the psychological and social habits of readers and writers is William Carlos Williams. In his long poem *Spring and All* (1923/1970), Williams describes his own attempts at writing as separating "things of the imagination from life . . . by using the forms common to experience so as not to frighten the onlooker away but to invite him." Here and elsewhere in his writings, Williams speaks of the paradox that while things of the imagination must be drawn from real life, they may not be so "common to experience" that they bore or frighten readers. Through their independent approaches to the text, the writer and reader are interdependent in their relations both to the text and to what are either unanswerable questions or already-answered questions about life.

Producing and interpreting written texts involves philosophical and psychological challenges for both readers and writers. Many adults do not handle these challenges well. How then do children begin to grasp the role of image maker so critical to their futures as readers and writers? This chapter addresses this question through considering imagination as the process by which readers and writers verbally express ideas about objects, actors, and events that they have never before wholly perceived; imagination thus recombines past experiences to produce a new synthesis. The imaginer can manipulate past images of nature or accumulated knowledge but can never create a whole new nature, set of images, or body of knowledge. This chapter also provides interpretations of some current research on reading and writing as background for the description and analysis of oral language collected from three groups in the Piedmont Carolinas: Mainstream families and two working-class communities—one black, the other white. The analysis identifies several ways in which early and persistent oral language habits affect individuals' readiness to be invited into a text or to become writers and readers who can separate "things of the imagination" from life to produce either written text or oral discourse which reflects an understanding of how written texts are separate from life.

CURRENT RESEARCH REINTERPRETED ON IMAGINATION

In the research of cognitive psychologists, linguists, and anthropologists in the 1980s, relatively few studies discuss imagination as a direct research topic. Instead, cognitive and developmental psychologists touch on imagination as we have defined it here through studies which ask questions about children's understanding of metaphors (Gardner, 1981; Vosniadou & Ortony, 1982); compare their recall of stories and narratives (Goelman, 1982) and their written and oral productions across genres (Hidi & Hildyard, 1983); describe their role as self-teachers (Bissex 1980, 1984); and outline their development of story-telling abilities (Sutton-Smith, 1980). Linguists focus on specific language features which appear critical to the construction and understanding of narrative: creating information categories (Snow & Goldfield, 1982), understanding past and future reference (Harner, 1982; Kaper, 1980), responding to the scaffolding interaction of bookreading (Snow, 1983), and fictionalizing the self (Scollon & Scollon, 1981). Anthropologists treat the social context of literacy habits and the roles adults and peers or siblings play in modeling, teaching, and questioning younger children about oral and written texts (Heath, 1982; Ochs & Schieffelin, 1984; Snow, 1983). Children's play—its forms, functions, content, and occasions—is a major focus of interest for linguists, psychologists, and anthropologists, and several researchers have specifically related certain types of play, such as dramatic play, to children's performance in tasks which surround reading and writing in school (Pellegrini, 1980, 1984; Pellegrini & Yawkey, 1984; Sutton-Smith, 1980).

Running through these and numerous interdisciplinary studies of readin g and writing are four major themes:

1. Good readers and writers approach a text with a learned frame, script, or

schema which acts as a monitor as they progress through the piece of written text. Readers and writers thus use a previously established framing system to guide them through the text and to organize and link incoming information to previously known information.

2. Reading and writing are dynamic, interactive, reiterative processes in which successful readers and writers actively engage with a text, hypothesizing about the future development of the text and testing incoming information against previously known sources; a one-time, single-stage linear movement through text is not the usual practice of good readers and writers.

3. Those who would comprehend written texts and produce comprehensible writing must continually transmute past experiences through the current text with a strong sense of future image. The form of this future image varies. For readers, it may be a developing "envisionment" of the meaning of the text for storing and later discussing the meaning, taking a test, or answering questions (Langer, 1986). On some occasions, this meaning envisionment is supplemented by the reader's projection of actions or regulations of behavior (e.g., to fly a kite or to become a Boy Scout) which drive the transmutation of the text into specific behavioral outcomes. For writers, the future image is "what the piece will look like" or what the piece will do (e.g., issue an invitation, anger a relative, or bring fame as a poet).

4. Talking about language as a topic and referent, about "language as such" (Olson, 1984), facilitates the transition from oral to written language. Particularly for those individuals whose early language socialization has included performance of metalanguage, the act of writing may bring to awareness individuals' language strategies and intensify their acceptance of language as object.

Langer (1986) provides a detailed analysis of how readers of reading comprehension tests create changing envisionments which record the sense of meaning that the messages from the text allow the reader to construct while reading. This sense of the need to "work ahead," building within a frame or organizational system a cumulative coherent text world, stays with good readers. They ask questions of the text as they try to resolve uncertainties they feel are warranted by text-based inferences or by inferences triggered by the text and fed by personal experience or previously acquired knowledge. Good readers also make predictions about "where the text is going," linking pieces of content and their knowledge of the genre form which the text will follow in order to reach a conclusion. Assumed to have a conclusion or to reach an end, texts go on or exist beyond their reading only to the extent that readers extend them.

I argue here that it is though imagination—the recombining of ideas into new wholes—that writers create texts and readers interpret them, and critical to imaginative powers is an ability to create future images verbally. The appropriateness of this statement is perhaps obvious when we think about the importance of imagination for writers: Their very act of creation depends on their expectation of producing a future verbal product. But I propose that imagination is equally necessary for readers. Imagination enters far more into the interpretation of texts than into their comprehension; it is with interpretation that readers do something with texts, that texts are, for example, allowed to achieve illocutionary or performative force. The direction and content of images and information recombined depend on the significance or meaning the reader assigns to a text.

Comprehension refers to the reader's understanding of a text, and judgments of comprehension are usually based on determining whether or not the reader grasped the message of the writer. Comprehension is, then, writer-dependent. Interpretation is reader-dependent, for in interpreting, the reader gives significance and meaning to a text and often translates this interpretation into action or belief. Literary theorists of the deconstructionist school who enter the "reading the reader" debate are forced to consider the extent of freedom readers have in interpreting a text versus the power over interpretations which the author holds. Some theorists maintain that the text contains a "linguistic imperative" and thus gives the *author* central power over interpretations of written works. Other theorists try to locate the knowledge and learned behaviors that enable *readers* to interpret texts.[1] My concern here is to try to identify the precursor oral habits which enable readers to become interpreters—or imaginers—of written texts; to what extent do these habits precede and supplement interactions around written texts?

THREE COMMUNITIES

Reported elsewhere is a full ethnography of communication of the Trackton, Roadville, and mainstream communities of the Piedmont Carolinas (Heath, 1983b). Trackton is a black working-class community whose older generations grew up farming the land but whose current members work in the mills. Roadville is a white working-class community of families steeped for four generations in the life of the textile mills. These two communities are only a few miles apart, and both are surrounded by neighborhoods of townspeople, black and white mainstreamers who have traditionally held power in the region's social retail businesses, mills, and schools. The language socialization habits of the three groups differ greatly, and only those of the mainstreamers seem to fit the expectations of the school and other mainstream institutions.

Roadville parents believe they should teach their preschoolers to talk and prepare them for school; they buy educational toys, read books with their children, and involve them in numerous do-it-yourself family leisure activities. Once the children go to school, however, parents become more spectators than participants, and their children do not extend their in-school activities to their homes or to their choices of leisure activities. Trackton parents believe children learn, and all but the "slow"

---

[1] The most comprehensive reviews of current reader-response literary theory are Suleiman and Crosman (1980) and Mailloux (1982). Both of these works consider the ambiguities and disagreements among critics regarding the extent to which a text authorizes a limited number of interpretations or multiple meanings. See Miller (1980) for a brief discussion of the imperative in the language of a text and the responsibility of readers. The work of Golden (1983) brings together the parallel strands of argument in semantic text analysis, cognitive science, and literary theory.

among their children will get along at school; they promote the belief that school will help move an individual ahead in life, and they wait for the power of schooling to "take" for their children. Mainstream parents begin early to "lesson" their children, providing educational toys, book reading, and leisure activities and voluntary memberships which support the school ideologically and, unlike Roadville parents, reinforce behaviors valued in schools once their children are enrolled (Heath, 1983a). Roadville and Trackton children usually do not maintain patterns of success throughout school; the children from mainstream families, with few exceptions, have successful school careers.

These general findings are not significantly different from traditional assumptions about the need for parents to take active roles in reinforcing school values and habits and to provide their children with literate models and incentives for school success. However, it would seem from these traditional assumptions that Roadville parents do provide a "good foundation" for their children, since their values and behaviors toward their preschoolers fit those prescribed in parent-education programs. Trackton parents would seem at least to demonstrate the positive attitudes toward schools and schooling which many parent educators advocate. Then why aren't these children successful in school? How are school-related values and habits actually instilled in the three different settings? By pulling apart the linguistic features characterizing the activities typically provided in each kind of home, we can identify how these children learn habits which relate to the four general conclusions noted in the previous section about good readers and writers.

I present here summaries of sample occasions in each community in which preschoolers and adults sustained face-to-face talk for at least five minutes; in Roadville and mainstream neighborhoods, such occasions occurred most frequently at mealtime or during rides in the car. In Trackton, families rarely sat down to the table as a group for a meal, and few individuals owned cars; sustained talk to preschoolers by adults occurred only on those rare occasions when either a single adult was left alone with a preschooler or when some action of the preschooler so caught the attention of a group of adults that they focused on the child in their subsequent talk. Siblings and peers in all three groups often held extended conversations with preschoolers, but compared to adult–child interactions, these occasions of peer talk were more frequent in Trackton than in Roadville or among the townspeople. During almost daily interactions over nearly a decade in Trackton and Roadville, I took field notes in homes and tape-recorded conversations which took place when adults and children were in my car. Mothers in mainstream homes tape-recorded their preschoolers at mealtime and annotated these recordings in their field notes and in discussions about the tapes with me (see Heath, 1982, for further discussion of data collection).

1. Excerpt of mainstreamer dinner conversation with 4-year-old Pat (who has spent the morning in the church nursery school with Mrs. L, the teacher):

Father: Pat, how did you like Mrs. L? Did she let you play with Robbie?
Pat: Me 'n Rob, we go to a zoo.

Father: You didn't go to a zoo; what are you talking about?

Mother: (starts giggling and looks at Pat): Tell daddy about the zoo.

Pat: Well, me 'n Rob, we got this plan, 'n we were gonna build a zoo for all the kids, so we took all the animals——

Father: Where'd you get the animals—and what did Mrs. L think?

Pat: Outta the toy box, and Rob went into the baby room to take the animals outta the cribs——

Father: But what did Mrs. L think?

Pat: Wait, lemme tell you what we did—we had this plan—we had it all worked out—we had decided—you know, we have this free time after the story and all—we were gonna build something *big*. It was gonna have a big gate, a park inside, parking lots, and lots of stuff. We's sell tickets to people who wanted to come look at the animals and see our park. They could have picnics too.

Father: Did your plans work out? Those sound like pretty big plans for just one Sunday School class.

Pat: No, that old teacher of the babies, the one from the crib room, found out that Rob had taken the animals from the empty cribs. She came and took 'em all back, so we just had to pretend then, but that wasn't so fun.

Father: Has Rob been to the zoo?

Pat: And we were gonna have a petting part too, you know, where the babies are.

Father: What would you kids have done if the teacher hadn't come to get the lost animals?

Pat: We would have taken 'em back.

Throughout the account of the morning's episode, Pat's parents use questions in an attempt to scaffold a narrative which will provide more details, describe the emotions of other key actors, and let them know the outcome. Pat steadily maintains the plan for the zoo as a central motif; she lets her parents know that she and Rob carried out their actions according to a plan for their dramatic play. They established scene, actors, props, and a subsequent plan for selling tickets and staging "three-ring" activities. The parents know they have just taken Pat to the new state zoo only last weekend, so they do not question the origin of her idea for recreating an imaginary zoo. They do question how Rob became interested in such a plan. Their questions also break into Pat's preferred way of telling the story—from beginning plan to executed end. Instead they ask for evaluations of onlookers, who are, in Pat's scheme for telling the story, not relevant until they intervene and stop the plan short of full execution. Pat's parents' questions spring from their past experience with this nursery school teacher, who keeps a "tight rein" on the children; Pat's relevant past experience for telling the story is her joint plan with Rob to build a zoo. She disregards what she knows of the teacher and possible consequences.

2. Excerpt of Roadville dinner conversation with 4-year-old Sally, her mother, teenage brother, and 10-year-old sister.

Mother: Can you tell your brother what you helped Mr. Jones do today?

Sally: We went to get gas, 'n there was this cricket, and he was in a field. I found some sticks to make one.

Mother: But wait, wait, why did we go to the gas station?

Sally:	Mr. Jones helped us?
Mother:	Yes, but why did Mr. Jones have to help us? Come on, you know what happened.
Sally:	We couldn't go to the store. The car broke, 'n I found a cricket.
Mother:	What broke on the car?
Sally:	The tire broke.
Mother:	And did you help Mr. Jones fix the tire?
Sally:	Yes. The cricket was fun, but I had to leave 'im; I took down the fence.
Mother:	Well, let me tell you what happened to us . . .
	[At this point, Sally's mother tells the events of the day, which included a flat tire on the way to the grocery store but near Mr. Jones' service station. She and Sally waited while Mr. Jones fixed the tire, and he let Sally help him count the lugs when he put them in the hubcap and put them back on the wheel. During her mother's account, the older daughter interrupts to ask how long they had to wait and if they ever got to the store. Sally's talk of the cricket refers to the fact that shortly after they arrived at the service station, Sally found a wounded cricket in the garage, and she built a fence of small sticks around the cricket and she talked to the cricket while Mr. Jones fixed the tire.]

In this discussion, Sally's mother asks her to tell about an event in which they both participated. As Sally offers pieces of information, her mother tries to structure the direction of the telling so that it fits the chronology of events and includes the points of action that the mother views important in the recounting she wants Sally to give. Sally's own contributions come in pieces, and she wants to tell about her play with the cricket. She thus tries to weave a ''side story'' into her answers to her mother's questions. When Sally does not produce an acceptable narrative, her mother give a full narrative of the day's events (omitting mention of the cricket), with interruptions from the older daughter who requests clarification.

3. Excerpt of Trackton conversation with three adults and Lem (4 years old); conversation takes place on porch where Lem has been playing.

[Lem stops playing and begins to pull the sole of his shoe off.]

Mother:	Boy, what you doin'?
Lem:	This shoe broke.
Mother:	What you mean that shoe broke? You broke it. Now stop that.
Mother's friend:	Lem, your mama gonna make you go barefoot, you tear your shoes up. What you want? You wanna go to school barefoot, have all the children laugh at you? Huh? Is that what you want?
Lem:	No.
Older female neighbor:	You goin' to school soon, Lem? What you gonna do at school? You gonna learn to be smart like Tony? Well, you better not tear up your clothes, do you be gettin' a switchin'—you gotta be a good boy, so you can go to school, learn to read, play games, learn to spell, and do all those things like Tony. You bring home homework, you see Tony doin' his homework?

Lem (standing up on the porch):	Yea, I'm 'a go to school, and I'm gonna do *all* (spreading his arms wide) my work, and I'm gonna eat hot dogs in the lunchroom everyday, and I'm 'a be like Tony and wear boots, and I'm 'a go to see—what's that man's name down at the office?—I'm 'a see 'im, and I'm play football (running around the chairs on the porch), and I'm—do they give you ice cream there? when you spell? (Trying an imaginary block tackle in front of his mother)

The adults interrupt his story with laughter. They have begun by scolding Lem, but he has so entertained them that his earlier misbehavior seems forgotten. One of his mother's friends sets a future scene and series of event for Lem, if he continues his current behavior. The older female neighbor takes up this scene suggestion and talks about the activities and the roles Lem will play at school, modeling after his older brother. Lem's performance picks up pieces of the scene, adds to these from past experience, and tells about himself as fictionalized actor in the future scene he has created from past and recent-past content supplied by others. He successfully deflects their attention from his tattered shoe, and he is rewarded by the adults' laughter at his performance.

When we examine these three episodes of early language socialization to find specific components which fit into the four general conclusions noted earlier for good readers and writers, we find wide differences. We analyze these episodes to see what they can tell us about how these preschoolers are learning: (a) to frame or script a narrative and to monitor their telling by guidelines that their schema for the narrative has established; (b) to participate orally in an interactive reiterative process of building and testing hypotheses; (c) to bring past events to bear on the present with a sense of mingling the two in a future imagined context—as verbal performance or as action; and (d) to accept talk about language and genre forms as an appropriate reason for interrupting a narrative.

A useful way of making distinctions among types of narratives which may result from these aspects of learning narratives is to distinguish among four types of narrative: recounts, accounts, eventcasts, and stories (see Heath, 1986, for further details). *Recounts,* usually the first of these narratives to appear in mainstream children's development of discourse forms, are given either voluntarily or in answer to questions from adults. These questions provide a scaffold for experiences or information known to both teller and listener; for example, a parent asks a child to tell about a shopping trip they had together, and as the child recounts episodes, the parent asks questions which direct the child to include missing information or to make given information clear. As children grow older, teachers ask for recounts of stories read in reading books, passages from social studies texts, and experiences on a class fieldtrip. Schooling is filled with requests for recounts—the telling of information already prescripted in the head of the listener(s). Dependent upon a power differential, recounts are given in response to the request of a parent, older sibling, or teacher who wants the child or student to tell someone what he has experienced or what he knows. In the telling of recounts, the child is expected to provide a match for the narrative in the head of the listener; the intrusion of imagination, evaluation, or experiences not known to the individual requesting the recount will meet with disapproval by those who expect recounts to adhere to a chronological replay of facts (cf. Michaels, 1981).

Accounts are narratives into which children may put their imagination and evaluative interpretations. These are narratives volunteered by the teller to provide new information to listeners or to give new interpretations of information which may already be known to both teller and listener. Examples include children sharing with parents the tale of the runaway dog at a friend's birthday party or the field trip to the science museum. Adults model accounts for children when they tell about events of their day at work or describe an automobile accident seen on the way home from work. Since tellers volunteer accounts, they must plan them as narratives which will be accepted by other parties in an ongoing conversation or by parties who are silently engaged in other activities. Accounts often have opening frames which announce an unfolding narrative: "Mom, you won't believe what Tad's dog did at his birthday party today!" Once the precursor announcement has been made and acknowledged, the teller usually has control of the floor, until the account moves through a chronologically arranged set of events to an end.

Eventcasts provide running narratives on events that are currently in the attention of both teller and listeners; the events may be simultaneous with the telling or may follow the eventcast. In mainstream homes, mothers model eventcasts for their infants when they talk about their nurturing actions as they carry them out. Young children give eventcasts when they verbalize their actions as they put puzzle pieces into place, build a castle of blocks, or describe what they will do at their birthday party or in some coming event. Familiar eventcasts are a sportscaster's running narrative on a game during play, parent's preplays of Christmas vacation or a family trip, and a teacher's forecasts of activities which will take place during a class hour or throughout the day.

The most familiar narrative is the *story,* which includes an animate being who moves through a series of events with goal-directed behavior (Stein, 1982). Fathers tell stories about what happened at the office; these tales may contain considerable accounting of facts, but the end point or certain twists and exaggerations within the tales make them more than an account. Children retell stories read to them from books or oral tales they have heard from their grandparents, remembering old times or fellow campers spinning ghost stories. Language arts textbooks as well as a large proportion of social studies and science textbooks contain stories, placed within the expository text to increase students' interest and to provide variety in forms of genre.

Within the three episodes given above of children telling narratives in their homes, these four types of narratives are very differently represented. Pat's parents ask for a recount, but accept Pat's account. Pat has already told her mother an abbreviated form of the zoo episode, and her mother invites Pat to tell her father about the event. As she gives her account, however, her father asks questions, but without knowledge of the events, he has no basis for prescripting her narrative. Her mother, who does know the story, does not try to persuade Pat to tell the narrative as she has heard it before. She listens instead for the new information she is receiving in this version. Pat's father indicates by his questions, however, the basic framework by which he will evaluate her story. He asks about a past event for Pat ("What did you do?"), and his subsequent questions are based on his expectations of an *account,* a reiteration of events in which the teller, but not the listeners, took part.

Once they learn the name of the event that took place—a trip to the zoo—Pat's parents are especially interested in the response of the teacher to an activity generally regarded as inappropriate in a Sunday School class. Pat, however, is guided in her narrative by the plan she and Rob made, and her telling expands on that plan and details its fulfillment. In past recounts of actions or knowledge she shared with her parents, Pat was asked numerous questions about labels for items and events, descriptions of these, and assessments of motives or causes (cf. Snow & Goldfield, 1982; Ch. 7 of Heath, 1983b). In past accounts, Pat was asked questions by her parents which focused on what happened, who was there, and what her feelings were about the event (for example, a friend's birthday party). At this stage or for this story, she is telling about a narrative plan within a narrative—the imagined zoo and the playing out of the dramatic script in reality. She and her parents have the shared knowledge that they recently went to the real zoo together, and they will bring that knowledge to bear on her account of the imagined zoo. Thus, basic components of her zoo frame—animals, three rings, tickets, and visitors—do not need explication. She seems to have two guides to her narrative—telling "what happened" and telling how it came to happen as the result of a mental plan she and Rob had worked out prior to the actual events. Pat has a metaplan within her planned narrative. Moreover, while she is accepting of interruptions which indicate the listeners' need for recycling, she sets aside those which threaten to deflect her from her plan for telling the story (". . . lemme tell you what we did . . .").

In Roadville, the mother responds to each of Sally's statements with a question that tries to move Sally away from her focus on the cricket and her imaginary play and on to the flat tire and the aborted outing to the store. Sally's mother wants her to give strict *recount* of the events in which they both participated that day. Interruptions by Sally's mother and by the older daughter are attempts to "straighten out" the narrative, so it fits expectations of the genre and of real-world events. Both Sally's mother and her older sister have a genre model which demands that a chronological recount which begins with a statement of destination end with some indication of whether or not the destination was reached. For Sally, a single piece of the day—her play with the cricket—captures the day's events, and she tries to tell of her imaginary interlude with the cricket and the sticks for his "field." Tutored by questions to provide a straightforward recount of events, Sally is not in this episode finally called on to produce such a sustained recount, but her mother models one for her. She does not, however, hear in the recount mention of motivations of actors and direct statements of causes and events; adults do not give evaluative comments on the events of the day or question, "What if?" (the tire had gone flat at the store in town?, etc.)

In Roadville, neither children nor adults tell exaggerated tales of real events or fantasized stories; well-formed oral stories are usually told without interruption and are summarized by morals or aphorisms (see Heath, 1983b, chap. 5). There are few opportunities for scaffolding through questions which focus children's attention on recombining experiences or expressing evaluations of them. Through the scaffolding questions with which they interrupt children (and only rarely adults) during their narratives, parents tutor children in the overall structures that recounts and accounts based on actual events should have. However, they do not "lead children on" when children begin to tell fantasized accounts or recombine real events with their own emotional evaluations or imaginary embellishments.

Trackton's parents do not see young preschoolers as appropriate conversational partners, and occasions on which they engage these children in sustained talk are rare. Lem is, however, 4 years old, and the episode took place only a month before he entered preschool. In approximately 90% of those occasions recorded over a period of 12 months when adults and preschoolers sustained talk for as long as five minutes, adults open the episodes by questioning the child. In the first 3 to 5 turn occasions, children respond with monosyllables. Then either individual adults or adults in dialogue asked questions they themselves go on to answer immediately; their questions provide the actors, events, and objects of a narrative usually set in the future and usually including exaggerated details or outcomes ("go to school barefoot"). This adult question-and-answer routine provides preschoolers the basic components of a narrative, which preschoolers reiterate through performance after the adults have hesitated or fully stopped their question-and-answer routines.

Lem's narrative fictionalizes himself, and the components of his frame for school have been provided in the adults' talk. The reiterative process of stating something and then questioning it has been modeled through the question and self-answer episodes of the adults; Lem creates his imaginative tale by staying within the script they have created, but by exaggerating some components and by adding some of his knowledge from past experience. His older brother plays football at school, and Lem inserts this activity within the scheme of school activities. Neither during nor after the *story,* however, do adults question Lem about what, how, or why events are taking place in his narrative. He has created the tale to be fantastic enough to deflect attention from his misdeed, and he is rewarded by laughter. In essence, he is not called on to repair or to recycle parts of his story; neither is he asked to explicate verbally reasons for linkages between its parts or his own choice of components. Thus the metalinguistic strategies he has used remain unexplicated, and he goes to school with no experience in having his narratives stopped for questioning by listeners (cf. Michaels, 1981).

CONCLUSIONS

My analysis of these episodes draws heavily from the context of nearly a decade of fieldwork among the three groups. Generalizations such as those stated here about language socialization patterns cannot be made without long-term fieldwork and immersion in a variety of situations and with changing casts of characters for the communities. Thus the conclusions I draw derive from far more than these single episodes noted from each group, which are meant simply to illustrate my points.

Over an 8-month period when each of the preschoolers was 2 years old and again when they were 4 years old, I recorded in field notes those occasions in which adults and children sustained conversations for at least 5 minutes. The frequency of these occasions for the three preschoolers mentioned varied greatly. Table 1 indicates this comparison. The sharp differences in the number of such occasions speak first to the opportunities each child had for practice of narratives with adults. Pat's parents framed multiple, redundant, and repeated opportunities to tutor her in telling narratives of various types and in listening to and questioning the narratives of adults. For Sally and Lem, however, such occasions occurred rarely. Moreover, the nature of the role of the children in these occasions differed greatly.

Pat's parents habitually framed invitations to her to perform narratives; they relied on her verbal explication rather than on gestures or dramatic performance. When they were not clear about her message, they asked for clarification and challenged her telling. She learned to fictionalize herself and others, drawing from experiences she assumed were known to her parents and adding experiences only she had had. These she recombined into new accounts. The regularity of family meals and car trips to voluntary activities (such as attendance at church and play school or visits to museums and the zoo) helped ensure that these sustained conversations took place. During these events and interactions around toys and books, adults often gave eventcasts, running narratives which detailed ongoing actions (preparation of a meal) or forecast future actions (a trip to watch an older brother play ball). Moreover, Pat's life space included many more places than her home and community, and she had numerous occasions by the time she was 3 years old to participate in activities in which her parents were not present. Thus she had "something to talk about" with her parents, and she could provide them with information not known to them by recreating her common experiences at play school, at friends' birthday parties, etc.

Sally and her family had evening meals together and regular trips in the car for grocery shopping, visits to friends, and attendance at church and local church women's groups. Her mother solicited Sally's preferences, told Sally what they would do, and asked often about what Sally had done when she was not with her. Sally often went to visit with other preschoolers in the community, and she regularly at-

Table 1.   Relative Frequency of Sustained Adult–Child Discourse

Child	16–24 months	40–48 months
Pat (mainstream)	680	1533
Sally (Roadville)	24	54
Lem (Trackton)	3	23

tended the nursery school at church. Her accounts of these events usually went unchallenged, so long as they followed a predictable frame and a chronological development. Though her siblings often asked questions of Sally, her mother rarely interrupted Sally's accounts of her experiences away from home. During Sally's recounts of events she shared with her mother, however, her mother interrupted with frequent questions, ensuring that Sally tell the story "right." Deviation from the actual chronology or factual representation of events met with questions designed to move Sally back to the expected frame of events and schema for the telling. While engaging in activities with Sally, her mother did not use eventcasts extensively; she did not verbalize about her own current or planned activities by detailing ongoing actions or forecasting a specific chronology. When the adults around Sally participated in do-it-yourself activities (such as building an outdoor barbecue grill), they centered on accomplishing the task; actors did not accompany their movements with a verbalized account of what they were doing.

Lem's occasions for sustained narratives with adults were rare. Instead, most of the sustained talk directed at him came from peers, except when adults teased him. Teasing is a form of dramatic play, and Trackton children were frequently incorporated into adult performances through "teasing invitations" of adults. Challenged by adults with questions, children learned how to recognize "ordinary language" as teasing in association with certain nonverbal cues. They were intimately involved in the households of several families, and all these intimates had a similar degree of power over them—feeding, pushing, offering affection, and teasing. This wide exposure to many different individuals who had power over them and the wide variety of roles the children were allowed to play in response to verbal teasing, provided them with numerous opportunities and contexts for practicing the interpretation of motives, intentions, and predispositions of others. These teases, which usually began with a question, allowed practice in numerous dramatic roles within the frame of the tease.

Trackton encouraged children to fantasize in teasing encounters, in their narratives to adults, and, as they grew older, in their accounts of their experiences outside the community. The scaffolding for these occasions was, however, designed to evaluate both the content of the narrative and its performance, and not to focus on metalinguistic or genre features. Requests for "sticking to the story" or telling "what happened" were inappropriate during a telling. Questions asked about particulars of the story, assessments of how actors played their roles, or "What would have happened if . . . ?" did not occur. Thus, Trackton children learned to use common experiences in their narratives, but they were not asked to explain how they varied either the genre form or the content from an expected organizational schema or a predicted sequence of events.

Numerous psychologists have recently looked carefully at the role of children's dramatic play on preschoolers' performance in reading and writing tasks at school. They suggest that the opportunity to participate in sociodrama and pretend play—situations in which children have to explicate verbally their plan for the scene, action, and objects—is an important prerequisite for successful performance in some routines which surround reading in the early grades (Pellegrini, DeStefano, & Thompson, 1983). These occasions like teasing and book reading (cf. Cochran-Smith, 1984; Heath, 1982) allow children to lift themselves out of the ongoing stream of their activities and to bring common experiences into another frame. As they accompany their fantasy games with talk which frames their play as out-of-the-ordinary, children learn to become imaginators. For example, in dramatic play, they must tell their peers what to do, what real objects are to become in their fantasy, and how outcomes will be determined; such joint fantasy production involves intimate collusion (and often secrecy from others outside the play, cf. Kelly-Byrne, 1984). The way other children interpret or assign meaning to this talk is immediately evident through ensuing events. If the plans in dramatic play are not clear to all participants, or if there are different interpretations of the direction of the fantasy, the play will fall away into either disjoined episodes or other activities (Sachs, Goldman, & Chaille, 1984).

Bruner (1984) proposes that "what initially attracts children to reading and into mastering all the mechanics of it is the opportunity the text provides for penetrating possible worlds beyond the mundanities of here and now" (p. 196). Different patterns of oral language socialization offer more or less preparation for calling up the linguistic resources necessary to penetrate the "possible worlds" which text production and interpretation can offer. Neither occasions for imaginative play (Sutton-Smith & Heath, 1981) nor genre structures which force the narrator to work with an eye toward future narrative shapes of the recombination of past experiences are universally given across cultures.

Bruner (1984), citing the Latin American essayist Jorge Luis Borges, refers to occasions for imagining as "guided dreaming." Bruner goes on to suggest that the greater the number and types of opportunities for imagining, for personalizing one's experiences in future possible worlds, the better prepared children will be to approach reading and writing. He further suggests that children know some of these forms of using language (such as telling personalized stories and scripting out dramatic play) better than they know other forms (such as providing straightforward chronologies). Thus one approach of teachers of reading and writing who want to invite more children into successful school achievement is to use the forms with which they are familiar.

I suggest here that experience in their language socialization has *not* ensured that all children know how to create dramatic play or to tell personalized narratives which contain imagined worlds. Children from some language socialization backgrounds will not know these forms of discourse better than other forms such as dialogue or other types of language uses which do not sustain focus on either a single topic or incorporate questions about the form and future direction of a narrative. It may therefore be necessary to immerse children in their early school experiences in "guided dreaming" and to familiarize then with these genre forms through pedagogic dialogue. Children from some communities not have had frames or tutors to ensure their introduction to and practice of occasions for imagination. Uses of time and space, patterns of leisure activities, ways of remembering past events, beliefs about roles of adults as teachers and children as learners, and acceptance of different types of fantasy all work interdependently to determine ways in which children draw from their common experiences to separate themselves into imagination. Social structural factors—such as the lack of access to a single-family car or to multiple occasions for preschoolers to have experiences away from their homes—help maintain cultural patterns of time and space usage, social role expectations, and preferences for leisure time activities. Thus both cultural ways and social structural features combine to shape children's early experiences in either multiplying images or synthesizing past images and experiences to create anew. The extent of attention cultural groups give to creating future images and linking past and present experiences to these images, as well as their tolerance for pedagogic dialogue which interrupts narratives to focus on form and content, will, to an important extent, determine how prepared children are for using language to penetrate texts with imagination.

William Carlos Williams (1923/1970) has said of reader and writer relations: "In the imagination, we are from henceforth locked in a fraternal embrace, the classic caress of author and reader. We are one. Whenever I say 'I' I mean also, 'you'. And so, together as one, we shall begin." To allow some children to begin, practitioners and researchers need to examine more closely the ways in which social groups across cultures give children opportunities to move from "I" to "you" in their writing and reading of texts. They must learn the power of the schema of genres for leading listeners and readers to anticipate meaning and to hypothesize about "what's coming" in the text; they appear to learn about such schema when their listeners can interrupt to call attention to the direction of narratives or the underlying assumptions of their recombinations of experience into new creations. Within their peer groups, dramatic play, teasing, and pretend play provide practice occasions for lifting the speaker out of the stream of ongoing experience into an extra-ordinary or nonordinary realm or into a scene and set of actions projected toward the future.

Further attention to specific oral language habits such as these and their covariance in different social and cultural contexts will bring us closer to understanding how children are prepared for imaginative uses of language, both as readers and writers. Such microanalysis of longitudinal data set in broader descriptions of community contexts will enable researchers to identify points of connection between language at home and at school and help teachers to expand their ways of using language to promote imagination. Schools may then be able to invite what are now large groups of onlookers into the "fraternal embrace" of readers and writers.

REFERENCES

Bissex, G.L. (1980). *GNYS AT WRK: A child learns to read and write.* Cambridge, MA: Harvard University Press.

Bissex, G.L. (1984). The child as teacher. In H. Goelman, A. Oberg, & F. Smith (Eds.), *Awakening to literacy.* Exeter, NH: Heinemann.

Bruner, J.S. (1984). Language, mind, and reading. In H. Goelman, A. Oberg, & F. Smith (Eds.). *Awakening to literacy.* Exeter, NH: Heinemann.

Cochran-Smith, M. (1984). *The making of a reader*. Norwood, NJ: Ablex.

Gardner, H. (1981). *The development of metaphoric operations: Final report*. Cambridge, MA: Harvard University Project Zero.

Goelman, H. (1982). Selective attention in language comprehension: Children's processing of expository and narrative discourse. *Discourse Processes, 5,* 1–32.

Golden, J. (1983). If a text exists without a reader, is there meaning? Insights from literary theory for reader–text interaction. In B.A. Hutson (Ed.), *Advances in reading/language research* (Vol 2). Greenwich, CT: JAI Press.

Harner, L. (1982). Immediacy and certainty: Factors in understanding future reference. *Journal of Child Language, 9,* 115–125.

Heath, S.B. (1982). What no bedtime story means: Narrative skills at home and school. *Language in Society, 11,* 49–76.

Heath, S.B. (1983a). A lot of talk about nothing. *Language Arts, 60,* 999–1007.

Heath, S.B. (1983b). *Ways with words: Language, life and work in communities and classrooms*. New York: Cambridge University Press.

Heath, S.B. (1986). The book as narrative prop in language acquisition. In B. Schieffelin & P. Gilmore (Eds.), *The acquisition of literacy: Ethnographic perspectives*. Norwood, NJ: Ablex.

Hidi, S.E., & Hildyard, A. (1983). The comparison of oral and written productions in two discourse types. *Discourse Processes, 6,* 91–105.

Kaper, W. (1980). The use of the past tense in games of pretend. *Language in Society, 7,* 213–217.

Kelly-Byrne, D. (1984). The meaning of play's triviality. In B. Sutton-Smith & D. Kelly-Byrne (Eds.), *The masks of play*. New York: Leisure Press.

Langer, J. (1986). The construction of meaning and the assessment of comprehension: An analysis of reader performance on standardized test items. In R. Freedle (Ed.), *Cognitive and linguistic analyses of test performance*. Norwood, NJ: Ablex.

Mailloux, S. (1982). *Interpretive conventions: The reader in the study of American fiction*. Ithaca, NY: Cornell University Press.

Michaels, S. (1981). "Sharing time": Children's narrative styles and differential access to literacy. *Language in Society, 10,* 423–442.

Miller, J.H. (1980). Theory and practice: Response to Vincent Leitch. *Critical Inquiry, 6,* 613–614.

Ochs, E., & Schieffelin, B. (1984). *Acquiring communicative competence*. London: Routledge Kegan & Paul.

Olson, D. (1984). "See! Jumping!" Some oral language antecedents of literacy. In H. Goelman, A. Oberg, & F. Smith (Eds.), *Awakening to literacy*. Exeter, NH: Heinemann.

Pellegrini, A. (1980). The relationship between kindergarteners' play and achievement in prereading, language, and writing. *Psychology in the Schools, 17,* 530–535.

Pellegrini, A. (1984). The effects of classroom ecology on preschoolers' functional uses of language. In A. Pellegrini & T. Yawkey (Eds.), *The development of oral and written language in social contexts*. Norwood, NJ: Ablex.

Pellegrini, A., DeStefano, J.S., & Thompson, D.L. (1983). Saying what you mean: Using play to teach "Literate language." *Language Arts, 60,* 380–384.

Pellegrini, A., & Yawkey, T. (Eds.). (1984). *The development of oral and written language in social contexts*. Norwood, NJ: Ablex.

Sachs, J., Goldman, J., & Chaille, C. (1984). Planning in pretend play: Using language to coordinate narrative development. In A. Pellegrini & T. Yawkey (Eds.), *The development of oral and written language in social contexts*. Norwood, NJ: Ablex.

Scollon, R., & Scollon, S. (1981). *Narrative, literacy, and face in interethnic communication*. Norwood, NJ: Ablex.

Snow, C.E. (1983). Literacy and language: Relationships during the preschool years. *Harvard Educational Review, 53,* 165–189.

Snow, C.E., & Goldfield, B.A. (1982). Building stories: The emergence of information structures from conversation. In D. Tannen (Ed.), *Georgetown University Round Table on Languages and Linguistics*. Washington, DC: Georgetown University Press.

Stein, N. (1982). What's in a story: *Discourse Processes, 5,* 319–336.

Suleiman, S., & Crosman, I. (Eds.). (1980). *The reader in the text: Essays on audience and interpretation.* Princeton, NJ: Princeton University Press.

Sutton-Smith, B. (1980). Introduction. In *The folkstories of children.* Philadelphia, PA: University of Philadelphia Press.

Sutton-Smith, B., & Heath, S.B. (1981). Paradigms of pretense. *The Quarterly Newsletter of the Laboratory of Comparative Human Cognition, 3,* 41–45.

Vosniadou, S., & Ortony, A. (1982). *The emergence of the literal-metaphorical-analogous distinction in young children.* Cambridge, MA: Bolt, Beranek, & Newman.

Williams, W.C. (1970). *Spring and all.* In *Imaginations.* New York: New Directions. (Original work published in 1923)

8

Home Background and Young Children's Literacy Development*

William H. Teale
University of Texas at San Antonio

William Teale addresses the relations between home background and preschool children's literacy development. Using results from naturalistic observations of low-income families, he describes the extent and nature of the children's literacy experiences across different participant structures and domains of activity. He concludes, like Heath, that both cultural and social structural factors affect preschool children's orientations to literacy. Teale discusses implications of the research for home and school intervention.

A lesson learned from child language studies—that language development begins long before a child ever utters his or her first words (Bruner, 1978)—has been taken to heart by researchers seeking to understand the emergence of literacy. The extreme importance of elucidating what happens during the preschool years, before a child is able to read and write independently, has been realized. As a result, we are in a period during which unparalleled attention is being given to studying what Yetta Goodman (1980) has called the roots of literacy.

In this chapter I discuss research I have been conducting which centers upon one aspect of the attempt to understand the roots of literacy: the relation between home background and young children's literacy development. More specifically, the aim of the work has been to shed light on the relations between children's preschool experiences with written language and their knowledge about and skills in reading and writing. Results from the research are presented. Also, special attention is given to integrating the findings with the research of others in the field and to discussing the directions and topics for further study of home background and literacy development in early childhood.

METHODOLOGY

Posture of the Research
The paradigm employed in my attempts to study children's preschoool literacy experiences is that of naturalistic inquiry (Guba, 1982). This approach was utilized for

---

* This research was supported in part by The National Institute of Education (Grant 79-0135) and The Spencer Foundation and by a Faculty Research Grant from The University of Texas at San Antonio.

several reasons. Historically, the study of emergent literacy is still in its infancy. We are at the point of working out what count as data, of determining the parameters of inquiry in the area, and how literacy development interfaces with oral language and cognitive development. In short, the field is very much involved with description, with building a sound theory of just what is being researched. Naturalistic inquiry, with its tendency toward the use of qualitative methods such as observation, interview, and documentary analysis, permits one to locate the relevant variables as they emerge from the situation and thereby construct ecologically valid descriptions.

Furthermore, we know that literacy and literacy learning are fundamentally social processes (Heath, 1980; Reder & Green, 1979; Scollon & Scollon, 1981; Scribner & Cole, 1981; Szwed, 1981). A naturalistic approach facilitates observation of the process as it occurs in the everyday contexts of home, community, and social institutions. A frequent shortcoming of research on the effects of home background is its correlational design. Children are tested in, for example, various aspects of literacy development (usually referred to as reading readiness), and their achievement levels are then correlated with particular home background characteristics. Such research provides no direct evidence for cause–effect relations. Yet, frequently, these studies put forth implications for instruction or home intervention programs. The naturalistic paradigm at least enables one to document what is actually occurring in the home and to observe links between these practices and effects on the child's developing reading and writing abilities.

Children's progress in reading and writing is the product of (a) adult–child (or sibling–child) interactions, which involve literacy, (b) the child's independent explorations of written language and (c) observations of others using written language. Naturalistic inquiry enables one to gather data on all of these contributors to literacy development so that a truly comprehensive description of home literacy background can be developed. Such completeness is of crucial importance when it comes to implications for instruction or home intervention programs. Without a firm understanding of the context, what seem to be well-formed curricula for literacy development often go astray, because they have neglected part of what is entailed in the home environment.

Thus, because it fits into, rather than disrupts, the patterns of family life, naturalistic inquiry is particularly well-suited for gathering data on the effects of home background on children's developing knowledge about reading and writing.

The San Diego Study
The initial project with which I was involved that examined home background influences on young children's literacy development was the systematic observation of 24 preschool children over a period of 3 to 18 months.[1] All of the children were from low-income families.[2]

---

[1] These children were observed as part of "Literacy Resources: How Preschoolers Interact with Written Communication," a research project funded by The National Institute of Education and conducted

Low-income families were focused upon because, as a group, children from these families tend not to achieve as well in reading and writing as their middle class counterparts (Bulcock, 1977; Grant & Lind, 1975; St. John, 1970; Stein, 1971; Thorndike, 1973), and it was hoped that the systematic observation of these children's home literacy backgrounds would give some insight into why this is the case.

The study addressed a broad, descriptive question: What is the nature of the home literacy experiences of these 24 children? We reasoned that, since literacy is a social process and the home is a primary socializing influence in young children's lives, detailed descriptions of the reading and writing which occurred in this setting would provide insight into the orientations to literacy with which the children entered school. In short, we were attempting to describe what the children learned about reading and writing and how they learned it.

Subjects. The children who took part in the longitudinal naturalistic observations were between approximately 2 ½ and 3 ½ years of age when they began to be observed. Children in this age range were chosen because, although initial encounters with print typically occur before this time, it is generally in this age range that (a) children begin to explore reading and writing on a more extensive basis, and (b) the bulk of what will be children's preschool literacy experience begins.

In addition to attending to the family income factor, we were extremely interested in how cultural background would affect the literacy activities to which each child would be exposed. Heath (1983) provides evidence of particular ways in which culture affected the preschool literacy experiences of working class Anglo and Black preschool children in the Piedmont, Carolinas. Therefore, Anglo, Black, and Mexican American[3] children were included in our sample so that we might also investigate cultural influences on the children's literacy socialization. In all, 8 Anglo, 8 Black, and 8 Mexican American children and their families were included in the sample.

Finally, an attempt was made to include, as subjects in the study, equal numbers of girls and boys so that any relation between sex of the child and home background literacy experiences could be examined. Table 1 provides a summary of certain major characteristics of each child and his/her family.

---

through the Laboratory of Comparative Human Cognition at the University of California, San Diego. In addition to myself, Rosalie Bennett, Elette Estrada, Linda Forest, Joe Martinez, Shelley Stokes, and Billy Vaughn worked on the project, Lonnie Anderson directed it, and Michael Cole kept it going in the right direction. Thanks to them and to other members of the L.C.H.C., most notably Peg Griffin and Bud Mehan, for the insights gained from this study have contributed immeasurably to any conclusions I draw about literacy development in early childhood.

[2] Low-income was defined for purposes of this study as being below $10,000 annual income for a family of four.

[3] The term *Mexican American* is used in the same way it was by Laosa (1977), referring to persons born in Mexico who now hold United States citizenship or otherwise live in the United States or whose parents or more remote ancestors immigrated to the United States from Mexico. It also refers to persons who trace their lineage to Hispanic forbears who resided within the Spanish or Mexican territory that is now part of the southwestern United States.

Table 1. Basic Information on Subjects and their Families

Focal Child	Age[a]	Adult(s) in Home	Other Children in Home (age)[b]	Parental Education (years)	Ethnicity[c]
Mike	3;10	F, M[d]	S(1;1)	F = 12 M = 12	A
Bobby Barbara	2;8 2;8	F, M, A, U	B(18), S(13), S(11), C(4;5)	F = 12 M = 11	A
Kristin	2;4	F, M	—	F = 9 M = 12	A
Alex	2;6	F, M	S(5)	F = 12 M = 12	A
Becki	3;4	M	B(9), B(5;10), S(5;10)	M = 12	A
Paul	3;2	M	B(5;1) B(2;0)	M = 12	A
Holly	3;7	F, M	S(1;4)	F = 9 M = 12	A
Myeesha	3;0	F, M	B(0;3)	F = 11 M = 12	B
Natalie Amin	3;5 2;8	F, M	B(8), S(5), B(2;8)	F = 12 M = 12	B
Denise	2;8	F, M	S(6;9)	F = 12 M = 12	B
Harvey	2;10	M	S(0;11)	M = 10	B
David	3;9	M	B(11), B(9)	M = 12	B
Alethia	2;5	M, SF, A	—	M = 12	B
Lori	3;7	F, M	B(16), B(12), B(4;8)	F = 12 M = 12	B
Alma	3;5	F, M	B(11), S(9), B(6), B(4;10)	F = 12 M = 1	MA
Luis	2;9	M, RM	S(5;9)	M = 12 RM = 0	MA
Juan	3;0	F, M	B(7), B(5)	F = 6 M = 7	MA
Maria	3;2	F, M	S(5), B(4)	F = 7 M = 6	MA
Terri	3;2	M, GM, GF, A, U	—	M = 11	MA
Roberto	3;3	F, M	—	F = 6 M = 0	MA
Ronnie	3;0	F, M	S(6;3), B(2;9), B(0;3)	F = 12 M = 12	MA
Miguel	2;5	F, M	B(6;5), B(4;7)	F = 12 M = 10	MA

[a]At the start of observations.
[b]S = sister; B = brother; c = cousin.
[c]A = Anglo; B = black; MA = Mexican/American.
[d]F = father; M = mother; A = aunt; U = uncle; GF = grandfather; GM = grandmother;
SF = stepfather; RM = resident male.

It should be noted that although there were 24 focal children for our observations, we worked in only 22 different households. This is because in one household we observed a pair of twins, Bobby and Barbara, and in another household, Natalie and Amin's, both children were within the desired age range.

Data Gathering Techniques.   The main method of data collection in this study was field notes. Selected interactions were also audio-taped and transcripts of these interactions, as well as information gathered through interviews and conversations with the families, were used to augment the field notes. Observations were spread over the hours of the day during which the focal child was typically awake and over the seven days of the week. Raw field notes taken during the observations were transformed into "cooked" notes (Spradley, 1980), and the cooked notes were used for the analysis.

As researchers, we assumed the role of observer participants when in the home collecting data. That is to say, we attempted to interfere as little as possible in the normal activities of the families, but at the same time were not completely passive presences. Thus, for example, we responded to conversation directed at us but initiated no interactions during the observations. This role compares with the type of participation which Spradley (1980) describes as moderate participation.

There were two foci for the observations. One was the preschool child in the family (the focal child, or FC). The observer would follow the FC wherever he or she went and took notes on what the FC observed and/or experienced directly. The other focus of the observations was on literacy. Detailed notes were taken for any occasion upon which a person produced, comprehended, or attempted to produce or comprehend written language. Any time the focal child or anyone in the FC's immediate environment looked at a book, wrote a note, signed his or her name, "scribbled," or was otherwise engaged with written language, the event was characterized as fully as possible. When there was an activity mediated by literacy, we attempted to describe the actions which took place, the context out of which the activity arose and was played out, the participants, the activities which co-occurred or alternated with the activity involving literacy, the reasons why the activity ended, and what occurred immediately subsequent to the activity. In this way we sought to develop a picture of the focal child's direct literacy experiences as well as the literacy which she or he had the opportunity to observe. Observations of individual focal children were conducted for periods of from 3 to 18 months. The number of home visits per child ranged from 5 to 47 with the total number of hours of observation per focal child ranging from 14 to 142. The total hours of observation in the homes of all the children approached 1,400.

Analysis

Field notes provided descriptions of both the physical literacy environment of the homes (the written language which existed there) and, more significantly, the social literacy environment (what was done with written language; i.e., the instances of reading and writing). The physical literacy environment is reported as observed.

Both quantitative and qualitative analysis of the actual reading and writing which occurred were performed in the attempt to understand better the relations between home background and young children's literacy development. Specifically, the observations of the children in their homes and communities were analyzed quantitatively to determine both the average number of activities per hour which were mediated by literacy and the average amount of time per hour spent in such activities.

More important, however, were the qualitative aspects of the analyses. In fact, a major aspect of describing the home literacy environments of the 24 children involved determining just what the analytic categories would be. We had no prespecified categories to guide us; our data were not derived from checklists. Thus, the initial step in this phase of the analysis consisted of developing a system for capturing the relevant dimensions of all that we had seen going on with written language in the homes of these preschool children.

Once these dimensions were determined, it became possible to analyze other factors to see if they were significant predictors of the child's home literacy background. As was mentioned earlier, income level, ethnicity, and sex were used in selecting subjects for the research. In addition, it was possible to analyze for level of education and family size. Previous social science research has indicated that these factors play a significant role in reading readiness and school achievement. (See White, 1982, for a review.)

RESULTS

Literacy Materials in the Homes

Space limitations prohibit reproducing a description of the reading and writing materials found in each of the households. An apt word for characterizing the home backgrounds of these children with respect to the amount and nature of literacy materials present, however, was variety. Environmental print—product labels, signs in the community, and so forth—was relatively similar for all the families (with the exception that for several of the Mexican American families many environmental print items were in Spanish).

On the other hand, examples of connected discourse varied widely. In 8 of the households (Mike's, Kristin's, Becki's, Holly's, Denise's, David's, Luis's, and Terri's,) there were numerous printed materials appropriate for and available to the focal children. Few children's books or other examples of materials written for children existed in the other 14 homes. In Bobby and Barbara's home we could find no printed materials written specifically for children.

The amount and types of adult material varied similarly. Kristin's, Becki's, Richard's, and Terri's mothers were all "readers" in a broad sense of the term. Accordingly, there were many books, magazines, and newspapers generally available in these homes. (Even in a family like Kristin's which could not really afford to buy materials because the father was frequently unable to find work, the mother made extensive use of the library and borrowed from friends so that she always had paperbacks and magazines around.) In the other 18 households magazines and newspapers appeared with greater frequency than books written for adults; however, even the magazines and newspapers were not found in great supply. Only the guide to television programs occurred with a high degree of regularity in the 22 homes.

An interesting pattern in adult printed materials was observed in the homes of Natalie and Amin, Lori, Juan, and Maria. In none of these four homes was there a great deal of material to be found beyond the typical environmental print (in Natalie and Amin's there was much more than in the other three), but relative to the other households they had considerable numbers of religiously oriented books and pamphlets. In fact, in Lori's, Juan's, and Maria's homes, by far the bulk of written language to be found was of a religious nature.

As well as the written language itself, the materials for producing written language were of interest, especially the writing materials available to the children. In all of the homes there were some writing instruments and some paper. It was common in most families, however, that when the focal child wanted to write, a pen, pencil, or, more often, paper was difficult to locate. Often the search which ensued in such cases resulted in the child's losing his or her desire to write. Only in three homes—Alex's, Holly's, and Natalie and Amin's—had there been established a special place (or special places) for writing materials to which the focal children had easy access. Furthermore, it was noted that these 4 children also tended to write more than the others in the sample.

Quantitative Findings

Table 2 summarizes by focal child the average frequency per hour of occurrences of literacy and the average number of minutes per hour spent in activities mediated by literacy. These figures indicate the total "amount of literacy" to which the child was exposed (i.e., that in which the child participated directly or which he or she had the opportunity to observe). The range in frequency was from .34 events per hour to 4.06 per hour, and in number of minutes per hour from 3.09 to 34.72. Estimating that the children in this sample were awake about 13 hours per day, we calculated that on average they experienced reading or writing from approximately 5 to 53 times per day and spent an average of between approximately 40 minutes and 7.5 hours per day in such activities.[4]

These quantifications of the literacy environment of the home indicate two points. First, every child in this sample was somehow involved with reading and writing during the course of everyday home experiences. Given these findings, even Harvey who experienced literacy comparatively less frequently than the other chil-

---

[4] The figure for the average number of minutes spent in activities mediated by literacy does not represent the amount of time spent in activities which involved literacy. For example, Alex's mother was observed using the Yellow Pages to find someone to repair her stove. Although her actual reading time was considerably less, the activity was recorded as lasting 22 minutes because that was the time she spent in reading and telephoning.

Table 2.   Average Frequency and Duration of Literacy

Focal Child	Average *n* of Occurrences of Literacy per Hour of Observation	Average *n* of Minutes per Hour Spent in Activity Involving Literacy
Mike	.85	5.42
Bobby	.66	4.75
Barbara	1.03	8.23
Kristin	1.15	7.72
Alex	.77	3.36
Becky	4.06	26.29
Paul	1.92	6.53
Holly	2.48	17.00
Myeesha	.54	4.68
Natalie	.69	15.90
Amin	.60	14.08
Denise	.98	11.85
Harvey	.47	5.78
David	.71	6.68
Alethia	3.23	34.72
Lori	.34	4.98
Alma	.64	5.62
Luis	.98	4.74
Juan	.89	4.10
Maria	.79	12.07
Terri	1.24	6.06
Roberto	1.18	7.21
Ronnie	1.03	3.09
Miguel	1.66	6.04

dren observed, would encounter reading or writing over 2,000 times and for almost 500 hours in the course of a year.

Second, there was considerable range in the amount of literacy occurring in these 22 homes. Both in terms of frequency and amount of time, the low and high results differ by a factor greater than 10. Although there are no ''normative data'' by which to judge these results, from personal experience we quite confidently report that these figures indicate that there was, compared to the overall population of the U.S., a great deal of reading and writing going on in some of these homes and very little in others.

Qualitative Findings

As we analyzed field notes of each of the approximately 1300 occurrences of literacy observed in the homes, we found certain qualitative variables of special theoretical significance to children's literacy development and success in school. Two of these variables, the *participant structure* of the event and the *domain of activity* in which the literacy occurred, especially pertain to the discussion in this chapter.

Participant Structure.   Our observations of reading and writing centered on the preschool children who were the subjects of the research, and thus one participant with whom we were concerned was the focal child (FC). But these focal children were obviously not the only participants in the literacy which took place in the homes and communities. Parents, siblings, relatives, and friends also engaged in literacy activities. Analysis of these activities revealed variation in participants in several respects.

On some occasions the FC was actually involved in the reading and/or writing which occurred. (These events were labeled FC Involved.) At other times she/he had the opportunity to observe literacy but did not actually become directly engaged in the activity. (These events were labeled FC Observing.) Both types of situations were of theoretical interest, for children learn about reading and writing through direct experiences and from observing others (Smith, 1981a, 1981b; Teale, 1982).

Furthermore, we found participant structure variation within the two major categories, FC Involved and FC Observing. Sometimes when the FC was directly involved, he or she acted alone—as when looking through a book or magazine, writing the letters of the alphabet, or 'scribbling,' for example. (Remember that we considered occasions upon which a person *attempted* to produce or comprehend written language as instances of literacy.) Sometimes the FC interacted with another person or persons. These variations were regarded as significant because, though not mutually exclusive, they offer opportunity for different effects on the child's literacy development. Interacting with literate others in such situations provides the FC with direct experience in the motives, actions, operations, and routines of literacy, all of which help the child develop new understandings about the functions, uses, and "how-to" of reading and writing. The solitary literacy experience is an excellent opportunity for polishing and refining what is learned through social interaction (i.e., for "practicing"). But also in these FC alone activities the child can try out solutions to the perturbations, or dilemmas, which she/he meets in the course of literacy development.

Finally, there is one more variation of theoretical significance to the discussion of participant structure: the literacy ability of the persons around the FC who engaged in reading/writing, whether in interaction with the FC or by themselves. Some of these persons were fully literate (parents, for example). Others were, like the FC, not yet to the point of being able to read and write independently. Furthermore, among the children in this latter category whose literacy was emergent, we found differing degrees of sophistication. Younger siblings, for instance, were generally not as accomplished as the FC, whereas certain older siblings (a first grade sibling, for example) might most accurately be described as being "on the edge" of becoming fully literate.[5] It was quite important to the analysis to attempt to account

---

[5] In the truest sense we are all continually in the process of becoming literate. Here, however, I am referring to those other children who were just at the phase in their literacy development where they were becoming able to read and write independently.

for these differences, because it seemed likely that the FC would have the opportunity to learn more about reading and writing from interactions with or observations of a literate other than from a child whose reading and writing abilities were no further advanced than the FC's.

Because of problems with characterizing and reliably categorizing the children "on the edge" of becoming literate, the UNESCO (1952) definition of literacy ["A person is literate who can with understanding both read and write a short, simple statement on his everyday life" (cited in UNESCO, 1957, p. 20)] was used, and each person observed was classified as either literate or preliterate. This definition successfully excluded our preschool focal children and their younger siblings from the category of literate people, yet accurately described the ability level of most of the school-age siblings and friends of the focal children.

Thus, the participant structures of the reading and/or writing events can be summarized as follows:[6]

FC Involved	FC Observing
Literate (s)/FC Interactive	Literate (s) Alone
FC Alone	Literates Interactive
	Literate (s)/Preliterate(s) Interactive

Tables which report quantitative summaries of the frequency of occurrence and amount of time spent in activities mediated by literacy for each of the categories of participant structure are included as Appendix A and Appendix B. All aspects of these results will not be discussed; instead, findings will be highlighted. First of all, as with previous results, there was considerable variation among the families. Becki had the opportunity to observe literate persons reading or writing (either alone or in interaction with each other) over 20 times a day on average, while Myeesha, Lori, and Luis had such opportunities less than twice per day on average. The results for 19 of the remaining 20 children were between 3 and 7 times per day on average. Thus, the variation is not merely found in extreme cases but occurs across the sample. A similar range was found for the amount of time literates in the households spent in such activities: in Paul's, Roberto's, and Ronnie's homes it averaged less than 20 minutes per day; in Becki's, Natalie's, and Amin's, more than 2 ½ hours each day on the average.

The picture does not change when we observe the frequency and duration of events in which the focal child was directly involved. In fact, there was not one time in 42 hours of observation when Harvey was seen interactively engaged in reading or writing with a literate person. Becki, Holly, and Alethia, on the other hand, averaged more than 8 such events per day. Five children (Alex, Myeesha, Harvey, Lori, and Maria) spent an average of less than 5 minutes per day in such interactive activi-

---

[6] There were other participant structures observed (e.g., pre-literate(s) interactive, literate/preliterate interactive, FC/preliterate interactive), but they occurred so rarely that they have been omitted from this discussion.

ties, whereas seven children (Kristin, Becki, Holly, Denise, Alethia, Terry, and Roberto) averaged over half an hour per day interacting with literate others.

The FC Alone category shows over a 10-fold difference in average frequency and duration between Amin and Harvey, on the one hand, and such children as Holly and Alethia, on the other, with a considerable range of increments in between.

In short, we found that in this low-income population there was considerable variation in how often and for how long in various participant structures the focal children experienced reading or writing.

We looked across participant structure categories to see if there were some discernible patterns to the frequency and amount of literacy and to note how activity in each subcategory compared with the overall frequency and amount of literacy to which the FC was exposed. Again, having no "standard" or "norm" with which to compare our frequencies, we relied on what was relatively high or low for the sample and our intuitive sense as researchers of homes in which there was considerable or little literacy activity. The relationships were by no means straightforward. The results from Becki's family were high in all categories: the mother read and wrote a lot; she engaged Becki and her siblings in a great deal of literacy; and Becki was very active in reading and writing on her own. In Natalie and Amin's home another pattern was observed: not much in the way of Adult-FC Interactive or FC Alone literacy but high on the amount of reading/writing done by the parents. For Kristin, the findings were high on Adult-FC Interactive and on the adults' frequency/amount of literacy but low on FC Alone.

The more we looked at the numbers, the more apparent the limitations of these quantifications became. It was possible to develop an interpretation of these patterns in Natalie and Amin's and Kristin's households, but not without a knowledge of how each family worked. For instance, the bulk of considerable adult activity in Natalie and Amin's house could be traced to a single source: religious-oriented reading/writing. There were regular Bible study sessions as well as frequent discussions between the mother and her church sisters which involved reading and writing related to religious materials. Kristin engaged in comparatively little reading/writing on her own because she preferred to do these activities with her mother.

Thus, the participant structure categories themselves were of great value because they help to describe more fully the nature of the literacy interactions which occurred in the preschool children's homes. Also, a quantitative report on each of these participant structures for each of the focal children did reveal some significant results:

1. Not only is there a great range overall in the frequency and amount of literacy in the homes; there is a comparable range in the various participant structures.
2. In some homes there are numerous demonstrations (Smith, 1982) of literacy available to the children; in other homes, very few.
3. Some of these parents interacted a great deal with their preschoolers in activities mediated by literacy; others only rarely did so.

4. Some of the focal children "read" and "wrote" considerably; others hardly ever did.

However, these were the limits of what such data could tell us. Another qualitative variable which emerged as we examined the field notes helped in understanding the literacy backgrounds in the homes even further.

Domain of Activity.   Perhaps the most striking feature of the literacy observed in these 22 homes was its social nature. For the most part, reading or writing functióned not as isolated events but as components of the social activities of the persons in their homes and communities. That is to say, the literacy occurred within particular socially assembled situations and the vast majority of the time was engaged in for reasons other than the reading or writing itself.

For example, the following observation was made in Bobby and Barbara's home:

1 June
    12:01—Bobby and Barbara have been playing outside. They come inside to the kitchen where their mother, Andy (their 18-year-old brother), Gail (their 22-year-old married sister who lives next door), Tanya (Andy's fiancee), and Tanya's mother are all sitting around the table. The group is involved in making a list for Andy and Tanya's upcoming wedding and reception. Tanya is doing the actual writing of the list. She organized and initiated the activity to "make sure that we don't forget anything." Writing items for the list alternates with discussion (sometimes a great deal, sometimes a little) about each item. From time to time Tanya reads items on the list to the others around the table because there is a need to 'review' what they had done so far. This activity continues for 21 minutes while Bobby and Barbara are in the room playing, talking to people around the table, climbing on laps, and so forth. The activity ends when the adults decide the list is complete and that they are now organized. (12:22)

Note that the writing and reading which occurred on this occasion were not done merely for the sake of writing and reading. Rather, the list which was constructed functioned as an integral aspect of organizing an event in their lives, a wedding reception.

The finding that literacy functioned primarily to mediate domains of human activity (rather than as an isolated skill) is significant for several reasons. First, as Soviet psychologists (Leont'ev, 1981; Vygotsky, 1978, 1981) have pointed out, there is a direct link between society and mind. In other words, the foundations of cognition are themselves social. Thus, there is more to literacy than merely reading and writing. In fact, recent anthropological, psychological, and linguistic research has indicated that even though literacy invariably involves people interacting with the written word, there is more than one way to be literate (Ferguson, 1971; Scribner & Cole, 1981). We can expect, therefore, that the ways in which literacy enters into the social life of a family will affect how it is incorporated into the mental life of the members of the family.

Therefore, a major task for our analysis was developing a scheme for describing the types of activities which were mediated by literacy in the 22 households. When

(a) the material (type/content of written language) used, (b) the action of the partici-
pant(s), and (c) the names typically attributed by members of our society to the actions were taken into account, nine domains of activity mediated by literacy were
identified. They are as follows:

(1) *Daily Living Routines:* This domain of activity is concerned with the ongoing
recurrent practices of everyday life: obtaining food, maintaining shelter,
participating in what is required by social institutions, maintaining the social organization of the family, and so forth. Literacy was often a part of daily living routines
such as shopping, cooking, paying bills, traveling from one place to another, maintaining welfare assistance, washing clothes, getting appliances or automobiles re-
paired, and so on.

(2) *Entertainment:* Literacy was also on occasion found to be a facet of the activities that passed the time of the participants in an enjoyable or engaging manner.
More specifically, it was observed that literacy mediated entertainment activities in
three different ways. Sometimes the literacy itself was the *source* of the entertainment (reading a novel, doing a crossword puzzle).

On other occasions the reading or writing itself was not entertaining but did relate intimately, either in an *instrumental* or *incidental* way, to the activity which
was entertaining. Literacy was considered instrumental to entertainment when it
was used to select or find out about, or in some other way facilitate or maintain
one's participation in an enjoyable or engaging activity. Examples observed of literacy as instrumental to entertainment were reading the TV guide to find out what
programs were on, reading the rules for Backgammon, and reading movie listings in
the newspaper.

Literacy was considered incidental to entertainment in an event like the following: Mike is watching cartoons on television, and there are several written signs
which appear at various times during the cartoon. The written language in this case
was embedded in an activity which was not essentially a reading or writing activity
(such as reading a novel or doing a crossword puzzle would be), and was not necessary for the a activity to be an entertaining one.

(3) *School-Related Activity:* This domain of activity is directly related to the social institution of school. We observed two general ways in which the school was
linked to activity mediated by literacy in the homes. Where there were school-age
siblings of the focal children, written language often came directly from school (letters from the principal, consent forms, announcements, and so forth, as well as
homework which involved reading and/or writing).

Second, members of the families labeled certain of their activity as being school
related. Cecelia, Alma's 9-year-old sister would often "play school" with Alma
and her brothers. Holly's mother would often "have school" with her. In another
family which unfortunately could not participate for very long in the observations
(and which is not reported on in this chapter) the father organized the 1-year-old, the
2-year-old, the 3-year-old, the 4-year-old and the kindergartner almost every night
for a "school lesson."

Thus, some of the reading and writing which we saw occurring in the homes was
intimately tied with school.

(4) *Work*: Sometimes the literacy which occurred in the homes related directly to employment. On most occasions the reading or writing was associated with performing one's actual job (filling out order forms for Avon or receipts for rent collected, reading a technical manual), but literacy related to securing or maintaining employment (reading classified advertisements, reading a flyer from the employer explaining work-force cutback procedures) was also observed.

(5) *Religion*: Literacy also mediated family members' religious activities linked directly to the social institution, church: We observed, for example, Bible reading, Bible study sessions (which involved both reading and writing), the use of Bible study/interpretation guides, and reading of children's pamphlets brought home from Sunday School.

(6) *Interpersonal Communication:* Literacy was also used to communicate with friends, relatives, or other persons physically or temporally distant. Examples of interpersonal communication through literacy we observed included sending Christmas and birthday cards with handwritten messages on them, reading a letter from a friend in another state, and writing a letter to "Nana."

(7) *Participating in "Information Networks"*: On occasion we observed people reading and thereby gaining information for which there was no immediately discernible use and which did not link directly to any of the previously mentioned social institutions (school, church, work, etc.). For example, a few of the fathers in the sample regularly or irregularly read the sports section of the newspaper. Such events could not really be said to be mediating entertainment activities. The readers were not being entertained; they were gaining information. But information for what? We had great difficulty deciding what domain of activity was being mediated by literacy on these occasions. Some questioning of the participants helped to clarify their motives.

Our findings can be summarized in the following way. Sometimes people read "just to find out what's going on" or in the case of Kristin's mother "to get the real story." One father also commented that he frequently used information from the sports pages in conversations with friends and coworkers. In a sense, then, there are various "information networks" out there: perhaps a sports network (or even a football network, a baseball network, etc.) a politics network (local politics, national politics, etc.), a gardening network—who knows what else? It depends how we slice the pie, but the important point for analysis (and for understanding the nature of literacy) is that reading is done for the purpose of acquiring information so that people can participate in discussions of sports, computers, real estate, or whatever in various settings in which they are interacting socially with others. Reading can contribute to helping a person achieve or maintain membership in certain groups or merely keep up with developments in that particular field of information.

(8) *Storybook Time*: Book-reading episodes which involve parents and preschool children have been shown to have, within certain limits, a characteristic structure (Teale, 1984; Snow, Nathan, & Perlmann, 1985). Three of the families in the study regularly engaged in adult–preschool-child book-reading episodes. Such instances of literacy were categorized as being the activity of storybook time because of the

characteristic structure just mentioned and because participants in such events have a well-developed schema for such occasions (namely, they themselves identified the context as storybook time).

Of course, not all of the events classified as storybook time involved books which contained a narrative (story). Many were "label books" (each page would contain a picture or pictures with the name of the object(s) depicted), picture books, or alphabet books that contained no story line at all. Thus, the category storybook time is employed somewhat generically here because of widespread use of the term in our society and in the professional literature.

(9) *Literacy for the Sake of Teaching/Learning Literacy*: This category stands apart from the preceding eight, for which it was stressed that the reading or writing was engaged in for reasons other than the reading or writing itself. On certain occasions, the focus of the activity was to help another person (usually the focal child) learn to read and write.

These events focused sometimes on very basic skills such as letter formation or identification, at other times on more complex reading or writing skills or knowledge (information) about literacy. In any case the activity was not so much mediated by literacy as it was about literacy. That is to say, literacy became the context.[7]

Thus, particular types of written materials and even the operations employed in comprehending or producing those materials to a certain degree were associated with the domains. For example, lists, bills, short forms, and checks were among the materials typically mediating Daily Living Routines. Such texts differed in several respects from the extended prose found in the Bible and the Bible study books used to mediate religious activities by three of the families. Also, certain of the operations involved in processing a shopping list were the same as those used by Maria's mother when she read and analyzed the Bible, but the operations differed in significant ways also. The distribution of literacy across the domains, then, provided some insight into qualitative aspects of the literacy environments of the homes.

All occasions for literacy for which the participant structure was Literate(s) Alone, Literates Interactive, Literate(s)/Preliterate(s) Interactive, or Literate(s)/FC Interactive were classified according to domain of activity. (Events involving only preliterates and/or the FC were not so classified because it was felt that the young

---

[7] Sapir (1921) once said that "all systems leak," and so it is with this system for categorizing the domain of activity mediated by the reading and writing which we observed. For example, when notes were written to maintain the social organization of the family, these events were categorized under the "Daily Living Routines" category. Obviously, however, there is interpersonal communication involved in such activities. Also, a connection between the "Literacy for the Sake of Teaching/Learning Literacy" and "School-Related" domains can be noted. Often the focus of homework activities was literacy itself. For instance when Andy's sister Sally would do her reading homework (a school-related activity) with mother, the motive for the activity was certainly to develop Sally's reading skills.

It seems impossible, and is probably not even desirable, to develop strictly mutually exclusive categories for describing the literacy which occurred in the 22 households, however, and the use of the system just outlined reveals many interesting insights into the reading and writing that went on.

child's motive for engaging in the reading or writing could not be inferred, whereas there were ample cues for making such determinations when literates were involved.) Table 3 summarizes the frequency and amount of time (and relative percentage for each) spent in literacy in each domain for the 24 children. The domains most frequently mediated by literacy for the 24 children were Daily Living Routines, Literacy for the Sake of Teaching/Learning Literacy, Entertainment-Source, and School-Related. The greatest amount of time in literacy is spent in the domains Entertainment-Source, Daily Living Routines, Religion, School-Related, and Literacy for the Sake of Teaching/Learning Literacy.

Comparatively little literacy mediated the Entertainment-Incidental, Work, and Interpersonal Communication categories. In addition, little reading for Storybook Time was observed in the 22 households; storybook reading was simply not a regular part of the practices of everyday life in most of these homes.

Further examination of the frequency and duration of literacy in the different domains helped clarify the findings reported in Table 3. First, among the domains in which literacy activity was high for the 24 FCs as a group, we find variation in the extent to which these levels were consistent across families. Reading or writing was used by all of the families to mediate Daily Living Routines and served as Entertainment-Source for all but two. However, in 4 homes there was no activity in the School-Related domain (with 4 additional homes having only one such event). In 8 homes, literacy was never observed to mediate the Entertainment-Instrumental domain. There were instances of Literacy for the Sake of Teaching/Learning Liter-

Table 3.   Average Frequency and Duration of Literacy for All Focal Children[a]

Domain	Frequency		Duration	
	Average *n* of Occurrences per Hour in All Households	%[b]	Average *n* of Minutes per Hour Spent in Activity In All Households	%
Daily living routines	.168	25.5%	1.29	19.3%
Entertainment				
Source	.113	17.2	1.41	21.2
Instrumental	.037	5.6	.25	4.0
Incidental	.007	1.0	.03	0.5
School-related	.074	11.2	.87	13.0
Work	.015	2.3	.09	1.4
Religion	.025	3.8	1.26	18.9
Interpersonal communication	.023	3.5	.13	2.0
Information networks	.060	9.1	.42	6.3
Storybook time	.006	0.9	.13	1.9
Literacy for the sake of teaching/learning literacy	.130	19.8	.77	11.6

[a]These data are also reported in Anderson and Stokes (1984).
[b]May not total exactly 100% because of rounding.

acy for 11 of the 24 focal children and for only 7 children was literacy used to mediate religious activities.

What happened in the cases of Literacy for the Sake of Teaching/Learning Literacy and Religion, then, was that the considerable reading or writing occurring in a small number of the homes in the sample accounted for the overall high averages. In fact, as far as the Religion domain is concerned, 73% of the frequency and 97% of the time is accounted for by three families—Natalie and Amin's, Lori's and Maria's.

Also, closer examination of the literacy in different domains revealed interesting patterns of participant structure. Literacy in Daily Living Routines and Entertainment-Source activities tended to be distributed across the main participant structures; sometimes a literate performed the reading or writing alone; other times, in interaction with another literate. Also, there were numerous occasions on which a literate interacted with the FC in such activities. Reading and writing in the Entertainment-Instrumental domain, on the other hand, tended to be done by literates, with the FC observing. Literacy for the Sake of Teaching/Learning Literacy was just the opposite—almost all events observed in this domain were instances in which the FC interacted with an adult or older sibling.

Thus, variation is again a striking characteristic of the ways in which literacy functioned in the lives of the 24 focal children. As has already been pointed out, there was variation in the extent to which literacy mediated the nine domains of activity. Simultaneously, there was variation within the individual domains. For example, even though Religion ranked second among the domains in terms of amount of time spent in literacy, this time was, for all intents and purposes, accounted for by three families. On the obverse of the coin, relatively little was observed in the way of Storybook Time or Interpersonal Communication for the focal children. Yet, in Erin's home, an average of approximately 26 minutes per day and 20 minutes per day, respectively, was spent in these domains.

Embedded within the variation, however, was consistency. Literacy mediated Daily Living Routines to a high degree across the families. Such a finding should not be surprising when we consider that in contemporary American society "Get it in writing" is not merely a saying; it is the accepted legal practice. When governmental officials communicate, they generally do so in print. Thus, written language serves an important function in keeping this country running, and virtually all people become involved in this vast network of reading and writing. Literacy is also used extensively by businesses in their dealings with the public. Advertising, product labels, and billing systems, for example, all make extensive use of written language. In many respects, then, it is impossible to escape the necessity of utilizing the literacy in one's Daily Living activities: bureaucratic communication to individuals comes largely in the written form, a good deal of advertising is conducted through the print medium, receiving and giving out the family income is often accomplished by using written language. These seem to be the consequences of living in a literate society such as ours.

Also, there was a paucity of literacy associated with the domain of Work. As was mentioned, the parents who worked were generally employed in unskilled or semi-skilled jobs. We do not know how much literacy was involved in their actual activities while at work because we did not observe the parents in that setting; however, when we considered the nature of their jobs and what we have learned through interviews about the literacy connected with those jobs, we hypothesized that it is actually quite little. One thing that was certain is that almost no reading or writing associated with work ''spilled over'' into the home environment. Virtually the only instances of literacy activities conducted in the domain of work were occasional uses of reading and writing in conjunction with the selling of Avon or other such products.

As the distributions across the domains of activity mediated by literacy were examined, one fact about home literacy background became very clear: The literacy environment of these homes was greatly influenced by relations which the members of the family had with other institutions of society beyond the family itself. Government, church, school, work—any of these can have a profound influence upon the literacy home background, depending upon how the family interacts with them.

On the other hand, activity in some domains cannot be so decidedly linked to the various institutions of society. Storybook Time, participating in Information Networks, and Interpersonal Communication, for example, seem closely related to what Heath (this volume) calls the ''cultural ways'' of the home. The extent to which literacy mediated activities in these domains reflected, to a large degree the language socialization practices of the homes.

Thus, the domain analysis helped bring to light the significance of the domains in terms of the factors which affected the home literacy background of these 24 children, as well as the distribution of literacy practice in the homes across the nine domains of activity.

Analyses of Major Social Variables

In an attempt to shed further light on the substantial diversity in the practice of literacy among the 22 families in the study, we conducted additional analyses. Clearly, since only low-income families were included in the research, economic factors, in and of themselves, did not account for the differences in literacy orientation.

There are a number of social variables which are often used as indicators in research, and we examined these also to see if they might provide insight into why it was that these families varied in terms of their literacy environments.

The first of these social variables which were investigated was ethnicity. We examined the frequency and amount of literacy for the three ethnic groups—Anglo, Black, and Mexican American—in terms of both participant structure and domain of activity. The results showed no clear differentiation of literacy practice in the families when examined according to ethnic groups.

Let us first examine the issue of frequency and amount of literacy by participant structure. Analyses of the six major participant structures discussed earlier (and reported in Appendices A and B) revealed only one statistically significant ethnic difference: Frequency in the Literates Interactive category was higher ($p = .03$) for Anglos than for either Blacks or Mexican Americans. Little of practical or theoretical importance could be linked to this result. In addition, there were no significant differences ($p > .05$) when the overall average frequency and amount of literacy for each ethnic group was analyzed. Inspection of the results across the six participant structures in each ethnic group revealed one trend that was characteristic of all analyses by ethnicity which were carried out: There was generally as much within-group variation as there was among groups.

Such a situation was certainly apparent in the ethnicity by domain of activity analyses. Statistically significant differences of $p \leq .05$ were found in two domains. First, for Religion, Black and Mexican American families more frequently used reading and writing to mediate religious activities than did Anglo families. However, as has already been pointed out, these differences were accounted for almost totally by a small number of families in each ethnic group. Second, in the domain of Daily Living Routines, it was found that Anglo and Black families spent greater amounts of time mediating these activities with print than did Mexican American families. (But the Anglo and Black families' frequencies were not significantly different.)

Thus, the analyses by ethnic group revealed no consistent pattern which could account for the variations observed in the home literacy backgrounds of the families. In other words, the families' ethnicity could not predict the overall level of literacy activity, the participant structures of the reading and writing that went on, or the domain of activity which literacy was used to mediate.

Similar analyses were also conducted using sex of the focal child, educational level of the parents, and indicators of family structure as independent variables. Results similar to the analyses by ethnicity were obtained: Nothing in the way of theoretically or practically significant patterns emerged.

The overall amount of time spent in activities mediated by literacy was significantly higher for female focal children than for male ($p = .049$). Inspection of these results according to participant structure revealed that this difference was accounted for by the fact that in homes where the focal child was a girl, the literate members of the family spent signficantly more time in such activities. Thus, girls did not spend more time in interactions with literate others or reading/writing by themselves than did boys. Also, analyses by domain of activity revealed no sex differences for the focal children.

For the level of education analyses, families were categorized as either high or low because a bimodal distribution existed in the sample. (See Table 1.) High was defined as 10.5–12 years of schooling on average for the parents: 19 focal children came from families in this category. The remaining 5 focal children came from families defined as having a low level of education, 6.5 years or fewer. No significant differences were found for overall literacy activity or according to participant structures. For differences in domain of activity mediated by literacy, only duration in the Daily Living Routines domain was significant, with the level of high education families using literacy in such activities more than those in the low groups.

Family structure was investigated by analyzing two factors, family size and the presence or absence of school-age siblings. Eight FCs came from large families (4 or more children); 7, from medium families (3 children); and 9, from small families (1 or 2 children). No statistically significant differences were found when the data were analyzed according to family size. The same was true of focal children with school-age siblings versus those without any. No significant differences in home literacy background were accounted for by this factor.

CONCLUSIONS

These investigations point to several conclusions about home background and young children's literacy development. First, the observations of the low-income children provide additional evidence for the contention that virtually all children in a literate society like ours have numerous experiences with written language before they ever get to school. The research of Heath (1983), Taylor (1983), Harste, Woodward, and Burke (1984) and the studies reviewed by Goodman (this volume) also support such a conclusion.

Furthermore, we can see that these children experienced literacy primarily as a social process during their preschool years. In approximately 80% of the reading and writing activities observed and for almost 90% of all the time spent in these activities, the focus of the activity (i.e., the motive for engaging in it) was not literacy itself. Thus, it was generally the case that reading or writing occurred as aspects of activities which enabled family members to organize their lives, both with respect to each other and to the community and larger society beyond the doors of their immediate household.

A predominant theme which arises from the observations is that of variation in home background literacy experiences of the 24 children. In sheer quantitative terms, some children had the opportunity to observe much more reading and writing going on around them than did others. Furthermore, there was a similar quantitative range in the actual experience children had interacting with parents or older siblings in activities which involved literacy. Also, some children "read" or "wrote" by themselves a great deal more than others. This range in experience extended to qualitative dimensions as well. The reading and writing which took place mediated nine different domains of activity, and the patterns of occurrence of literacy among these domains certainly varied across households.

These findings should prompt a reconsideration of traditional wisdom which has it that children from low SES backgrounds come to school with a dearth of literacy experience. Some low-income children have considerable contact with literacy and are well on their way to become competent readers and writers by the time they get to school.

In a recent meta-analysis of almost 200 studies of the relation between socioeconomic status and academic achievement, White (1982), raises a related issue. He found, contrary to what is believed by many, that when the individual is the unit of analysis, the correlations between traditional measures of SES and academic achievement are relatively weak (.19–.33). White comments, "It may be *how* parents rear their children . . . and not the parents' occupation, income, or education that really makes the differences" (p. 471). The data from the present study certainly indicate that this is the case.

A question of theoretical and practical importance, then, is what causes the variation in this population which is, in the usual terms of measures of SES (occupation of breadwinner, source of income, quality of housing, and status of dwelling area) fairly homogeneous? Our analyses indicated that the answer does not lie in explanations which make use of variables like ethnicity, sex of the child, level of education, or family size, which are traditionally employed in social science research.

Rather, in order to understand why there is considerable literacy activity in some homes and little in others and why the functions and uses of literacy vary across families, we must "unpackage" terms such as SES and ethnicity and keep at the forefront of our considerations that literacy is a social process and a cultural practice.

Home background plays a significant role in a young child's orientation to literacy. But home background is a complex of economic, social, cultural and even personal factors. For example, a factor such as income can have a dramatic effect on the home literacy environment. Our observations showed that this factor is significant in several ways. Of course, families with greater amounts of spendable income can afford to buy more literacy materials for the home; but, also, more income generally means more purchasing of goods, services, and entertainment. The fact that one family can afford to buy or travel more than another can actually increase the literacy activity of the home because of the literacy associated with buying or traveling. For example, there is reading of product ads in magazines, newspapers, catalogues, or the Yellow Pages; trips to stores and restaurants with the associated exposure to the environmental print and texts present there, planning which involves reading tour booklets and maps, or writing for information. See also Heath's discussion (this volume) of sustained face-to-face talk for Roadville and mainstream families which often occurred during car rides. She points out that many Trackton families did not have cars. This serves as a related example of how economic circumstances affect language and literacy interactions of the family. Thus, as well as directly affecting the literacy environment in the home, income has "indirect" effects because of the constraints it places on, or opportunities it affords for, interaction with various facets of society. It can be said that the middle-income family is at an advantage because its members come in contact with more print in this way, simply as a consequence of being middle income. If you cannot afford to eat out, you usually spend little time reading restaurant ads, let alone the menus which actually are in the restaurants. But by the same token, the data clearly showed that economic circumstances need not in any way restrict the amount of richness of literacy experiences for preschool children. We observed instances of what other writers have described as "highly literate" homes among these low-income families.

Also, as the analysis by domain of activity revealed, of tremendous significance to home literacy background is the interface between various social institutions (school, workplace, government, or church, for example) and the home. As was discussed earlier, for instance, certain literacy activities conducted in the home arise as virtually unavoidable consequences of participating in a literate society. Utility bills, tax forms, advertisements—they came into every home we observed, and reading and writing resulted.

Other activities arising from contact with social institutions are not so much unavoidable as they are products of the fact that the family elects to interact with the particular institution. The church, for example, was a potent source of literacy in some families. Literacy that mediated the domain of religious activities typically utilized distinctive types of texts with a particular range of content. Thus, practicing a religion actively and participating in church activities greatly affected the literacy environment of some homes and consequently the literacy orientations of the young children there. It should be emphasized, though, that there was no simple relation between practicing religion and the home literacy environment. Certain faiths promoted a particular relation between reader and text. Two of the families in the study, for example, were Jehovah Witnesses. Their faith placed a great deal of importance on the individual's reading and interpreting scripture. Consequently, we observed many instances of adults performing textual analyses and discussing interpretations, as well as involving the children in Bible study sessions. However, in other families that were "equally religious," we did not observe similar effects on the reading and writing activities of the home. It would appear, therefore, that the particular religion and the role which text/reading/writing play in it must be understood in order to account for how an institution like the church can affect the home literacy background.

A finding like this one serves to illustrate another conclusion prompted by the domain analysis: The home literacy environment is influenced by more than social structural factors. The extent to which literacy mediated a particular domain of activity for a particular family and the distribution for each family of reading and writing across the different domains was also affected significantly by cultural practices, the recurrent, goal-directed activities constructed and maintained by particular groups of human beings. That is to say, cultural as well as social structural factors influenced how, to what ends, by whom, and when literacy was used.

It may be recalled that our analyses revealed that ethnicity could in no significant way account for substantial quantitative and qualitative differences we found among the 24 focal children's home literacy experiences. But such a finding should not be taken to indicate that cultural factors play no role in home literacy background. To the contrary, Heath (1983) provides compelling evidence that culture significantly affects young children's socialization into language and literacy, and we observed that, within domains of activity, families structured the actions and roles which participants assumed in reading or writing differently. Thus, their concepts of the functions, uses and means of accomplishing reading and writing combined with concepts of childhood and child rearing greatly affected their children's socialization into literacy. How is our finding of no ethnic differences to be interpreted, then?

First, it indicates that ethnicity is not identical with culture. Ethnicity certainly relates in important ways to culture, but cultural practices are not merely the product of one's race.

Also, a significant difference between Heath's study and the San Diego project should be noted. Each of the communities in which Heath worked had a long tradition which "held them together." Roadville, the white working-class community, consisted of families which had been a part of mill life for four generations. The families in Trackton, the black working-class community were also part of the mill life, though only for the past 20 to 30 years. But the older generations of this community also shared a common history, being brought up on the land, either as farmers on their own or as tenant farmers (Heath, 1983, chap. 1). The families in each of the respective communities worked, played, and socialized with each other. Several of the Roadville families were blood relations. Each of the communities was relatively small (approximately 25 to 30 members). In short, these were genuine communities held together by history, tradition, and cultural practices.

We, on the other hand, gathered subjects from various neighborhoods around metropolitan San Diego. We did not work in any well-defined communities. Even the families within each ethnic group lived miles from each other and did not know each other or, to any great extent, share similar histories of experience. Thus, the variable ethnicity only tapped culture in its most general aspect, and this general aspect proved not sufficient for describing the variations seen among homes. However, this finding should not be interpreted as an indication of an absence of cultural influences on home literacy background.

To this point, then, we have discussed the variations among the homes. However, the similarities were important also. Three stood out. First is the consistent use of literacy to mediate Daily Living Routines. As has been reported in other studies for other populations (Heath, 1980; Taylor, 1983), literacy served a significant role of accomplishing numerous such everyday tasks for these low-income families. A widespread use of literacy in our society, then, is mediating the ongoing, recurrent practices of daily life, like shopping, working, paying bills, and so forth. In this respect, reading and writing played a very utilitarian role in the social organization of the family.

The second consistency across families was the dearth of literacy associated with the domain of work. This stands in sharp contrast to naturalistic research conducted in middle-class homes. For example, Taylor (1983) found that "literate pursuits (were) an integral part of the working routine" for each of the parents employed outside the home in the six families she studied, and Hoffman (1982) cites numerous examples of how literacy associated with her and her husband's work filtered into the everyday activities of their home. An example from Hoffman illustrates this point nicely: At age 4; 3, David found one of his lawyer father's legal papers on the desk where he was playing. He held the paper upright in front of him and "read" dogmatically, "the law says to stop on red" (p. 70). Such experience was clearly not available to the 24 children in the present study.

Instead, results are more consistent with what Heath (1983) observed in the white and black working-class communities in the Carolinas. She found very little reading or writing associated with the parents' work in the mills. In fact, she even comments that employers organized it such that they actually performed most of the literacy for the workers—filling out forms and so forth for them, thus eliminating the necessity to read and write.

The absence of storybook reading also deserves note. Storybook Time was of special interest for the study, simply because there is such widespread agreement in the research and teaching communities that experience in being read to contributes directly to early literacy development. (See Teale, 1984, for a review of this literature.) In fact, Wells (1981, 1982) concluded from his longitudinal Children Learning to Read Project that participation in storybook reading is "probably the best way" of helping young children become literate because it provides experience with decontextualized language and the opportunity to learn some of the essential characteristics of written language, as well as helping the child to cope with the reflective, disembedded thinking so necessary for success in school.

Thus, it was particularly interesting to note the extent to which the 24 children were read to. Unlike Heath's (1982) findings for working-class white homes but like what she observed in working-class Black homes, we found little evidence of parent–child reading in the low-income homes in San Diego. In only three of the families–Kristin's, Becki's and Terri's—were there parent–child interactions around books which occurred with sufficient regularity so that it might be said that a domain of activity recognizable to participants and observer alike as Storybook Time had been established. There were occasional adult–focal-child interactions around books for 6 of the remaining 21 children, but such interactions were quite infrequent. Mike, for instance, was involved in book reading with an adult on three occasions in the course of 70 hours of observation over a period of almost two years. Once his father read him *Things in my House,* once his mother read him a Little Golden Book *Wizard of Oz,* and once his mother's friend who was visiting the house read the *Wizard of Oz* to a group of three children—Mike, Mike's 15-month-old sister Megan, and the friend's own 4-year-old daughter.

Storybook reading, then, was not a widespread practice among families. Becki and Kristin, however, were read to an average of approximately 4 times per week; and Terri, an average of approximately 5 times per week. Also, these three children were judged, on the basis of observer opinion and results from informal print awareness and book handling interviews, to be among the most highly developed of the 24 focal children in terms of emergent literacy abilities. These results reaffirm the long-standing contention that storybook reading experiences further children's literacy development. Although, perhaps not absolutely necessary for becoming literate, storybook reading has an extremely facilitative effect on children's emergent literacy abilities.

But possibly even more interesting were the results of qualitative analyses of the book-reading episodes themselves. As field notes and transcripts of the episodes were analyzed, it became clear that parents read books to their children in qualitatively different ways. A finding like this one raised the question of whether differential storybook reading practices have differential consequences for children. Unfortunately, there were not sufficient data available from this project to resolve the question. Because the focus of the study was not storybook interaction per se, we had mainly field notes rather than tapes of the episodes and thus could not hope to develop the full-blown transcripts necessary for analysis. Also, Kristin moved to another state after only a few months in the study, leaving us with longitudinal (nine months) data for only two children. However, what was available indicated interesting variations and suggested a profitable research slant.

As an exploratory study, audio-taped storybook readings were gathered from three mother–child pairs not among the families in this study. Analyses of the transcripts confirmed variety in social interactional and language factors in the episodes. (See Teale, 1984, for examples.) These results, taken in concert with Heath's description of developmental trends in storybook reading practices (Heath, 1982, 1983), suggested that researchers still have much of theoretical and practical significance to learn about the practice of reading to young children.

FURTHER RESEARCH ON HOME BACKGROUND AND YOUNG CHILDREN'S LITERACY DEVELOPMENT

Recent research has verified the appropriateness of the naturalistic paradigm for conducting studies of home background and literacy development. A naturalistic approach promotes the development of thorough descriptions—descriptions of what is going on in homes and what children are learning about reading and writing. Such descriptions are particularly appropriate at this point in time, because they allow us to get beyond merely calculating correlations. From thorough descriptions we can infer causal relations between home background and the child's emerging literacy abilities while maintaining sufficient ecological validity for testing further (e.g., experimentally), whatever hypotheses are indicated by results of the observations.

Specifically, I see several directions which would be profitable for research on this topic in the immediate future. First, and perhaps foremost, is the need to conduct additional longitudinal studies of literacy development in early childhood. Aside from a few case studies of mainstream children (e. g., Baghban, 1984; Hoffman, 1982) we have precious little descriptive, longitudinal information on literacy development in early childhood. Heath's (1983, this volume) and Taylor's (1983) projects stand as notable exceptions. Longitudinal research affords a unique look at the learning processes. Especially interesting for studying home background and literacy development is the opportunity such research provides for observing how parent–child interactions vary over time. Vygotsky (1978) has argued that cognition is internalized social interaction. Longitudinal studies offer opportunities to test this theory directly. Furthermore, longitudinal research is indispensible for constructing accounts of typical patterns of development which children go through in their progress in writing and reading during the first few years of life.

A second area which warrants further study is that of the domains of activity in the home mediated by literacy. Szwed (1981), in the tradition of Hymes (1972), and Basso (1974), called upon researchers to document "the social meaning of literacy" (p. 14). Papers by Heath (1980) and Taylor (1982), for example, and the results reported earlier indicate that Szwed's message has been taken to heart. We now have a good deal of observational information on the functions and uses of reading and writing in the lives of children and adults. But much remains to be studied in this area. We need to discover more about how text types and people's mental operations on those various types of text cluster under the various domains of activity mediated by literacy. As we understand better the various patterns involved in producing or comprehending texts associated with the different domains, we shall be able to see more clearly the effects which experience or lack of experience with literacy in these different contexts can have on development.

Also, the research reported in this chapter suggests several domains of activity which are potentially of special interest in research on home background and young children's literacy development. Religion is one. It was obvious from our data that the way in which a family practices religion can have a profound influence upon the home literacy environment. More needs to be documented regarding the roles played by reading and writing in various religions, the types of operations which are typically performed on texts, and the very status of texts itself in the religion.

Work is another domain where much remains to be learned. We found extremely little work-related literacy spilling over into the homes of our 24 children. We also have strong reason to suspect that there was very little reading and writing done by the working parents in these families on their jobs. Study of work-related literacy in homes where such activity is present could tell us much about the literacy orientations of the parents and could also afford opportunities for observing if, and in what ways, preschool children are involved in these activities. Closer attention to job-related reading and writing for working-class parents would also help us understand the factors which influence the degree to which literacy is a part of one's work.

The domain of Participating in Information Networks was, in my estimation, for a long time more or less a catchall category in our analytic scheme. As I look back on that, I suspect it was because, as originally conceived, it had considerably less theoretical justification than the other categories did. In fact, it had once been termed "General Information." However, the phenomenon that it now represents—gaining information that enables one to participate in certain social networks—has been verified by audiences at conferences and research colloquia who have heard it proposed and by researchers seeking to describe the functions and uses of literacy. (Compare, for example, Guthrie's, 1983 category "Keeping Abreast.") Although it is perhaps a function of literacy not on the typical checklist, it is nevertheless a powerful motivator for involving people in reading and writing—it represents one way of achieving or maintaining group membership.

My hunch is that the frequency and amount of literacy in this domain will be a key factor in describing varying home background orientations to literacy. Where we see considerable activity in the Information Network domain, we shall see a very literacy-oriented family. But also, it would be interesting to note patterns of interrelation with other domains of activity and patterns in the type of family engaging in such activity, as well as the types of operations involved in literacy associated with this domain. Participating in information networks is a powerful motive for engaging in reading and writing for many individuals; we should not underestimate its importance or its effects in studies of home background and literacy development in early childhood.

Finally, there is Storybook Time. So much has been written about parent-child book reading interactions in the last few years that it seems almost redundant to say that this is a domain of extreme importance. Recently, I reviewed the literature on this topic (Teale, 1984). I shall not reiterate the details of that review here, but I should like to emphasize certain points made there as they pertain to the subject of this chapter. I already discussed above the need for more longitudinal research on young children's literacy experiences; nowhere is this need more acute than in studies of parent–child storybook-reading episodes. Longitudinal studies allow us to view development across time. We can see how the language and social interactional characteristics vary as the child becomes more familiar with a particular book (for example, the first versus the fifth versus the twentieth time the book is read) and as the child becomes more experienced with literacy in general (compare, for instance, Heath's (1982) description of the typical pattern of book-reading episodes involving 3-year-olds in mainstream homes with Ninio and Bruner's (1978) analysis of the pattern of a mainstream mother and her 1-year old).

Additional longitudinal studies and more synthesizing of the information that is already available are both necessary. We now have considerable data documenting variations in the language and social interactional patterns involved in such episodes (see the earlier discussions on storybook reading). Moreover, we have evidence that being read to leads to young children's displaying literacy skills, uses of language, and information structures which they have previously encountered in book reading interactions (Baghban, 1984; Holdaway, 1979; Snow & Goldfield, 1982; Sulzby, 1985; Taylor, 1983; Snow & Ninio, this volume). Finally, we have indications that there are social class and cultural differences in storybook reading practices (Heath, 1982a; 1982b; Heath & Thomas, 1984; Ninio, 1980). But we are still in a period in which the area of research itself is lacking in coherence. Descriptive research of this nature is very labor-intensive, and longitudinal study of storybook reading is even more so. I doubt there will ever be large-scale research of this type; Elizabeth Sulzby and I have eight families in a 3-year study we are conducting (Sulzby & Teale, 1983), and we find this to be a tremendous amount of data to deal with. Rather, the work will continue to be conducted as case studies, or with relatively small numbers of families. Thus, we need additional, careful longitudinal studies. But we are also at the point where some meta-analyses would be most useful—not meta-analyses in the Glassian sense (Glass, 1977), but analyses which could draw data from many different sources and apply a consistent analytic framework.

There is much more to be learned about the variations in language and social interaction of storybook reading, as well as the roles which social and cultural factors play in the variations and the effects such experience has on children. This domain of activity is an extremely important one in the study of home background and young children's literacy development. It deserves all of the attention it has been given recently—and more.

The reference just made to the roles which social and cultural factors play in young children's literacy experiences suggests an area to which considerable attention should be paid in future research. Heath's (1983, this volume) work and that of Scollon and Scollon (1981), among others, indicate important cultural aspects to home literacy background. I interpret the research reported on in this chapter as giving additional evidence of cultural factors in literacy socialization. But we must also be careful to sort out what are social structural influences on the reading–writing environment of the home. The challenge is to explore more completely how economic, cultural, social structural, ethnic, and other factors blend to create the orientation to literacy which exists in a home.

Such understandings have important implications for school and home intervention programs. The Kamehameha Early Education Program (Au, 1980; Tharp, 1982, Tharp et al., 1984), for instance, is an example of a school's adjusting instruction in light of the cultural needs and patterns of interaction of Hawaiian children. The results show significantly better reading achievement for children in this program than for controls or for children in the same school who had been through traditional instruction which did not take such cultural factors into account.

Also, an understanding of cultural and social structural factors can help in designing home intervention programs. Typically, such programs seek to change two things: (a) the patterns which parents employ when interacting with their children, and (b) the amount of literacy which occurs in the home. All too frequently, however the approach to effecting such changes ignores the social structural factors facing the family or cultural factors which affect parent–child interactions. As a result, many home intervention programs simply attempt to overlay mainstream interactional patterns on lives which are not mainstream. Long-term effects are not pronounced in such situations. It would seem that the secret to developing more literacy oriented homes is, in essence, to get the families to 'need' more literacy. The research reported in this chapter clearly indicates that nonmainstream families use reading and writing to mediate certain activities in their everyday lives. Broadening and deepening the extent to which literacy mediates activities means simultaneously affecting the patterns of daily activities. The marketplace, the workplace, the church—these are three avenues through which long-lasting changes in home literacy background might be introduced.

In other words, it is not enough simply to try to get parents to change *how* they do something. Reading and writing are at once social processes and cultural practices. Changes in the home literacy environment imply changes in the ways the family organizes its everyday activities.

This is not to say, however, that adult–child interactions are not important. To the contrary, the language and social interactional patterns of parent and child are of great significance and need to be researched much more thoroughly. It is apparent from the data reported above that parents and their children differ in the extent to which they participate in interaction involving reading and writing. Also, however, we found varying patterns to these interactions. On some occasions, a structure similar to the Initiation-Reply-Evaluation (IRE) sequence Mehan (1979) reports as being typical of school lessons was employed; the majority of the time it was not. Furthermore, it was observed that many of the parent–FC interactive events were initiated by the child rather than by the adult, a result corroborated by Schickedanz and Sullivan (1984), who found that the majority of literacy events that parents noted in the six middle-class homes they studied were child-initiated. Finally, there is the issue of how effectively the child's zone of proximal development (Vygotsky, 1978) is negotiated in such interactive events. Vygotsky's theory implies that the more successful the parent and child are at accomplishing this, the better the child will progress in learning to write and read.

Thus, many questions about adult–child interactions involving literacy remain to be answered. For example, to what degree do children initiate interactive literacy activities? Why do they initiate the activities they do? Does whoever initiates the event (adult vs. child) make a difference in how it is carried out? What differences are there among families in the extent to which IRE patterns are employed in adult–child interactive events? How does such an interactional pattern relate to cultural practices or social structural factors? Are there other identifiable interactional patterns? Are particular domains of activity associated with particular parent–child language or social interactional features? We still have much to learn about an extremely important facet of home-literacy-background–parent–child interactions in activities mediated by literacy.

Finally, there is one additional aspect of preschool literacy experience which deserves much greater attention: writing. We observed considerable writing in the homes of the 24 children in the San Diego study. In fact, of the total literacy that took place during the 1,300-plus hours of observation, almost half of it was writing. The focal children wrote on many occasions, both in interaction with an adult and by themselves. Thus, our results confirm what researchers like Clay (1975), Read (1975), and Bissex (1980) helped us realize: Writing plays a significant role in young children's literacy development. The legacy of research in the language arts is largely a legacy of reading research. Furthermore, reading is a well-established subject in school. Partly because of these facts and partly as a result of the traditional approach to the language arts which has it that listening precedes speaking which precedes reading which precedes writing, historically we have tended to overlook writing during the early years. Perhaps nowhere is the importance of the concept of emergent literacy more evident than with young children's writing. Their writing is unconventional, but it is writing nonetheless. Even the early "scribbles" of very young children exhibit the distinctive features of the culturally elaborated writing system to which they are exposed (Clay, 1975; Ferreiro & Teberosky, 1982; Harste et al., 1984). Also, children distinguish between writing and drawing quite early on (Clay, 1975; Harste et al., 1984; Sulzby, 1981, 1985), and although their spellings may not be correct according to adult standards, they are consistent and logical (Read, 1975; Henderson & Beers, 1980). We are coming to realize the importance of early writing behaviors (Farr, 1984). Now we need additional descriptions of what children are learning about writing during these early years and how they are learning it. Such information would help greatly in understanding better how home background affects children's writing competencies.

In summary, a formidable task lies ahead. We have broken through an important barrier, providing convincing evidence that literacy development does begin very early in life and that children's early reading and writing experiences are of considerable importance in their overall literacy development. It remains now to conduct additional studies, especially longitudinal ones which will help us understand better the relations between home background and literacy development.

REFERENCES

Anderson, A.B., & Stokes, S.J. (1984). Social and institutional influences on the development and practice of literacy. In H. Goelman, A. Oberg, & F. Smith (Eds.), *Awakening to literacy.* Exeter, NH: Heinemann Educational.

Au, K.H. (1980). Participation structures in a reading lesson with Hawaiian children: Analysis of a culturally appropriate instructional event. *Anthropology & Education Quarterly, 11,* 91–115.

Baghban, M.J.M. (1984). *Our daughter learns to read and write: A case study from birth to three.* Newark, DE: International Reading Association.

Basso, K. (1974). The ethnography of writing. In R. Bauman & J. Sherzer (Eds.), *Exploration in the ethnography of speaking.* Cambridge, England: Cambridge University Press.

Bissex, G.L. (1980). *GNYS AT WRK: A child learns to write and read.* Cambridge, MA: Harvard University Press.

Bruner, J.S. (1978). Learning the mother tongue. *Human Nature, 1,* 43–49.

Bulcock, J.W. (1977). Evaluating social facts related to school achievement in Sweden and England. *Scandinavian Journal of Educational Research, 21,* 4–12.

Clay, M.M. (1975). *What did I write?* Exeter, NH: Heinemann Educational.

Farr, M. (1984, April). *State of the art: Children's early writing development.* Paper presented at American Educational Research Association Annual Meeting, New Orleans.

Ferguson, C.A. (1971). Contrasting patterns of literacy acquisition in a multilingual nation. In W.H. Whitely (Ed.), *Language use and social change.* London: Oxford University Press.

Ferreiro, E., & Teberosky, A. (1982). *Literacy before schooling.* Exeter, NH: Heinemann Educational Books.

Glass, G.V. (1977). Integrating findings: The meta-analysis of research. *Review of Educational Research, 5,* 351–379.

Goodman, Y.M. (1980). The roots of literacy. In M.P. Douglass (Ed.). *Claremont Reading Conference Forty-fourth Yearbook.* Claremont, CA: Claremont Reading Conference.

Grant, W.V., & Lind, C.G. (1975). *Digest of educational statistics.* Washington, DC: U.S. Department of Health, Education and Welfare.

Guba, E. (1982, April). *The search for truth: Naturalistic inquiry as an option.* Paper presented at the 27th Annual Convention of the International Reading Association, Chicago, IL.

Guthrie, J.T. (1983, May). *Comprehension: What's the use!* Paper presented at the 28th Annual Convention of the International Reading Association, Anaheim, CA.

Harste, J.C., Woodward, V.A., Burke, C. (1984). *Language stories and literacy lessons.* Portsmouth, NH: Heinemann Educational.

Heath, S.B. (1980). The functions and uses of literacy. *Journal of Communication, 30,* 123–133.

Heath, S.B. (1982a). Questioning at home and at school: A comparative study. In G. Spindler (Ed.). *Doing the ethnography of schooling: Educational anthropology in action.* New York: Holt, Rinehart & Winston.

Heath, S.B. (1982b). What no bedtime story means: Narrative skills at home and school. *Language in Society, 11,* 49–76.

Heath, S.B. (1983). *Ways with words: Language, life and work in communities and classrooms.* Cambridge, England: Cambridge University Press.

Heath, S.B., & Thomas, C. (1984). The achievement of preschool literacy for mother and child. In H. Goelman, A. Oberg, & F. Smith (Eds.), *Awakening to literacy.* Exeter, NH: Heinemann Educational.

Henderson, E.H., & Beers, J. (Eds.). (1981). *Developmental and cognitive aspects of learning to spell.* Newark, DE: International Reading Association.

Hoffman, S.J. (1982). *Preschool reading related behaviors: A parent diary.* Unpublished doctoral dissertation, University of Pennsylvania, Philadelphia.

Holdaway, D. (1979). *The foundations of literacy.* Sydney, Australia: Ashton Scholastic.

Hymes, D. (1962). The ethnography of speaking. In T. Gladwin & W. Sturtevant (Eds.), *Anthropology and human behavior.* Washington, DC: Anthropology Society of Washington.

Hymes, D. (1972). Models of the interaction of language and social life. In J.J. Gumperz & D. Hymes (Eds.), *Directions in sociolinguistics.* New York; Holt, Rinehart & Winston.

Laosa, L.M. (1977). Socialization, education, and continuity: The importance of the sociocultural context. *Young Children, 32,* 21–26.

Leont'ev, A. (1981). The problem of activity in psychology. In J.V. Wertsch (Ed.). *The concept of activity in Soviet psychology.* White Plains, NY: Sharpe.

Mehan, H. (1979). *Learning lessons.* Cambridge, MA: Harvard University Press.

Ninio, A. (1980). Picture-book reading in mother-infant dyads belonging to two subgroups in Israel. *Child Development, 51,* 587–590.

Ninio, A., & Bruner, J.S. (1978). The achievement and antecedents of labelling. *Journal of Child Language, 5,* 5–15.

Read, C. (1975). *Children's categorization of speech sounds.* Urbana, IL: National Council of Teachers of English.

Reder, S., & Green, K.R. (1979, December). *Literacy as a functional component of social structure in an Alaskan fishing village.* Paper presented at the 78th Annual Meeting of the American Anthropological Association, Cincinnati, OH.

Sapir, E. (1921). *Language.* New York: Harcourt, Brace & World.

Schickedanz, J.A., & Sullivan, M. (1984). Mom, what does U-F-F spell? *Language Arts, 61,* 7–17.

Scollon, R., & Scollon, S.B.K. (1981). The literate two-year-old: The fictionalization of self. In R. Scollon & S.B.K. Scollon (Eds.), *Narrative, literacy, and face in interethnic communication.* Norwood, NJ: Ablex.

Scribner, S., & Cole, M. (1981). *The psychology of literacy.* Cambridge, MA: Harvard University Press.

Smith, F. (1981a). Demonstrations, engagement and sensitivity: A revised approach to language learning. *Language Arts, 58,* 103–112.

Smith, F. (1981b). Demonstrations engagement and sensitivity: The choice between people and programs. *Language Arts, 58,* 634–642.

Snow, C., Nathan, D. & Perlmann, R. (1985). Assessing children's knowledge about bookreading. In L. Galda & A. Pellegrini (Eds.), *Play, language, and stories.* Norwood, NJ: Ablex.

Snow, C.E., & Goldfield, B.A. (1982). Building stories: The emergence of information structures from conversation. In D. Tannen (Ed.), *Analyzing discourse: Text and talk.* Georgetown University Round Table on Languages and Linguistics. Washington, DC: Georgetown University Press.

Spradley, J. (1980). *Participant observation.* New York: Holt, Rinehart & Winston.

Stein, A. (1971). Strategies for failure. *Harvard Educational Review, 41,* 158–204.

St. John, N.H. (1970). Desegregation and minority group performance. *Review of Educational Research, 40*, 111–134.

Sulzby, E. (1981). *Kindergarteners begin to read their own compositions: Beginning readers' developing knowledges about written language project*. Final Report to the Research Committee of the National Council of Teachers of English. Evanston, IL: Northwestern University.

Sulzby, E. (1985). Kindergarteners as writers and readers. In M. Farr (Ed.), *Advances in writing research. Vol. 1: Children's early writing development*. Norwood, NJ: Ablex.

Sulzby, E., & Teale, W.H. (1983). *Young children's storybook reading: Longitudinal study of parent–child interaction and children's independent functioning*. Proposal to The Spencer Foundation, Northwestern University, Evanston, IL.

Szwed, J.F. (1981). The ethnography of literacy. In M. F. Whiteman (Ed.), *The nature, development, and teaching of written communication*. Hillsdale, NJ: Erlbaum.

Taylor, D. (1982). Children's social use of print. *The Reading Teacher, 36*, 144–148.

Taylor, D. (1983). *Young children learning to read and write*, Exeter, NH: Heinemann Educational.

Teale, W.H. (1982). Toward a theory of how children learn to read and write naturally. *Language Arts, 59*, 555–570.

Teale, W.H. (1984). Reading to young children; Its significance for literacy development. In H. Goelman, A. Oberg, & F. Smith (Eds.), *Awakening to literacy* . Exeter, NH: Heinemann Educational.

Teale, W.H., Estrada, E., & Anderson, A.B. (1981). How preschoolers interact with written communication. In M. Kamil (Ed.), *Directions in reading: Research and instruction*. Washington, DC: The National Reading Conference.

Tharp, R.G. (1982). The effective instruction of comprehension: Results and description of The Kamehameha Early Education Project. *Reading Research Quarterly, 17*, 503–527.

Tharp, R.G., Jordan, C., Speidel, G.E., Au, K., Kline, P.W., Calkins, R.P., Sloat, K.C.M. & Gallimore, R. (in press). Product and process in applied developmental research: Education and the children of a minority. In M.E. Lamb, A.L. Brown, & B. Rogoff (Eds.), *Advances in developmental psychology, Volume 3*. Hillsdale, NJ: Erlbaum.

Thorndike, R. Reading comprehension in fifteen countries. *International Studies in Education* (Volume III). New York: John Wiley.

UNESCO. (1957). *World illiteracy at mid-century*. Westport, CT: Greenwood Press.

Vygotsky, L.S. (1978). *Mind in society*. Cambridge, MA: Harvard University Press.

Vygotsky, L.S. (1981). The genesis of higher mental functions. In J.V. Wertsch (Ed.), *The concept of activity in Soviet psychology*. White Plains, NY: Sharpe.

Wells, G. (1981, October). *Preschool literacy-related activities and success in school*. Paper presented at the Cognitive Consequences of Literacy Conference, Ontario Institute for Studies in Education, Toronto.

Wells, G. (1982). Story reading and the development of symbolic skills. *Australian Journal of Reading, 5*, 142–152.

White, K.R. (1982). The relation between socioeconomic status and academic achievement. *Psychological Bulletin, 91*, 461–481.

Appendix A.   Frequency of Literacy (Average Number of Occurrences per Hour) by Participant Structure

	FC Observing				FC Involved	
	Literate(s) Alone	Literates Interactive	Literates/ Pre literates Interactive	Pre literates Alone	Literate(s)/ FC Interactive	FC Alone
Mike	.24	.08	.03	.04	.24	.22
Bobby	.16	.20	—	—	.08	.22
Barbara	.25	.30	—	.07	.04	.37
Kristin	.45	.30	—	—	.25	.15
Alex	.27	.15	—	—	.09	.26
Becki	1.02	.63	.25	.68	.63	.81
Paul	.17	.23	.08	.18	.26	1.00
Holly	.28	.12	.04	.25	.73	.98
Myeesha	.11	.03	—	—	.07	.33
Natalie	.31	.11	—	—	.10	.17
Amin	.32	.13	—	—	.05	.10
Denise	.40	.04	—	—	.23	.31
Harvey	.38	.02	—	—	—	.07
David	.22	.21	—	—	.13	.15
Alethia	.22	.28	.21	.15	.74	1.63
Lori	.15	—	.01	—	.05	.13
Alma	.17	.09	.02	.02	.18	.15
Luis	.08	.04	.02	.02	.12	.24
Juan	.30	.24	.03	—	.18	.14
Maria	.13	.07	.26	.07	.06	.20
Terri	.23	.06	.02	.02	.61	.30
Roberto	.13	.16	.06	—	.40	.39
Ronnie	.18	.02	.10	.11	.35	.23
Miguel	.17	16	.15	.11	.50	.48

Appendix B.   Duration of Literacy (Average Number of Minutes per Hour Spent in Activities Mediated by Literacy) by Participant Structure

	FC Observing				FC Involved	
	Literate(s) Alone	Literates Interactive	Literates/ Preliterates Interactive	Preliterates Alone	Literate(s)/FC Interactive	FC Alone
Mike	1.07	.56	.49	.30	1.69	1.31
Bobby	.70	2.63	—	—	.50	.92
Barbara	1.43	3.58	—	.85	.73	1.64
Kristin	3.62	.73	—	—	3.65	.26
Alex	1.12	1.14	—	—	.18	1.00
Becki	13.13	1.51	1.13	2.51	3.37	4.53
Paul	.55	.92	1.10	.54	1.25	2.17
Holly	.92	.75		.61	5.64	7.97
Myeesha	2.41	.52	—	—	.33	1.42
Natalie	6.54	6.79	—	—	1.30	1.17
Amin	5.70	7.03	—	—	.91	.44
Denise	5.71	2.43	—	—	2.42	1.29
Harvey	4.64	.38	—	—	—	.76
David	2.43	2.80	—	—	.82	.63
Alethia	5.63	2.14	4.80	.37	9.78	12.00
Lori	3.71	—	<.01	—	.38	.89
Alma	1.41	.68	.24	.03	1.87	1.39
Luis	1.42	.23	.69	.22	.49	1.57
Juan	.92	.81	.03	—	1.07	.84
Maria	1.05	8.14	1.67	.27	.14	.80
Terri	1.13	.85	.11	.04	3.03	.90
Roberto	.82	.20	.53	—	4.05	1.34
Ronnie	.79	.04	.44	.21	1.28	.27
Miguel	1.23	.61	1.09	1.32	1.31	.35

About the Authors

Emilia Ferreiro, born in Argentina, is now full professor at the Department of Educational Research of the Center for Research and Advanced Studies (CINVESTAV) of the National Politechnical Institute, Mexico. She has been Professor at the National Universities of Buenos Aires and Montevideo and Visiting Professor at the Universities of Geneva and Rome. Professor Jean Piaget directed her Ph.D. thesis (in 1970) and wrote an important introduction to the published version of it. She published several papers on developmental psycholinguistics with Hermine Sinclair. Then she focused her attention on literacy development. Her contributions in this field are widely referred to in the current literature (mainly in Spanish, English, Italian, and French).

Yetta M. Goodman, Professor of Education in the Program in Language and Literacy at the University of Arizona, conducted pioneering research on young children's print awareness in the early 1970s. She has continued work on literacy development in early childhood, and her papers, "Learning to Read is Natural" (co-authored with Kenneth Goodman) and "The Roots of Literacy," have been influential in directing theoretical and research attention toward the knowledge children have about literacy prior to schooling. Professor Goodman served as president of the National Council of Teachers of English for 1979, chaired the Early Childhood and Literacy Development Committee of the International Reading Association from 1981 to 1984 and, in collaboration with Dorothy Strickland, organized the joint IRA-NCTE IMPACT conferences which focused on translating recent child language and literacy research into classroom experience.

Shirley Brice Heath, anthropologist, linguist, social historian, and Associate Professor of Anthropology and Linguistics in the School of Education at Stanford University, conducted ethnographic field work on young children's literacy development in communities in the Piedmont Carolinas for almost 10 years. The book which resulted from this study, *Ways with Words: Language, Life, and Work in Communities and Classrooms* (1983), has made a major contribution to the understanding of literacy development in early childhood. Professor Heath has lectured in Europe, Asia, Australia, and Latin America in addition to the U.S., and taught in primary and secondary schools in bilingual and bidialectal communities. In recent years, she has often collaborated with classroom teachers as coresearcher on problems of oral and written language use.

Jana Mason is Associate Professor of Educational Psychology and Research Associate Professor at the Center for the Study of Reading at the University of Illinois. Her work with young children includes experience as a kindergarten teacher, Assistant Director of the Nursery School at Carnegie-Mellon University, and Director of Day Care and Preschool in the Children's Research Center, University of Illinois. She has also taught at Mount St. Vincent, Halifax, Nova Scotia, Canada. She is best known for her research in linguistic awareness and its influence on children's reading development. More recently, she has been turning her attention to institutional interventions. In addition to numerous journal articles, chapters in books and technical reports on the subject of early literacy, she recently published "Early Reading: A Developmental Perspective" in the *Handbook of Research in Reading*.

Christine E.M. McCormick, Assistant Professor in the Psychology Department at Eastern Illinois University, has been collaborating with Jana Mason on research in early reading for the past six years. Her previous experiences as a Montessori preschool teacher and a school psychologist have influenced her research interests toward an emphasis on the educational implications of recent theoretical descriptions of early reading skills.

Anat Ninio was born in Budapest, Hungary, and immigrated to Israel in 1957. She is Senior Lecturer in the Department of Psychology at the Hebrew University, Jerusalem. While doing postdoctoral study at Oxford University, England, she began studying picture-book reading between mothers and their infants in collaboration with Jerome S. Bruner. She has visited the United States on a Fulbright-Hayes Travel Grant, and the United States–Israel Binational Science Foundation funded a 3 year collaboration for Dr. Ninio and Carol Eckerman of Duke University to study mother–infant interaction. Her article, "Joint Bookreading as a Multiple Acquisition Device," appeared in *Developmental Psychology* in 1983.

Catherine Snow, Associate Professor at the Harvard Graduate School of Education, is perhaps most widely known for her work on child language acquisition. In recent years, however, she has focused increasingly on literacy development in early childhood. In the period leading up to the publication of her book (with Charles Ferguson), *Talking to Children: Language Input and Acquisition* (1977), she taught and did research at Erasmus University and the University of Amsterdam, The Netherlands, and the University of Cambridge, England. In recent years, her attention on parent–child interaction has turned toward the context of book reading, and she has published widely on this topic.

Elizabeth Sulzby is Associate Professor of Education at Northwestern University, where she also teaches in the Department of Linguistics and in the Interdisciplinary Program in Language and Cognition. She has taught children in grades K–7 in the United States. Her early research on metalinguistic awareness has for the past eight years turned increasingly toward emergent literacy, or the reading and writing behaviors of young children that develop into conventional reading and writing. Her book, *Emergent Reading and Writing in 5 to 6-Year-Olds: A Longitudinal Study,* will be published soon (also by Ablex). She is continuing research in young children's storybook reading with William H. Teale, in a 3-year study supported by The Spencer Foundation.

Denny Taylor is an author and researcher whose writing focuses upon language, literacy, and learning in family contexts. Her initial research, which is described in *Family Literacy: Young Children Learning to Read and Write,* has provided some valuable insights into the many complex and interrelated ways that children's literate activities are mediated and affected by multigenerational family patterns and by their personal experiences of everyday life. Taylor has taught in England, New Zealand, Spain, and the United States. She has also taught in the Early Childhood Department, Kean College, NJ, and has been a Senior Research Fellow at the Institute of Urban and Minority Education, Teachers College, Columbia University. At the present time she is writing a book with Catherine Dorsey-Gaines which focuses upon the social contexts of literacy learning in inner-city families. The research on which this text is based received the Elva Knight Research Award from the International Reading Association.

William H. Teale is Assistant Professor of Education at the University of Texas at San Antonio. His work on early literacy development began in Melbourne, Australia, where he was Lecturer at La Trobe University. He has been Research Specialist at the Laboratory of Comparative Human Cognition, University of California, San Diego, studying the family literacy contexts of low-income children and has continued his work in family literacy with low- and middle-income English and Spanish speaking families in the San Antonio area. Currently, he and Elizabeth Sulzby are conducting a longitudinal study of young children's storybook reading funded by The Spencer Foundation. His article, "Toward a Theory of How Children Learn to Read and Write Naturally," originally published in *Language Arts,* has recently been reprinted in the NCRE/ERIC volume *Composing and Comprehending.*

Author Index

SUBJECT INDEX